METAPHYSICS: ITS STRUCTURE AND FUNCTION

STEPHAN KÖRNER

EMERITUS PROFESSOR OF PHILOSOPHY
UNIVERSITY OF BRISTOL, AND EMERITUS PROFESSOR
YALE UNIVERSITY

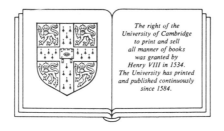

The right of the
University of Cambridge
to print and sell
all manner of books
was granted by
Henry VIII in 1534.
The University has printed
and published continuously
since 1584.

CAMBRIDGE UNIVERSITY PRESS

CAMBRIDGE
LONDON   NEW YORK   NEW ROCHELLE
MELBOURNE   SYDNEY

Published by the Press Syndicate of the University of Cambridge
The Pitt Building, Trumpington Street, Cambridge CB2 1RP
32 East 57th Street, New York, NY 10022, USA
10 Stamford Road, Oakleigh, Melbourne 3166, Australia

© Cambridge University Press 1984

First published 1984
Paperback edition 1986

Printed in Great Britain at the University Press, Cambridge

Library of Congress catalogue card number: 83–26294

British Library Cataloguing in Publication Data
Körner, Stephan
Metaphysics
1. Metaphysics
I. Title
110   BD111

ISBN 0 521 26496 0 hard covers
ISBN 0 521 33802 6 paperback

Der Metaphysik . . . ist das Schicksal bisher noch so günstig nicht gewesen, daß sie den sichern Gang einer Wissenschaft einzuschlagen vermocht hätte, ob sie gleich älter ist, als alle übrige, und bleiben würde, wenn gleich die übrigen insgesamt in dem Schlunde einer alles vertilgenden Barbarei gänzlich verschlungen werden sollten.

Kant, *Kritik der Reinen Vernunft* (BXIV)

Vergangnem nachzusinnen, Raschgeschehenes
Zurückzuführen, mühsamen Gedankenspiels,
Zum trüben Reich gestaltenmischender Möglichkeit.

Goethe, *Pandora* (Nacht)

CONTENTS

PREFACE

This book is the last of a series, the plan of which I formed about forty years ago. Although closely related to its predecessors, it is meant to stand and to be understandable on its own. An earlier monograph – *Categorial Frameworks*, published in 1970 – is a first attempt at dealing with some of the problems considered in the present essay.

In this brief preface I can do no more than mention my general indebtedness to my family, teachers and friends, as well as to colleagues and students at Bristol, Yale and Graz Universities. My friends John Cleave and David Hirschmann kindly undertook the arduous task of reading the typescript of the book. I am grateful to them for their labours and for assisting me in the struggle against philosophical error and stylistic infelicity. My sincere thanks are also due to the referee who read the book for Cambridge University Press and made some perceptive and helpful comments.

INTRODUCTION

Most people would, it seems, agree without much argument that what they experience is partly a public world of intersubjectively given particulars with intersubjectively ascertainable attributes, partly a private world which cannot be experienced by anybody else; and that what they experience may differ from the world as it exists in itself, i.e., independently of anybody's experience of it. This does not mean that they would necessarily agree on what in human experience is private and what public or how far what they experience coincides with, or resembles, the world in itself. The public world is the subject matter of commonsense thinking, as well as of the sciences and the humanities. It is the sphere of human actions, of practicabilities and, hence, of practical attitudes, prudence and morality. It also constitutes the main theme for one of the two branches of metaphysics, which in some accord with tradition will be called "immanent", as distinguished from its other branch, which will be called "transcendent".

A person's immanent metaphysics comprises the principles to which every proposition about the public world must conform if it is to be acceptable. These principles are thus less general than the principles of his logic, to which not only propositions about the public world, but every proposition whatever must conform. In expressing conditions which every proposition about the public world must satisfy, the principles of a person's immanent metaphysics define the borders between his private and his public world. They also, as will be shown, indicate the manner in which what is subjectively given in perception is interpreted as intersubjective or, to put it more emphatically, in which intersubjectivity is conferred. A person's transcendent metaphysics comprises his speculative conjectures about the relation between the – private or public – world of experience and the world in itself or transcendent reality.

It is not the purpose of this essay to expound and to defend a particular system of immanent or transcendent metaphysics, but to inquire into the common structure and function of such systems, whether explicitly formulated, e.g., by philosophers, philosophically minded theologians or

1

scientists, or only implicitly accepted. Such an inquiry appears no less worthwhile than are more familiar inquiries into the common structure and function of, say, geometries, scientific theories or legal systems. It resembles them in method and should, if properly executed, counteract the tendency towards an intolerant metaphysical dogmatism without supporting a boundless pluralism. For it is intended not only to exhibit the possible variety of metaphysical systems, but also the strong constraints on it.

The essay falls into three parts. The first examines the organization – whether imposed or found — of a person's beliefs about the public world of his experience. It also considers the organization of his practical, including his moral, attitudes towards this world, as well as the nature of aesthetic attitudes and of aesthetic representation. The organization of a person's beliefs about the public world involves, *inter alia*, a differentiation of his experience into particulars and attributes; a deductive organization of the judgments by which he assigns or refuses attributes to particulars; a method of conferring intersubjectivity on what is subjectively given; a classification of intersubjective particulars into maximal kinds; a ranking or stratification of beliefs into classes of different epistemic strength. As a result of this organization of his beliefs about the public world of his experience, a person accepts a more or less definite system of logically and nonlogically "necessary" or supreme principles which together constitute his "categorial framework". This notion is intended to replace the less precise notion of an immanent metaphysics. Yet because of their similarity the two notions can, and will, in many contexts be used interchangeably.

It may not be immediately obvious why an essay on metaphysics should require a discussion of practical and aesthetic attitudes. The need for a discussion of practical attitudes arises, as has been mentioned earlier, from the observation that the world of public experience is not only a world of unchangeable fact, but also of practicabilities the realization of which appears to depend on practical attitudes. Another, connected reason is the fairly frequent occurrence of arguments in which the propounder of a metaphysical thesis appeals to a prudential or moral attitude which he shares with his opponent. Further reasons for a preliminary discussion of practical thinking and morality are problems of transcendent metaphysics, especially the problem of the sense in which and the extent to which man is a finder or a maker of his world; and the problem whether and in what sense he is free to choose between different actions.

The reasons for including a consideration of the nature of aesthetic attitudes and aesthetic representation may be even less clear. One is the occasional reference to the aesthetic appeal of transcendent speculations and of immanent principles which, other things being equal, may make their acceptance preferable to the acceptance of aesthetically less appealing alternatives. A more important reason is the need to discuss the strong conviction of some philosophers that any attempt at grasping and characterizing the nature of transcendent reality through the application of concepts is doomed to failure, that it can be apprehended only through mystical experience and, at best, conveyed only through aesthetic representation. It seems in order to point out that whereas the chapter on the organization of practical attitudes is a brief summary of a book with the contents of which I still agree, the chapter on aesthetic attitudes constitutes the sketch of a book which is unlikely to be written.

The second part of the essay begins by illustrating the variety and function of categorial frameworks. The function of categorial frameworks consists chiefly in providing their acceptors with criteria of "meaningfulness", as opposed to mere linguistic intelligibility, of "coherence", as opposed to mere logical consistency, of "explanatory power", as opposed to mere descriptive or prognostic effectiveness. Loyalty to these criteria, which may be combined with ignorance or confusion about their origin in their acceptor's immanent metaphysics, plays an important part in the choice of theories or the direction of research. The procedure of exhibiting the actual and potential variety of categorial frameworks is endowed with some orderliness by showing that, and how, principles of immanent metaphysics may have their origin in special disciplines or regions of thought: logic; mathematics; predictive and instrumental thinking within and outside the sciences; thinking about persons and mental phenomena; thinking about social phenomena and history.

After exemplifying the great variety of accepted and acceptable categorial frameworks two questions arise which, within the confines of this essay, call for, and are given, answers. The first question is a request for clarification of statements to the effect that a categorial framework, a metaphysical principle or, quite generally, a proposition has *as a matter of empirical fact* been accepted by a person. The second question concerns the relation of a person's accepted categorial framework, as well as of other categorial frameworks, to a reality which exists independently of being experienced by him or anybody else. It raises the problem whether this reality is capable of being apprehended and, if so, whether it can be characterized by concepts or in some other way. The discussion of metaphysics ends with a rebuttal of antimetaphysical errors and illusions, which imply its nonexistence or its avoidability in human thinking.

Whereas the first two parts of the essay are mainly devoted to an inquiry into the static structure of systems of metaphysical beliefs, the third part inquires into their changes as a result of internal strains and external pressures. The latter are exerted by appeals to philosophical methods which are claimed to yield absolutely valid premises for the derivation of the one and only true system of metaphysics, as well as by more modest arguments which try to transfer the convictions felt by their proponents to those to whom they are addressed. An examination of these arguments, which results in rejecting arguments of the first type and in accepting arguments of the second, leads to a critique of various concepts of progress, be it progress within a system of metaphysical beliefs or progress of metaphysics itself.

Although this critique might well have concluded the essay, I thought it appropriate to add a chapter indicating in the barest outline my own categorial framework and transcendent metaphysics. It is meant to enable readers to judge how far I have avoided the danger of confusing my metaphysics with metaphysics in general. The final summary of theses will, I hope, also be useful to them. The frequent cross-references are not essential to the understanding of the text.

PART I

ON THE ORGANIZATION OF BELIEFS
AND ATTITUDES

CHAPTER 1

ON THE COGNITIVE ORGANIZATION
OF EXPERIENCE

It is one of the central aims of this essay to show that and how a person's immanent metaphysics depends on the organization of his experience into a system of beliefs and to show that and how his transcendent metaphysics expresses speculative conjectures about the relation of this system to a reality which exists independently of his apprehension of it. The present chapter will be devoted to the cognitive organization of a person's experience and the structure which is thereby imposed on his beliefs, the second and third to the evaluative organization of his experience and the structure thereby imposed on his practical and his pure, especially his aesthetic, attitudes. The fourth chapter will in a general and preliminary way explain the notions of immanent and of transcendent metaphysics. A discussion of all the ways in which experience is cognitively and evaluatively organized is here obviously neither needed nor possible. What, however, can and will be attempted, is a discussion of those aspects of cognitive and evaluative organization which are relevant to the understanding of the structure and function of metaphysics.

The topics of the present chapter, which examines the cognitive organization of experience, are the distinction between particulars and attributes (1); the deductive organization and epistemic stratification of beliefs (2); the interpretative stratification of beliefs and the origin of *a priori* concepts (3); in particular of concepts of intersubjectivity and objectivity (4); the distinction between dependent and independent particulars and attributes (5); and the notion of a categorial framework (6).

1 On the distinction between particulars and attributes

To classify – literally to make classes – is to determine (find or make) in one's experience attributes which are instantiated by instances. The instances of any attribute constitute its extension, i.e., the class or set of the instances by which it is instantiated. From the relation between an attribute and its instances, one must distinguish the relation between a whole and its parts. There is no need to exhibit the differences in detail, especially as this has been done in various works by logicians who have, in sufficient agreement with each other and with common usage, formalized and contrasted class-logic and mereology.[1] Two rather subtle contrasts might be mentioned. First, in class-logic one distinguishes between a class and the class having the aforementioned class as its only member. No such distinction is made between a whole and this whole considered as a part of itself. In the former case we are presented with two classes, in the latter with only one whole. Second, the logical impossibility of instantiating internally inconsistent attributes leads to the natural assumption of empty classes, whereas the assumption of empty wholes would, to say the least, be unnatural. Quite apart from such comparative subtleties, it will henceforth be taken for granted that there are many cases in which there is no doubt whether one is faced with a part–whole or an instance–attribute relation, e.g., parts of a whole apple or instances of the concept of being an apple.

Neither the subtle nor the down-to-earth differences between attributes and their instances on the one hand and wholes and their parts on the other are meant to imply that even the most primitive tribes distinguish between the two kinds of aggregation or that some very sophisticated tribe of logicians could not for most or all of our purposes make do with only one of them. It is, however, more important to note that neither the subtle nor the down-to-earth distinction between the two kinds of aggregation exclude doubtful and controversial cases. Before mentioning some of them, it will be useful to define the concept of a particular: an entity is a particular if, and only if, it is instantiating but not instantiated. A particular, moreover, has component parts (spatial parts, temporal parts, parts of either or of neither kind) or is capable of being a component part of some other particular. Thus Democritean atoms, if any, can be spatial parts of a material object during some or all phases of its existence; and Leibnizian monads, if any, can be nonspatial and nontemporal parts of a society of monads. In parallel fashion, an entity can be defined as an attribute if, and only if, it is instantiated. An attribute, moreover, has subattributes (determining extensions, included in the extension of the attribute) or is a subattribute. Only the universal attribute, the extension of which comprises all particulars, has subattributes without being one.

Among the entities the status of which as particulars or attributes has given rise to philosophical controversy are some which are by no means the special preserve of philosophy. They include space, time and the bearers of natural and other numbers. According to Newton and Kant space is a

[1] See, for example, A. Tarski, "Foundations of the geometry of solids", in *Logic, Semantics, Metamathematics* (Oxford, 1956).

particular which exists independently of any particulars which are in space and, *therefore*, stand in spatial relations to each other. Just as an object filling a volume in space can be divided into component parts, so can the unoccupied or empty volume itself be divided into subvolumes. According to Leibniz, on the other hand, space is the class of all relations holding between coexistent things, *qua* coexistent. There is according to him no empty space – an assumption which would imply a class of relations without *relata*. Again, according to Newton and Kant time is a particular, whereas for Leibniz it is the class of all relations holding between temporally ordered things, *qua* temporally ordered.

The controversy extends to the concept of number. Thus for Kant and Hilbert numbers are attributes of simple or complex particulars, e.g., of singles, couples, triples, etc., whereas for Russell and Whitehead they are attributes of classes, e.g., the class of singles, the class of couples, the class of triples, etc. The class-conception appears to be more fertile in producing infinities of ever greater cardinality by using, e.g., the method of forming the class of all subclasses of a given class. But finitists and others will regard this fertility as a curse rather than a blessing. As matters stand at present, it seems that both an approach which regards numbers as attributes of classes and an approach which regards numbers as attributes of particulars can do justice to their use in counting and to their rôle in developing large parts of mathematics in a rigorous manner.

That in geometry, chronometry or arithmetic the line between particulars and attributes can be drawn in different ways does not mean that the status of an aggregate as a compound particular or as a class must – or can – be made clear in every case. A good deal of commonsense thinking about the place, time or number of things or occurrences can proceed very well without this. For a philosopher to require of a baker that, before the price of two loaves of bread is paid, it must be determined whether what is called "two loaves" is a compound particular or a class of particulars would be a waste both of the baker's and of the philosopher's time. The latter should be aware of the distinction between particulars and attributes and, hence, between a compound particular and its component parts on the one hand and a class of an attribute's instances on the other; he should know that the status of some aggregates cannot without further determination be judged to be that of a particular or that of a class (see chapter 6, section 1).

2 On the deductive organization and epistemic stratification of beliefs

Deductive organization and epistemic stratification constitute constraints on all thought and thinking. To organize one's thinking deductively or logically is to conform to principles of consistency and principles of deductive inference, defined in terms of logical implication between compound propositions, the components of which are combined by means of connectives, quantifiers and, sometimes, modal or other operators. There are more ways than one of deductive organization, i.e., more than one system of logic. Yet all the various systems have a common core and differ from each other by mutually incompatible principles added to it.

The common core is, or at least contains, what may be called "the weak principle of noncontradiction". It can be formulated as the thesis that not all propositions are acceptable or – for propositions in which attributes are applied to particulars – as the thesis that there is, at least, one attribute which has positive cases, to which it is correctly applicable but not correctly refusable, and negative cases, to which it is correctly refusable but not correctly applicable. A more detailed discussion of the notions of accepting a proposition and of applying or refusing an attribute to a particular will form part of the discussion of alternative principles of logic (in chapter 5). Discussion of the relation between accepting a proposition and accepting it as true is best postponed until the acceptance of alternative logical *and nonlogical* principles has been exemplified (see chapter 10).

Rejection of the weak principle of noncontradiction would render the acceptance and rejection of propositions as well as deduction pointless: there would be no inconsistent set of propositions and no invalid deduction from an acceptable premise to a conclusion which is not acceptable. Acceptance of the weak principle of noncontradiction leaves open the question whether there are "inexact attributes", which apart from having positive and negative cases, also have neutral cases to which they are correctly applicable and correctly refusable (but not both correctly applied and refused). It is compatible not only with an exact logic conforming to Frege's requirement "that the definition of every concept determine for every object whether or not it falls under it",[2] but also with a logic of inexact concepts, a logic without the principle of excluded middle and other "nonclassical" systems of logic (see chapter 5). Each of them can be characterized as a set of principles or criteria of consistency and deducibility and, hence, as including the weak principle of noncontradiction. For our purpose it is not necessary to decide which, if any, of the two notions – consistency or deducibility – is the fundamental logical concept.[3]

Philosophers have often rightly insisted that certain nonlogical principles and other beliefs of lesser generality may share the dominating position

[2] *Grundgesetze der Arithmetik* (2 vols, Jena, 1903, reprinted Hildesheim, 1962), vol. 2, pp. 69f.
[3] See Tarski, "On the concept of logical consequence", in *Logic, Semantics, Metamathematics.*

with a person's logical principles. To make this more precise, one may define a person's system of beliefs as epistemically stratified if, and only if, it contains at least two sets of beliefs, say, α and β, such that α epistemically dominates β in the sense that if he acknowledges that a belief belonging to α is inconsistent with a belief belonging to β, he rejects the latter and preserves the former. In terms mainly of domination one may define the important notion of epistemic supremacy as follows: a set of a person's beliefs, say, α, is his supreme set of beliefs if, and only if, α cannot be divided into two sets, say, α_1 and α_2, such that α_1 epistemically dominates α_2; and α dominates the set of all his beliefs not belonging to α.

Examples of beliefs which are accepted as supreme by individuals and societies are – apart from logical beliefs – religious beliefs and metaphysical beliefs, including beliefs claimed to express conditions which are satisfied by whatever exists or can be thought. It is important to emphasize that a logical or other principle which at one time is acknowledged as supreme by a person may lose its supremacy – and thus its status as a principle of logic or metaphysics – either by being rejected or by being demoted to a dominated principle of one kind or another. Such changes, of which there are many examples in the history of philosophy, may come about as the result of philosophical reflection based on the discovery of hitherto hidden inconsistencies, on the fear of future inconsistencies or on various kinds of intellectual discomfort. They may also be due to arguments against an old and in favour of a new metaphysical position (see chapters 14 and 15).

3 On the interpretative stratification of beliefs and on a priori concepts

In order to characterize the nature of supreme principles expressing conditions of intersubjective experience, it seems best first to explain and exhibit the interpretative stratification of concepts and judgments, second to show how it gives rise to a priori concepts and judgments, and third to characterize those a priori concepts whose application to subjective phenomena confers intersubjective or objective validity on them.

A few preliminary definitions and comments are likely to prove useful: a person's concept will be called "perceptual" if, and only if, it is applicable to something that is given to him in perception or imagination or, more precisely, as an appearance in space and time or in time only. That a concept is applicable to a spatio-temporal or temporal appearance, does not imply that it is descriptive of it. For example, whereas 'x is red' is applicable to, and descriptive of, such an appearance, 'x causes y' is never descriptive of such an appearance, even if it is applicable to it. Let us say that a person's perceptual concept has sensible or ostensive content *in so far* as it describes a spatio-temporal or temporal appearance. It is doubtful whether there are any perceptual concepts which have only sensible or ostensive content, since even concepts like '*x* is red' and '*x* is painful' are logically connected with concepts which like '*x* is an animal' are not merely descriptive of spatio-temporal or temporal appearances. And it is equally doubtful whether the ostensive and the non-ostensive content of a perceptual concept can be separated by an exact border.

However, what follows is independent of how these doubts are resolved or whether they are resolved at all, i.e., whether one assumes that there are purely ostensive concepts and that a sharp distinction can be made between the ostensive and the non-ostensive content of every perceptual concept; or whether one rejects one of these assumptions or both of them – as I am inclined to do. For each of these assumptions is compatible with the possibility of sometimes correctly judging that two perceptual concepts do or do not differ in their ostensive content or that, even though they differ in their ostensive content, they do not differ in their full content. Thus the concepts 'being a chair as conceived by Plato' and 'being a chair as conceived by Hume' are co-ostensive, however greatly they differ in their full content. It will further be convenient to say briefly that "one concept logically implies another" when it would be more precise to say that the applicability of the former concept to any particular (or any ordered set of particulars) logically implies the applicability of the latter to this particular (or ordered set of particulars).

A special – and in the present context crucial – case of two perceptual concepts which are co-ostensive and yet differ in their full content is the case where, as will be said, one of them is "interpretative" of the other. More precisely, a concept *P* is interpretative of a concept *Q* if, and only if, (i) *P* and *Q* are co-ostensive and (ii) *P* logically implies *Q* but *Q* does not logically imply *P*. Thus a Platonist would be right in asserting that his concept of a chair and the everyday concept of a chair stand in the relation which has just been defined, i.e., that his concept of a chair, which participates in a certain Form, is interpretative of the commonsense concept of a chair.

If a perceptual concept *P* is interpretative of a perceptual concept *Q*, i.e., if in spite of their co-ostensiveness *P* logically implies *Q* but *Q* does not logically imply *P*, then there may exist – and, e.g., in classical logic always exists – a concept *A* such that *A* does not logically imply *P*, *P* logically implies (*Q* and *A*) and (*Q* and *A*) logically implies *P*. The concept *A*, if any, whose addition to *Q* turns the unilateral logical implication between *P* and *Q* into the bilateral logical implication or logical equivalence between *P* and

(Q and A), may be called the "nonsensible" or "*a priori*" difference between P and Q. (The difference is nonsensible because P and Q, though different in their full content, are co-ostensive and therefore do not differ in their sensible content.) Thus if we assume that a Platonist and a philosophical layman agree about the commonsense meaning of 'x is a chair', then 'x is a chair as conceived by Plato' is interpretative of 'x is a chair' and the nonsensible or *a priori* difference between the two concepts is 'x participates in the Platonic Form of chairness.' This concept, whose content is nonsensible, is (for the Platonist) nevertheless applicable to something perceived, namely, to everything to which 'x is a chair' is applicable. A concept which, though applicable to what is perceivable or imaginable, lacks sensible content will be called a perceptual *a priori* concept. The use of the term "*a priori* concept" is meant to indicate its Kantian origins, even though Kant used it in an absolute sense which implied that there cannot be internally consistent, but mutually exclusive, sets of such concepts.

Perceptual *a priori* concepts must – again in Kantian fashion – be distinguished from ideal *a priori* concepts, which not only lack any sensible content but also are inapplicable to what can be perceived or imagined. Among the ideal *a priori* concepts two species should be distinguished which will respectively be called "idealizing" and "transcendent". The idealizing concepts (e.g., the concept of a Euclidean triangle), though not applicable to what can be observed, can be, and are, for certain purposes and within certain contexts used *as if* they were so applicable. Their most important employment occurs in the sciences, especially those involving more or less complex mathematical theories (see chapters 6 and 7). The transcendent concepts (e.g., the concept of an infinitely perfect being) refer to a reality which is not accessible to perception. While the Kantian Ideas are clearly transcendent, it might be reasonably argued that the Platonic Ideas or Forms are idealizing concepts.

A perceptual *a priori* concept which will prove particularly important for the purpose of this inquiry is the concept of intersubjective accessibility. In order to explain its content and function it will be helpful to consider a typical transition from a subjective to an intersubjective judgment. Consider the case where a person – correctly or incorrectly – judges that an object of his awareness, say, o, possesses a sensible or ostensive attribute P (e.g., 'being red'), the applicability of which to o, i.e., $P(o)$, neither logically implies that o is also perceivable by at least one other person nor that it is not so perceivable. Since the attributes of intersubjective accessibility, briefly $Int(o)$, and $P(o)$ are logically independent, a person may judge without contradiction that both $P(o)$ and $Int(o)$ (that the object of his awareness is

not only red but also intersubjectively accessible). If one defines a concept
$\mathfrak{P}(x)$ as logically equivalent with *(P(x) and Int(x))*, then clearly $\mathfrak{P}(x)$ and
P(x) are co-ostensive; *Int(x)* does not logically imply $\mathfrak{P}(x)$; $\mathfrak{P}(x)$ logically implies *P(x)* without being logically implied by *P(x)*; and *Int(x)* is the *a
priori* difference between $\mathfrak{P}(x)$ and *P(x)*. Indeed it is, even apart from the
preceding considerations, obvious that the concept of intersubjective accessibility – though applicable to what is perceived – lacks sensible content
because one can be perceptually aware of one's own perceiving or imagining,
but not of another's perceiving or imagining. The concept of intersubjective
accessibility is the simplest concept conferring intersubjective validity on
subjective phenomena.

4 On concepts of intersubjectivity and objectivity and their application to subjective phenomena

It is important to note that the transition from applying a subjective concept
P(x) to an object *o* of one's awareness to applying an intersubjective concept
$\mathfrak{P}(x)$ to it (e.g., the transition from '*o* is red' to '*o* is red and intersubjective')
may take a variety of different forms. It may, first of all, be that different
persons or groups of persons add the attribute of intersubjectivity to
different subjective concepts. Thus some people might add the concept of
intersubjectivity to any colour-concept so that for them every object of their
awareness which is correctly judged to be red would *eo ipso* be correctly
judged to be intersubjective. Others might add the concept of intersubjectivity not to colour-concepts, but to the concept of being heavy, others still
to the conjunction 'being coloured and heavy' (and not to its separate
conjuncts) or to more complex conjunctions of sensible concepts.

Second, the interpretation of a sensible concept *P(x)* by an intersubjective
concept $\mathfrak{P}(x)$ need not consist merely in the addition to *P(x)* of the concept of
intersubjectivity. It can, and normally does, lead to a concept $\Pi(x)$ – or a
number of such concepts – such that $\Pi(x)$ logically implies $\mathfrak{P}(x)$ and, hence,
P(x) without being logically implied by either and such that it is co-
ostensive with both $\mathfrak{P}(x)$ and *P(x)*. Thus the Platonic concept of a table
logically implies not only the sensible attributes which are characteristic of
tables and the concept of intersubjectivity, but also the nonsensible concept
of participating in a Platonic Form.

Third, different persons or the same person at different times may employ
different concepts of intersubjective accessibility, in particular concepts of
different strength. A very weak concept, which will here be mentioned only
this once, is '*x* is under realizable and more or less specified conditions

accessible to the awareness of at least one other person, with the *proviso* that these conditions do not include the condition of objective or mind-independent existence.' A strong concept which will henceforth be expressed by '*x* is intersubjectively accessible' differs from the weak concept in that 'accessibility to at least one person' is replaced by 'accessibility to a class of persons' (e.g., the class of all persons or the class of persons with normal vision). A still stronger concept, which will be expressed by '*x* is objective', means the same as '*x* exists independently of anybody's awareness of it.'

It is now possible to define concepts of intersubjectivity and of objectivity or, more briefly, intersubjectivity- and objectivity-concepts of any interpretative level as follows: a concept $I(x)$ is an intersubjectivity-concept if, and only if, (i) it is the concept '*x* is intersubjectively accessible' *or* (ii) it logically implies '*x* is intersubjectively accessible.' Moreover, $I(x)$ is an *a priori* intersubjectivity-concept if in addition (iii) it is *a priori*. Similarly, a concept $O(x)$ is an objectivity-concept if, and only if, (i) it is the concept '*x* is objective' *or* (ii) it logically implies '*x* is objective.' Moreover, $O(x)$ is an *a priori* objectivity-concept if in addition (iii) it is *a priori*. In the case of both these definitions the third condition is obviously satisfied by the concept '*x* is intersubjective' and the concept '*x* is objective' since, as has been pointed out, they are nonsensible but nevertheless applicable to objects of awareness, i.e., perceptual *a priori* concepts. The Kantian Categories are not only – as again has been mentioned earlier – *a priori* perceptual concepts. They are *a priori* intersubjectivity-concepts.

In admitting the possibility that there are different, mutually exclusive sets of intersubjectivity- or objectivity-concepts by whose application otherwise merely subjective phenomena are interpreted as intersubjectively accessible or as objective, one admits that different thinkers may have different conceptions of the intersubjectively accessible particulars contained in the common human world. Of special importance is the characterization of those intersubjectively accessible particulars which are ultimate in the sense that all other particulars are reducible to them while they themselves cannot be reduced to even more ultimate ones. This characterization may either imply that there is only one maximal kind (*maximum genus*) of such ultimate particulars, e.g., only things or only events, or that there are at least two maximal kinds, e.g., things and events or minds and material things.

From intersubjective particulars, whether ultimate or reducible to ultimate ones, one must distinguish particulars which, not being objects of awareness or subjectively accessible, are therefore also not intersubjectively accessible. These unreal, or fictitious, particulars are characterized not by perceptual *a priori* concepts, but by ideal *a priori* concepts, i.e., either by idealizing or by transcendent *a priori* concepts. It is possible that particulars which for one thinker are intersubjective (e.g., 'being a constellation of physical atoms' for Democritus) are fictitious for another (e.g., 'being a constellation of physical atoms' for Leibniz), in which case they may even be useful fictions (as were the physical atoms for Leibniz). This possibility is among the reasons why one thinker whose universe of intersubjective particulars differs radically from that of another can gain at least a partial understanding of it.

It may be worth emphasizing that what has been said about perceptual concepts and their interpretative stratification does not imply that, as has for example been held by Husserl, there is a clear, distinct and wholly determinate core of perceptual phenomena which is free from any interpretation and is the same for everybody. For if a person is on the one hand able to order some of his perceptual concepts in a sequence, say, $P_1, P_2, \ldots,$ P_n, in which every member, except the first, is interpretative of its predecessor, and if on the other hand he is unable to provide the first member with a predecessor, it does not follow that the first member describes a clear, distinct and wholly determinate phenomenon. Again, a person's application of an intersubjectivity-concept to a particular, as perceived by himself, does not imply that his perception of the particular (e.g., of a certain chair) must resemble everybody else's perception of it in all respects.[4]

5 On distinguishing between independent and dependent particulars and attributes

Just as the distinction between merely subjective and objective phenomena is central to the Kantian theory of Categories, so is the distinction between independent and dependent particulars and attributes to the Aristotelian. And just as Kant acknowledges only one valid objectivization, so Aristotle acknowledges only one correct way of distinguishing independent from dependent entities. An independent particular or, as Aristotle calls it in his famous definition, "a primary substance" is something that "can never be found in a subject, nor yet asserted of one – that man or horse for example", where the locution "can be found in a subject" means that "it cannot exist apart from the subject referred to" (*Categories*, II). Instead of objecting on Spinozistic, Leibnizian, Kantian or other grounds that a certain man or horse cannot exist apart from *deus sive natura*, apart from a society of monads, apart from a substance, subject to conservation laws or apart from some other simple or compound particular, one may try to clarify the general distinction between independent and dependent particulars and, thereby, the various ways in which it can be drawn.

It seems best to start with a definition of existential dependence and to define a particular *d* as existentially dependent on a particular *i* if, and only if, *d* cannot exist (in logic or in fact) without *i*'s existing, but *i* can exist without *d*'s existing. A particular *i* can then be defined as an existentially independent particular *in a certain universe of fact and discourse* if, and only if, *i* belongs to a class of particulars, say, *Ind*, none of whose members is existentially dependent on any particular. In Aristotle's universe of fact and discourse horses, men and other particulars belonging to clearly de-marcated classes and capable of being individuated with sufficient precision belong to *Ind*.

Two particulars may be existentially dependent on each other. This is so, for example, if one accepts an atomic theory in which material objects are regarded as constellations of atoms so that a certain material object exists if, and only if, a certain constellation of atoms exists. In this and similar cases one type of particular may be regarded as more fundamental than the other, e.g., because scientific prognoses or explanations (in some sense of this term) apply to one type rather than the other, because some supreme metaphysical principle accords one type a merely subsidiary status, etc.

Again, it may be that even though one particular is not existentially dependent on another, one is an idealization of the other, which is in practically or theoretically important contexts identified with it. An example is the relation between on the one hand the particulars of an idealizing mathematical or scientific theory and on the other hand the particulars of some range of commonsense experience to which the theory is applied through *as-if* identification. Here again there may be reasons for according fundamental status to the particulars of the theory and dependent – though not existentially dependent – status to the common-sense particulars or vice versa. It may for some purposes be important to distinguish between various kinds of nonexistential dependence-relations. Here it suffices to contrast two general kinds of dependence of one particular on another: existential dependence and what might be called "explanatory" or, simply, "nonexistential" dependence.

To the independence-relations between particulars there correspond what may be called "relations of applicative priority" between attributes, some of which are relevant to various doctrines of Categories. Thus we may define one attribute, say, *X*, as having strict priority of application over another attribute, say, Y, if and only if Y is not applicable (has no instances) unless – as a matter of fact or logic – X is applicable and if the converse relation does not hold. ('Being an animal' has strict priority of application over 'being human'. So – in contemporary common sense – has 'having a heart which is beating' over 'being capable of thinking'.) Again, we may define an attribute X as having weak priority of application over an attribute Y if, though not having strict priority, it is judged to be fundamental on scientific or other grounds. An attribute can then be defined as having applicative priority *in a certain universe of fact and discourse* if, and only if, it belongs to a class none of whose members stand in the converse of the priority relation to any attribute.

6 On the notion of a categorial framework

The results of the preceding discussion can be incorporated into the notion of a categorial framework, which will prove a useful and convenient tool in the subsequent inquiry. A categorial framework is a set of supreme principles which determine:

(i) a differentiation of experience into particulars and attributes and, hence, a logic containing at least the weak principle of noncontradiction without which the differentiation would be empty;

(ii) a set of intersubjectivity-concepts, i.e., concepts which, if applied to subjectively given particulars (particulars given in a person's perception), confer intersubjectivity upon them; and, consequently, a domain of intersubjective particulars, i.e., the instances of these concepts;

(iii) a categorization of the intersubjective particulars into maximal kinds (*maxima genera*);

(iv) for each maximal kind

(a) a constitutive principle according to which an object's being a member of the maximal kind logically implies its possession of a certain attribute or conjunction of attributes;

(b) in some cases, an individuating principle according to which a member's distinctness from every other member of a maximal kind logically implies its possession of a certain attribute or conjunction of attributes (e.g., according to Kant and others, specific spatio-temporal position of material objects);

(v) in some cases, a division of particulars and concepts into independent and dependent ones;

(vi) in some cases, the admissibility of various kinds of "auxiliary" concepts, i.e., concepts other than intersubjectivity-concepts, which (like, for example, mathematical or theoretical idealizations) serve the application of intersubjectivity-concepts.

In so far as a person thinks about intersubjective particulars and in doing so conforms to the principles which constitute his categorial framework, it will be convenient to refer to the subject matter of his thought as his "intersubjectively interpreted experience", his "intersubjectively interpreted world", "the world of his intersubjective experience" or, briefly, his "intersubjective world".

Borderline cases between maximal kinds are admitted. So, as has been emphasized, are borderline cases between particulars and attributes. The definition of a categorial framework does not explicitly cover a nominalism in which all classes are replaced by complex particulars or the opposite position in which all particulars are replaced by intersections of attributes. But the definition could be easily – though somewhat tortuously – adjusted explicitly to cover those extreme positions without substantially affecting the subsequent discussions.

Although it seems sufficiently specific for our purpose, it may well turn out that some further specification would add to its usefulness for this or some other philosophical purpose. Again, a person's adherence to a categorial framework may – like his adherence to a morality, a legal system, a scientific theory and other systems of beliefs and attitudes – be more or less explicit, more or less definite and more or less confident and he may even waver between one or more such systems. All this is no objection to the use of the notion of a categorial framework (a morality, etc.) since it is in general more useful to know than not to know that about which one is not explicit, indefinite, dubious or undecided.

CHAPTER 2

ON THE ORGANIZATION OF
PRACTICAL ATTITUDES

The world of our intersubjective experience is a world which we and others observe and a world in which we and others act. And since our actions depend not only on our beliefs, but also on our practical attitudes, their organization is part of the intersubjective world. It is also the origin of one of the central problems of transcendent metaphysics, namely, the problem whether and in what sense an agent is free to choose his actions.

A person's practical attitudes are directed towards practical possibilities, that is to say, towards possibilities which he believes himself to be able to realize *or to leave unrealized*. A person's pure attitudes are directed towards possibilities as such, i.e., independently of whether they are realizable or unrealizable, unrealized or realized. And there are mixed attitudes which combine practical and pure attitudes in a more or less complex manner. Among them are certain aesthetic attitudes, which are directed towards works of art as realized possibilities and, at the same time, as capable of being changed in ways which would make them more or less adequate to whatever it is that determines their adequacy. The present chapter is devoted to an examination of the general organization of a person's practical attitudes. It discusses practical attitudes as involving beliefs (1); the evaluative stratification of practical attitudes and the notion of evaluative supremacy (2); types of practical inconsistency and the deductive organization of practical attitudes (3); personally universal practical attitudes and practical principles (4); the concept of morality and different kinds of it (5).

1 Practical attitudes as involving beliefs about practicabilities

The practical and pure attitudes which concern us here fall, at least prima facie, into two groups. The first contains a person's preference for one possibility over another, his indifference between two possibilities, as well as other attitudes which are analysable in terms of preference and indifference and express a comparison between pairs of possibilities and ultimately an ordering of the members of a set of possibilities. The second group contains a person's pro-attitude (liking, loving, etc.), anti-attitude (disliking, hating) and indifference towards a possibility. For our present purpose it is not necessary to analyse the nature of these attitudes any further by characterizing the various types of ordering to which they give rise. Nor will it be necessary to raise and answer the question whether the attitudes of the first group can be analysed in terms of those of the second group or vice versa.[1]

A fundamental difference between practical and pure attitudes is their relation to beliefs. Let us, for example, consider a person who has a pure pro-attitude towards a possibility about the realizability of which he holds a false belief (e.g., the possibility of achieving eternal youth). If he discovers that the belief is false, his pure attitude does not thereby *become* groundless because as a pure attitude it was never grounded in a belief in its realizability. A pure attitude towards a logical possibility is grounded in the belief that what appears to be a logical possibility is a logical possibility. While the belief may obviously be mistaken, there is here no need to decide the question whether a person's discovery of such a mistake must in all circumstances affect his attitude.

A person's practical attitude is directed towards one of a number of options which he believes to be practicable and does, therefore, become groundless if he recognizes that what he believed to be a practicability is not realizable. For our present purpose there is no need to analyse in detail the notion of an action, a course of action or more generally a practicability (see chapter 8, section 2). But it is important to emphasize that having a practical attitude logically implies having a practical belief, as one might call beliefs in the practicability of options. Thus any feature of the practical belief which is logically implied by a practical attitude is also a feature of this attitude. In order to distinguish clearly between a practical attitude which is grounded in a false practical belief and a false belief as such, one might call the practical attitude "practically false".

There are many species of practical falsehood. A person's practical attitude may in particular be practically impossible because the belief in the realizability of an option, in which his attitude is grounded, is (a) logically impossible, i.e., logically inconsistent with his accepted principles of logic; (b) metaphysically impossible, i.e., logically inconsistent with the principles of his immanent metaphysics; (c) empirically impossible, i.e., logically inconsistent with his beliefs about the course of nature, especially the laws of nature; (d) effectively impossible, i.e., logically inconsistent with his

[1] See *Experience and Conduct*, (Cambridge, 1976), chapter 4.

beliefs about what he can effectively choose to realize or to leave unrealized. And there are other kinds of impossibility. Clearly, the logical impossibility of an option's being realized logically implies the metaphysical impossibility of its realization, which logically implies the empirical impossibility of its realization, which in turn logically implies the effective impossibility of its realization, whereas the converse logical implications are not valid.

To the various kinds of practical impossibility, i.e., the impossibility of beliefs in realizable options in which practical attitudes are grounded, there correspond various kinds of practical inconsistency. In order to distinguish them from other kinds of practical inconsistency which are not, or not only, based on the impossibility of beliefs, the latter will be called practical opposition. It will further be helpful to introduce some fairly obvious schematic representations of the practical attitudes which a person, say, S, can have towards an assumed practicability (described by a proposition, say, f). Let us write $(S + f)$, $(S - f)$, and $(S \pm f)$ to express respectively that S has a practical pro-attitude, a practical anti-attitude or a practical attitude of indifference towards f and let us write $(S * f)$ to express that S has one of these practical attitudes towards f, as opposed to his not having any such attitude towards f.

Two practical attitudes of a person are (practically) opposed to each other if, and only if, the practical belief in their joint realizability is (logically, metaphysically, empirically, effectively, etc.) impossible. Thus $(S + f)$ and $(S - f)$ are practically opposed and their opposition is logical. Again, if f and g are (logically, metaphysically, empirically, effectively, etc.) inconsistent with each other, then $(S+f)$ and $(S+g)$ are (logically, metaphysically, empirically, effectively, etc.) opposed. In terms of practical opposition, which is a species of practical inconsistency, a corresponding species of practical implication can be defined: a practical attitude of a person (logically, metaphysically, empirically, effectively) implies another of his practical attitudes if, and only if, the conjunction of the practical belief associated with the former and the negation of the practical belief associated with the latter is (logically, metaphysically, empirically, effectively) inconsistent.

2 On the evaluative stratification of practical attitudes and on evaluative supremacy

Because practical attitudes are grounded in practical beliefs, they are, to the extent to which they involve such beliefs, subject to the principles of logic. This is why one kind of inconsistency between practical attitudes, namely, practical opposition, depends only on the cognitive aspect of practical attitudes, i.e., the practical beliefs in which they are grounded, and not on their evaluative aspect. But there are other kinds of inconsistency between practical attitudes – and hence of implication and other relations between them – which are not or at least not wholly dependent on their associated practical beliefs. In order to understand these relations between practical attitudes it is necessary to consider the evaluative stratification of practical attitudes.

A person's practical attitudes may be directed towards practicabilities which do or do not themselves include his having a certain practical attitude. Practical attitudes of the latter kind will be called practical attitudes of "the first level", practical attitudes of the former kind will be called practical attitudes of "higher level". More precisely, a practical attitude directed towards a practicability of first, second, third . . . level is itself respectively a practical attitude of second, third, fourth . . . level. The possibility of a person's having practical attitudes towards practical attitudes is a characteristic of the human predicament and is as such acknowledged, e.g., by the biblical contrast between the weakness of the flesh and the willingness of the spirit, by Kant's distinction between the lower faculty of desire and the will or higher faculty of desire and in one way or another by everybody who suffers from the conflict between his inclinations and his duties.

If a person's practical attitude is directed towards (a practicability involving his having) another practical attitude, then the former attitude will be said to dominate the latter. This evaluative domination may be positive, negative or indifferent according to whether the higher practical attitude is a pro-attitude, an anti-attitude or an attitude of indifference. Just as a person may not have any practical attitude – i.e., not even a practical attitude of indifference – towards a practicability not involving a practical attitude, so he may also not have any higher-level practical attitude towards a practicability involving a practical attitude. In this case the latter practical attitude will be said to be (practically) undominated.

One can easily think of examples of practical attitudes of second level dominating practical attitudes of first level, e.g., when somebody has a pro-attitude towards his anti-attitude towards smoking or when somebody has an anti-attitude towards his pro-attitude towards smoking. In the latter case, as in all cases of negative domination, it may seem doubtful whether both the higher and the lower attitude are practical. Yet it is, for example, perfectly possible that a person has a practical pro-attitude towards drinking a pint of whiskey a day and a practical anti-attitude towards this practical pro-attitude: for he may realize the dominated, lower attitude by drinking a pint of whiskey a day and the dominating, higher attitude by undergoing a suitable aversion therapy. Although a person's practical attitudes may be stratified into more than three levels, there will be no need for us to go beyond the third.

If a person's practical attitudes are – unlike those of the *homo economicus* of classical economics – evaluatively stratified, then some of them must be (evaluatively) supreme in the sense of dominating one or more practical attitudes and of not being dominated by any. A person's moral attitudes are among his supreme practical attitudes, just as his metaphysical beliefs are among his supreme beliefs. Yet just as cognitive supremacy is only a necessary condition of a belief's being metaphysical, so evaluative supremacy is only a necessary condition of a practical attitude's being moral. For even before a more detailed analysis is given, it seems clear that, for example, a person's undominated second-level anti-attitude towards his first-level pro-attitude towards smoking is not *ipso facto* one of his moral attitudes.

Again, as in the case of cognitively supreme beliefs, a person may be uncertain as to whether or not a certain practical attitude is supreme or may be wavering between two practical attitudes. In dealing with such cases it is sometimes useful not only to consider pro-attitudes, anti-attitudes and attitudes of indifference of various levels, but also preferential orderings. The ordering of preferences which is most common and useful is the so-called "weak ordering" of options by means of a relation of preference-or-indifference which (like the relation of greater-or-equal when applied to the natural numbers) is transitive, symmetrical and complete.[2] The evaluative stratification of practical attitudes presupposes of course the logical, epistemic and interpretative organization of beliefs, since all practical attitudes and preferences are directed towards possibilities which are *believed* to be realizable in the world of intersubjective experience.

3 Types of practical inconsistency and the deductive organization of practical attitudes

By acknowledging the evaluative stratification of practical attitudes one is enabled to characterize two types of conflict between practical attitudes, which, unlike practical opposition, depend on the stratification. Because of their strong formal analogies to practical opposition and, hence, to the cognitive inconsistency of beliefs, they will be regarded as species of

[2] For details about this and other kinds of ordering see *Experience and Conduct*, chapter 4.

practical inconsistency and will be distinguished from practical opposition and from each other as (evaluative) "discordance" and "incongruence". The former, which, as has been indicated, is one of the sources of moral conflict and, hence, of morality, is a relation between practical attitudes of at least second level and the lower-level practical attitudes towards which they are directed. The latter holds between practical attitudes of the same level – with the exception of first-level practical attitudes – and combines opposition and discordance.

Two practical attitudes of a person are discordant if, and only if, one of them is negatively dominated by the other. Thus, if we consider only practical pro-attitudes, practical anti-attitudes and practical attitudes of indifference, discordance involves a practical anti-attitude of the person directed towards one of his practical attitudes which may be a practical pro-attitude, a practical anti-attitude or a practical attitude of indifference. In the case of the discordance between preferences, which will not concern us here, the person's higher-level preference is a preference for a lower-level preferential ordering of practical preferences which differs from his actual lower-level preferential ordering.

Before defining the incongruence between practical attitudes in terms of evaluative domination and opposition, it is necessary to define the relation of the complementarity of practical attitudes, which is stronger than practical opposition. Two opposed practical attitudes of a person are practically complementary if, and only if, his practical beliefs in their realizability imply (logically, metaphysically, empirically, effectively) that one of them will be realized. Practical complementarity and practical opposition are related as are contradictoriness and incompatibility of beliefs, i.e., the first member of each pair implies the second without being implied by it. Thus a person's practical pro-attitude towards taking a holiday and his practical pro-attitude towards not taking a holiday are practically complementary and, hence, practically opposed; whereas his practical pro-attitude towards taking a holiday only in January and his practical pro-attitude towards taking a holiday only in February are practically opposed but not complementary (provided, of course, that he believes that a holiday at some other time of the year is also a practicability).

The incongruence of practical attitudes can now be defined: Two practical attitudes of second (of nth, $n > 2$) level are incongruent if, and only if, (i) each of them positively dominates a first-level (n-1st level) practical attitude and the dominated attitudes are opposed or (ii) each of them negatively dominates a first-level (n-1st level) practical attitude and the dominated attitudes are complementary. Examples are (i) two practical pro-attitudes, one directed towards a pro-attitude towards taking a holiday only in January, the other towards a pro-attitude towards taking a holiday only in February (since the first-level attitudes are opposed); (ii) two practical anti-attitudes, one directed towards an anti-attitude towards taking a holiday during January, the other towards an anti-attitude towards working during January (since the first-level attitudes are complementary). Compared with practical opposition and discordance, practical incongruence is a fairly trivial relation and of little importance to what follows.

To each kind of practical inconsistency there corresponds a kind of practical implication. But it is for many purposes sufficient to employ a general concept of practical inconsistency (i.e., the concept 'practical opposition-or-discordance-or-inconguence') and a general concept of practical implication. In order to emphasize the analogy between cognitive and practical implication, it is necessary to have a suitable concept of negation. One may, for example, define the negation of a practical attitude, say, a, in symbols $\neg a$, as the disjunction of the practical attitudes with which a is practically inconsistent, that is to say not merely as the absence of a. One can then define that a practically implies b – in symbols $a \rightarrow b$ – if and only if a and $\neg b$ are practically inconsistent.[3]

Just as the logical implications between a person's beliefs make it possible to organize them into a deductive system in which each belief is placed into its proper position as a premise of other beliefs, as a conclusion from other beliefs or as being logically independent of all other beliefs, so the practical implications between a person's practical attitudes make it possible to organize them into an analogous practical system. Yet it must not be forgotten that both the deductive relations between the beliefs of a person and the deductive relations between his practical attitudes do *not* logically imply that he is aware of them. In the case of the deductive relations between his practical attitudes he may, moreover, be fully aware of them and yet not live by them. He may in particular realize a lower-level practical attitude which he knows to be practically inconsistent with his morality.

4 *On personally universal practical attitudes and on practical principles*

A person's awareness of his practical attitudes does not involve his awareness of anybody's sharing them. The position is no different from his awareness of what he perceives. In judging that his practical attitude is shared by at least one other person, he interprets a merely subjective attitude as intersubjective. This he does – as in any other case of passing

---

[3] *Experience and Conduct*, pp. 98–100.

from subjective to intersubjective phenomena – by applying the *a priori* concept 'x is intersubjective' or some other intersubjectivity-concept to the subjective phenomenon. From cognitive intersubjectivity, as one might call the result of applying intersubjectivity-concepts to the objects of one's subjective awareness, one must distinguish practical intersubjectivity or the personal generality of practical attitudes which is the result of having practical attitudes not only to one's own practical attitudes but to practical attitudes of others besides oneself.

Practical intersubjectivity presupposes on the one hand the stratification of practical attitudes, i.e., that a person has practical attitudes towards his own practical attitudes; and on the other hand cognitive intersubjectivity, i.e., that a person judges his practical attitude to be shared or capable of being shared by at least one other person, by a group of persons including himself, or by all human beings. A person's second-level practical attitude, e.g., his practical anti-attitude towards his practical pro-attitude towards smoking, is a subjective practical attitude of second level, which may be schematically represented by

(a) $S_0 - [S_0 + f]$.

It becomes, so to speak, minimally intersubjective if the person's second-level attitude is directed towards a first-level attitude of his which he judges to be shared or shareable with one other person, i.e., schematically,

(b) $S_0 - [(S_0 \text{ and } S_1) + f]$.

The class of persons sharing or capable of sharing the lower practical attitude may be larger and determined by some general characteristic. It may also be the class of all human beings, in which case the higher-level attitude will be called "personally universal", schematically,

(c) $S_0 - [U + f]$.

The example may, of course, be modified by any combination of $+$, $-$ and $\pm$ in the higher-level and the lower-level practical attitude and *mutatis mutandis* by substituting a preferential ordering for the first-level or the second-level practical attitude or both.

In so far as a person's second-level attitude is directed towards a practical attitude not only of himself but also of others, it may, but need not, be wholly practical. The scope within which such an attitude is practical depends on a person's beliefs about his ability to influence others. It will be wide in the case of a confident moral reformer and narrow in the case of a diffident recluse. (When speaking of universal or general *practical* attitudes, this qualification of scope will be tacitly assumed.)

That a person has a practical attitude towards *everybody's* having a certain lower-level practical attitude presupposes that he has some conception of the common humanity which he shares with everybody. And whatever this conception of the limitations and potentialities of his and everybody else's individual and social existence, it certainly does not call this existence into question. The point is particularly important for the understanding of moral principles which, besides being practical attitudes towards everybody's having certain lower-level practical attitudes, satisfy some further conditions.

The first is circumstantial generality, i.e., the requirement that the lower-level practical attitude be directed towards a kind of practicability rather than a strictly singular one (which cannot be characterized by a finite conjunction of general attributes). This does not mean that moral attitudes – as opposed to moral *principles* – may not be directed towards a unique practicability, i.e., one which arises only once and only for one person. The second condition which a moral principle, as well as a moral attitude which is circumstantially unique, must satisfy is freedom from domination. In other words, a moral attitude is not the object of any higher practical attitude or, to use Kant's terms, is not heteronomous, but autonomous. The third condition which a person's moral principles must fulfil is that they be practically consistent with each other. Moral principles in the strict sense, or strict moral principles, must be distinguished from moral principles in a looser sense or competing moral principles. The latter compete, and are acknowledged to compete, for application in certain special cases in which they are suspended in favour of a unique moral attitude which is expected to emerge. Lastly, a moral principle must not contain any irrelevant characteristics and not be decomposable into a conjunction of such principles.[4]

Moral principles, like all practical principles, are grounded in beliefs about what is practicable and, like all personally universal attitudes, are grounded in beliefs about the nature of man. Even though primarily directed to man as potentially active, they naturally give rise to questions about the status of men as passive objects of the actions of others. Among them are questions about the status of infants, as well as questions about other living things which resemble human beings in the capacity for pain and pleasure. All these are moral questions the general answers to which consist in the acceptance of moral principles.

---

[4] For a more detailed discussion of these requirements see *Experience and Conduct,* pp.118–20.

5 On the concept of a morality and on different kinds of morality

The distinction between moral principles, which are personally universal and circumstantially general practical attitudes, and moral attitudes, which are not moral principles because they are circumstantially unique – schematically, between $S * [U * X]$ and $S * [U * f]$ – is meant to be in accord with common usage and to cover a wide spectrum of philosophical views on the nature of morality. At one of its extremes lies an intuitionism which considers all circumstantial generalization as at best an approximation to practicabilities whose moral relevance cannot be characterized in general; at the other extreme lies a Kantianism which regards all morality as based on moral laws, i.e., as circumstantially general. In what follows, it will be assumed that men could live by a concrete morality, which contains no moral principles; by a general morality, which contains only moral principles or moral attitudes instantiating moral principles; and lastly by a morality which is partly concrete and partly general. Moreover, that people did in fact live by these moralities follows from the assumption that the philosophers who described morality as concrete, general or mixed did not deceive themselves about the kind of morality which they themselves acknowledged.

A general morality, or a morality which is at least partly general, may be deontic, axiological or a combination of the two. A person's morality is purely deontic if, and only if, it consists of one moral principle, namely an undominated practical attitude towards everybody's continued acceptance of a certain code of conduct, e.g., the decalogue. Schematically, a purely deontic morality can be represented by $S + [U + \mathcal{M}_0]$. To accept the code $\mathcal{M}_0$ is of course to accept all its regulations and all the obligations following from them. A code of conduct consists of rules of the form: 'If certain specified conditions are satisfied, then an action of a certain specified kind should be performed by one or more specified persons.' Its rules must be separately and jointly consistent, applicable in the actual world and practicable in it. The application of a code consists in the deduction from it of actions which *with respect to it* are obligatory, prohibited or permissible.[5] In a purely deontic morality, say, one governed by the code of conduct $\mathcal{M}_0$, an action is morally good or the object of a moral pro-attitude if, and only if, it is obligatory with respect to $\mathcal{M}_0$. Such a morality leaves no room for supererogatory actions, i.e., actions which are morally good but not obligatory.

[5] See *Experience and Conduct*, chapter 2.

A general morality is purely axiological if, and only if, all its moral principles are directed towards practicabilities independently of any accepted code of conduct. Although such a morality does not contain code-dependent moral obligations, it may nevertheless contain (code-independent) moral obligations. Thus, for example, the moral obligation not to lie may be analysed in such a morality as a moral pro-attitude towards everybody's pro-attitude towards telling the truth together with a moral pro-attitude towards everybody's pro-attitude towards *requiring* of everybody that he tell the truth, schematically, $S + [U + f]$ and $S + [U + Req f]$. A purely axiological morality has room for supererogatory actions, i.e., actions which are morally good but are not morally required. An example could be drawn from a morality according to which it is morally good to live the life of a saint but according to which it is not morally good to require of everybody that he should live such a life.

Even if a person's morality is purely axiological, a code of conduct may play an important auxiliary rôle in it. This is particularly so in situations in which a person who has every intention to live by his moral principles does not know which of two incompatible actions he should perform and in which postponing a decision may cause greater harm than making the wrong decision. In this and other cases of intellectual rather than moral weakness, it may be preferable to make a decision by consulting a moral code – which can only approximate an axiological morality – than not to make any decision or to postpone it. If it then turns out that the performed action was not moral, it may yet be morally excusable by an axiological moral principle, e.g., the undominated practical pro-attitude towards everybody's excusing an immoral action provided that it is derived from a certain code of conduct and employed as a means of overcoming one's intellectual weakness in the described manner.

It seems useful to note the following analogy between organized systems of beliefs and organized systems of practical attitudes: just as a person's categorial framework, if any, comprises those of his epistemically supreme beliefs which express cognitively supreme principles, so a person's general morality, if any, comprises those of his practically supreme attitudes which express moral principles. But a person may also have epistemically supreme beliefs which are not principles, but ungeneralized concrete beliefs. And he may also have practically supreme attitudes which are not principles, but (circumstantially) ungeneralized, concrete moral attitudes.

CHAPTER 3

ON AESTHETIC ATTITUDES

Aesthetic attitudes may be pure or practical. Moreover, a possibility towards which an aesthetic attitude can be directed may be pure for one person and practical for another. This obvious distinction applies in particular to works of art – whether finished, unfinished or in the making. Any person's capacity for aesthetic criticism of possibilities outruns his capacity for aesthetic creation, i.e., the capacity to implement his critical judgment. In God, if he exists, the scope of his critical and the scope of his creative power coincide and extend over all logical possibilities. The nature of the analogy between God's relation to the world and an artist's relation to a work of his own art is a frequent theme of transcendent metaphysics. This is one reason for a preliminary examination of practical and pure aesthetic attitudes. Another is the ubiquitous rôle of the general concept of representation which relates not only works of art and other aesthetic objects to the aesthetic meaning which they represent, express or embody, but relates whatever may have meaning – such as a word, a sentence, a formal system, a life, life, history, existence – to the meaning which it has.

The aim of this chapter is to distinguish pure from practical attitudes and some kinds of pure attitudes from each other (1); to analyse the general concept of representation and some of its varieties (2), especially aesthetic representation (3); to exhibit the structure of aesthetic attitudes (4); and to contrast aesthetic criticism with aesthetic creation (5).

1 On pure attitudes and some of their kinds

A pure pro-attitude, anti-attitude or attitude of indifference of a person is directed towards what he believes to be one of a number of possibilities – whether or not he believes them to be realized, realizable or unrealizable. As has been remarked earlier, a person may have a pure attitude towards an apparent possibility which is in fact a logical impossibility – a case in point being a scientist's or mathematician's pro-attitude towards the existence of an apparently consistent theory which is in fact inconsistent. So long as such cases are not forgotten, one may for our present purpose assume that the impracticable possibilities which are the objects of pure pro-attitudes, anti-attitudes or attitudes of indifference are all logical possibilities. Similar remarks apply to impracticable possibilities arranged according to pure preferential orderings. (Whenever it will be necessary to indicate the difference between pure and practical attitude in a schematic fashion, the former will be surrounded by a circle, so that $\oplus$, $\ominus$, etc., will stand for pure and so that, as before, $+$, $-$, etc., will stand for practical attitudes.)

Assuming that just as practical attitudes are directed towards practicabilities so pure attitudes are directed towards logical possibilities, we may, after the fashion in which the corresponding relations between practical attitudes were defined, define the relations of pure (nonpractical) domination, opposition, discordance, implication and other relations between pure attitudes. An example of pure discordance would be a situation in which a person has a pure pro-attitude towards his being faced by a pornographic picture and pure anti-attitude towards this pro-attitude. The stratification of attitudes may be mixed in the sense that a pure attitude may be dominated by a practical or vice versa. Thus a person's pro-attitude towards his being faced by a pornographic picture may be dominated by a practical anti-attitude, which he realizes by attending suitable classes in art criticism.

A person's pure and practical attitudes are alike in being directed towards situations or happenings rather than towards the things which are constituents of them. This seems perhaps more obvious for practical attitudes than for pure ones. Yet when we say that we like a thing we express a pure pro-attitude towards its existence, i.e., a preference for a situation in which it exists over a situation in which it does not exist or a preference for a situation in which it possesses certain attributes over a situation in which it possesses different ones. Once this is recognized clearly, one may without fear of misunderstanding allow oneself to speak loosely of pure attitudes towards things.

The possible situations or happenings towards which a person's pure attitudes are directed differ in a variety of ways, of which some are worth mentioning here. Thus a person's pure attitude may be directed towards an actual situation or one which he believes to be merely possible. This is so because every actual situation is also possible, though not merely possible. Again, a person's pure attitude may be directed either towards a singular or a general possibility. It is directed towards a singular possibility if, and only if, he would consider any modification of its characteristics as replacing the object of the attitude, and, hence, of the attitude itself, by another. A general possibility is characterized by a conjunction of characteristics, which can be instantiated in more ways than one. It is sometimes difficult to distinguish a person's pure attitude towards a general possibility, e.g., the performance of a play or symphony, from his attitude towards a disjunction or class of mutually exclusive possibilities none of which he prefers to any other. The distinction is impossible for attitudes which are common borderline cases of the two kinds of attitude. To acknowledge the difficulty or impossibility when it occurs is, however, not to imply a need for overcoming it.

In order to understand aesthetic and other composite attitudes, it is important to distinguish between pure or practical attitudes directed towards self-contained possibilities and possibilities the realization of which fulfils a certain function in one of a number of possible ways. With regard to the latter, one may have a pure or practical attitude towards both, the possibility as such, as well as towards the manner in which it fulfils the function which it is meant to fulfil. An example would be one's attitudes towards a hospital as a building and as a building which is to serve as a hospital.

2 On representation and some of its kinds

The term "representation" is often used in a narrow sense as meaning or, at least, as necessarily involving imitation. Using the term in this sense, art critics and others speak of portraits and still-lives as representational in contrast to nonrepresentational works of art; and empiricist philosophers of ideas as copies or representations of impressions. Before defining and using the term "representation" in a much wider sense it may be worthwhile to anticipate and dispel any suspicion of artificiality by an example of a common, technical use of the term in a sense in which it neither means nor necessarily involves imitation. Such an example is legal representation, which, like some kinds of representation involving imitation, will also have to be covered by the general definition of the term. Legal representation clearly does not involve imitation since, for example, a lawyer may legally represent a child in court without imitating the child and since, on the other hand, the child may imitate the lawyer in court without legally representing him.

It is trivially obvious that every instance of a representation involves what may for the moment be called a *representandum*, i.e., something that is to be represented, a *representans*, i.e., something that represents the *representandum*, and the relation '*x* represents *y*' which holds between them. The following definition of the relation seems general enough to cover the wide variety of disparate cases and to enable one to make useful distinctions between them: x represents y if, and only if, in a certain more or less definite context x can be treated *as if* it were identical with y even if in fact x and y are different. It is worth emphasizing that identity, i.e., identifiability in all contexts, is a limiting case of identifiability in some contexts. What distinguishes various kinds of representation from each other is the context in which *representans* and *representandum* are identifiable. The context may be determined by more or less precise rules stating the conditions in which such identification can or should be made, by the purpose of the identification or by both. The following characterization and exemplification of various kinds of representation is not intended to be exhaustive, but merely to prepare a brief analysis of 'aesthetic meaning' – a notion which will be employed in the discussion of transcendent metaphysics.

An example of a very largely rule-determined representation is linguistic representation, i.e., the identification of inscriptions or utterances with linguistic meanings in accordance with the syntactical and semantic rules of a language. In formal languages the context of identifiability is almost exclusively determined by these rules, whereas in natural languages pragmatic considerations play a much more important rôle in its determination. Another example of a largely rule-determined representation is, as has been noted before, the legal representation of a person by a legal representative, whose actions in certain contexts can, or must be, treated *as if* they were the actions of the person represented by him. The rôle played by rules and purposes in determining the context of identification varies from one legal system to another – the rôle of rules being naturally more important in systems with codified laws than in systems based on precedent and custom.

A kind of representation which is largely determined by explicitly or, at least, implicitly accepted purposes is imitative representation, e.g., when for the purpose of describing a person his facial features are identified with the facial features on his passport photograph. From imitative representation one must distinguish idealizing representation which allows or requires that in certain contexts, determined by one or more of a variety of purposes, a certain relatively complex entity be treated *as if* it were a relatively simple entity. A crude example is the representation of men or women by simple schematic drawings on cloakroom doors. Examples of great sophistication and subtlety are found in applied mathematics, when mathematical concepts and statements are identified with empirical ones; in science, when theoretical structures of a nonmathematical or not purely mathematical kind are identified with mathematical ones; and in practical thinking, when, e.g., a complex axiological morality is treated as if it were a simple deontic system or code of conduct.[1]

The last kind of representation to be considered may be called "evocative expression". Because of its special relevance to the present inquiry it will be described in what might seem an unnecessarily cumbersome way: the *representans* of evocative expression is a person's conduct or a product of his conduct (e.g., a gesture or a letter) which evokes a feeling in some other person (e.g., a feeling of joy, despair, hope, anxiety about some more or less precisely specified possibility). The *representandum* is a feeling which the conduct or product constituting the *representans* is intended to evoke and may evoke more or less imperfectly. The context of evocative representation, in which the evoked feeling is treated *as if* it were the feeling whose evocation was intended, is determined by a more or less clearly accepted purpose (e.g., attending a play, engaging in correspondence). As here characterized, evocative expression need not be self-expression (e.g., in the case of an actor making a gesture of despair or of somebody writing an insincere letter). It is self-expression if, and only if, the person who by his conduct or product intends to evoke a feeling in another person possesses this feeling himself. Evocative expression has some similarities with linguistic representation. It differs from it in that it conveys feelings rather than linguistic meanings and that its context of identifiability is determined more by purposes than by rules.

3 On aesthetic representation

Aesthetic expression, whether or not it ranks as art, is always and preponderantly evocative expression and, in so far as it is sincere, evocative self-expression. Conveying the linguistic information that one has a certain feeling may sometimes evoke a similar feeling. Yet the bare informative content of a statement must be distinguished from those of its noninformative features which may be more or less effective in evoking a feeling. The informative content of Shakespeare's sixty-sixth sonnet is that he was – like many other people before and after him – tired of life because of various injustices. The same informative content could be conveyed in different English sentences or sentences of some other language and might evoke feelings which are similar to those expressed in the sonnet. Yet it is the sonnet as a whole which evokes a highly specific feeling rather than the general kind of feelings which would be indifferently evoked by the bare

---

[1] For a discussion of mathematical and scientific idealization see *Experience and Theory*, (London, 1966) chapters 7–11; for a discussion of practical idealization see *Experience and Conduct*, chapter 15.

information that Shakespeare for such and such reasons felt tired of life. In other words, although there is some correspondence between bare information and a class of feelings which differ in kind and intensity from each other and can be evoked by the information, a person who tries to express a unique or highly specific feeling cannot do so by means of an informative statement which is arbitrarily selected from a class of statements with the same informative content. The art of evocative self-expression and the skill of conveying information are quite different.

Again, although aesthetic expression may be combined with imitative or idealizing representation, it differs from bare imitation or idealization. Thus the features of a portrait may imitatively or idealizingly represent the features of a person and, thereby, evoke some feeling in a person contemplating the portrait. Yet the element of self-expression which distinguishes a painting from a merely imitative representation demands a special evocative skill which goes beyond mere imitation or idealization. Similar remarks apply to the ballet, which, unlike, say, the usual ballroom dancing, is preponderantly self-expressive, or to musical self-expression, which, unlike, say, a military bugle signal, is preponderantly expressive of the composer's feelings.

The *representans* of aesthetic expression, or, as it will henceforth be called, the "aesthetic object", is thus a person's conduct or product in so far as it evokes a certain feeling. The *representandum*, or, as it will henceforth be called, the "aesthetic meaning", is the feeling which the aesthetic object is intended or meant to evoke. The aesthetic object represents or expresses aesthetic meaning for a person who treats the feeling evoked *as if* it were the feeling whose evocation was intended. The limits within which a person who makes this *as-if* identification can be regarded as having grasped *the* aesthetic meaning of the aesthetic object cannot be stated exactly. To require the full identity of evoked and intended feeling would clearly be to ask too much. At the other extreme, a feeling which is quite accidentally evoked by a person's conduct or product or which is evoked by what merely seems to be his conduct or product would clearly not be an aesthetic meaning expressed by an aesthetic object.

The feeling which is evoked by an aesthetic object and the feeling which is its aesthetic meaning may be more or less rich in content and more or less complex in structure. This is obvious if one notes that there is no sharp borderline between aesthetic objects which are and aesthetic objects which are not works of art; and if one remembers that works of art may express an unlimited variety of feelings. In attempting to characterize this variety one often says that the feelings may range from the superficial to the profound, from affecting some fairly unimportant aspect of one's life to affecting one's whole being, or one uses other metaphors, i.e., a mode of expression which, like all representation, depends on an *as-if* identification of different entities.

Because the term "feeling" or other terms one might use in its place, e.g., "emotion", "passion" or "state of mind", are used in many senses, some of which are quite incompatible with the sense intended here and because no other more suitable term seems to be available, it is necessary to characterize the feelings in point more specifically. This can be done by qualifying them as grounded, concrete and complete and by explaining these qualifications as follows: they are grounded in other conscious states of mind, such as being aware of something, assuming something, believing something, having a practical attitude towards something, and not groundless as, for example, a depression or euphoria which lacks any conscious foundation for its occurrence. They are concrete in that, like Othello's jealousy of Desdemona or like the feelings of a person attending a performance of Shakespeare's *Othello*, they are grounded in specific states of mind, and not abstract in the sense of being related to a merely general characterization of certain kinds of states of mind, for example, of general beliefs of the sort which generally or normally give rise to jealousy. Last, they are complete in the sense of including their grounds as essential components, i.e., in such a manner that a change in the grounds would amount to a change in the feelings. Thus Othello's jealousy would be a different feeling of jealousy if he had not believed that Cassio was his faithful lieutenant; and a spectator's feelings watching a correspondingly modified play would also be different from his feelings in watching the original one.

The feelings which are evoked or meant may be more or less "intellectual", depending on the states of mind in which they are essentially grounded. Thus the feeling evoked and meant by a piece of music may be grounded solely in one's awareness of the sequence and structure of its sounds and not in one's considering any possibilities or having any beliefs. The feeling evoked and meant by a painting may be grounded not only in one's awareness of its visual features but also in, for example, one's belief that the picture is a picture of something. Last, the feeling evoked and meant by a poem is normally and obviously grounded in something that is said in it and thus capable of being considered as true or false or at least as logically possible. Yet even those feelings which are most clearly grounded in the consideration of possibilities or beliefs are nevertheless still feelings.

4 On aesthetic attitudes

The term "aesthetic attitude" is here used in the narrow sense in which such an attitude is directed towards objects *meant* to represent or express something and not to aspects of nature such as mountains or sunrises. Aesthetic representation (like linguistic representation and, more generally, any human deed) has an internal aspect from the doer's point of view and an external aspect from that of the outside observer. As in the case of other deeds the agreement between the internal and external aspects of aesthetic representation depends on the doer's making use of his experiences as a mere observer, the observer's making use of his experiences as a doer and of both being aware of their own and each other's natural and traditional surroundings. Any full inquiry into aesthetic representation would have to examine in some detail the rôle played by these surroundings in the doer's and the observer's attempts at understanding each other. For what follows, however, the problem of agreement between the internal and the external aspects of aesthetic representation need not be considered further.

Because of the composite character of aesthetic representation – involving an aesthetic object in so far as it evokes a certain feeling, an aesthetic meaning, i.e., the grounded, concrete and complete feeling which is meant to be evoked, and an *as-if* identification of the evoked and the meant feeling – aesthetic attitudes are also compound. For such attitudes, whether practical or pure, are directed towards the aesthetic object, the aesthetic meaning and the representation or expression of the aesthetic meaning by the aesthetic object. In order to see this more clearly it will be helpful to make use of some schematic notation. Let us write

$$a \; Rep - P \; m \qquad\qquad (1)$$

for 'the aesthetic object a represents the aesthetic meaning m for the purpose or within the context P'. In doing so we assume that the purpose or context of the *as-if* identification of evoked and intended feeling are clear to both the originator and the observer and that in general the agreement between the internal and the external aspect of the representation is close enough for any differences between them to be negligible.

A person S may have a pure or practical attitude towards this representation. Considering only pure attitudes, we may indicate his attitude towards the aesthetic representation as a whole by

$$S \; \circledast \; [a \; Rep - P \; m] \qquad\qquad (2a)$$

He may have – and, in the cases which interest us here, usually does have – also a pro-attitude, an anti-attitude or an attitude of indifference towards a in so far as it evokes a certain feeling and towards m, which he takes to be the meant feeling. And he may even put a and m respectively into a preferential ordering involving other realized, realizable or unrealizable possibilities. Neglecting preferential orderings, we have

$$S \circledast a \qquad\qquad (2b)$$

and

$$S \circledast m \qquad\qquad (2c)$$

The attitudes which S has towards a and m may or may not be relevant to the attitude which S has towards a $Rep - P$ m, i.e., to the representation as a whole. They are relevant to his attitude if, and only if, a change in them, e.g., a change from $S \oplus a$ to $S \oplus a$, would involve a change in his attitude towards the representation as a whole, e.g., from $S \ominus [a$ $Rep - P$ $m]$ to $S \oplus [a$ $Rep - P$ $m]$ (or a change in the preferential ordering of possible representations of m by a or some other aesthetic objects). In a similar manner some features of a and m may be relevant to $S \circledast a$ or $S \circledast m$ and, thus, indirectly to $S \circledast [a$ $Rep - P$ $m]$.

Consider, for example, Rodin's statue of the thinker, which evokes and is meant to represent a certain feeling grounded in a complex combination of the awareness of a material object, of beliefs and practical attitudes. Its being a marble statue and not a statue made of iron is an aesthetically relevant feature for any person whose attitude towards the representation by the statue of its aesthetic meaning would be different if the statue were made of iron rather than of marble. For any person whose attitude towards the representation would be unchanged by replacing the marble statue by an otherwise exactly similar iron statue, its being a marble statue would be an aesthetically irrelevant feature. The test of the aesthetic relevance of a feature thus consists in an imagined or real substitution of this feature by another and in determining its effect on the aesthetic attitude towards the representation.

The aesthetically relevant features of the aesthetic object may exclude the possibility of its being reproduced, as is the case with some paintings, or may allow the possibility of reproduction, as is the case with literary works. The totality of those features of an aesthetic object which are aesthetically relevant to a person determine his aesthetic attitude to the representation by it of what he takes to be its aesthetic meaning. In other words, no single relevant feature or combination of relevant features can be changed without changing the person's aesthetic attitude, i.e., his pro-attitude, anti-attitude or attitude of indifference toward the representation or the place which this representation occupies in his preferential ordering of it in comparison with other possible representations of the same aesthetic meaning by different aesthetic objects.

5 On aesthetic criticism and creation in the arts

Whereas every artist is *ipso facto* a critic of his own work, an art critic may not have the capacity of putting his criticism into practice. In order to understand the nature of such pure criticism it is necessary to recall the distinction between pure and practical attitudes and between attitudes of different levels. Consider a person's pure attitude towards the representation of an aesthetic meaning by an aesthetic object, schematically,

$$S \circledast [a \ Rep - P \ m] \tag{3a}.$$

As in the case of practical attitudes, he may also have a second-level attitude towards the first-level attitude, schematically,

$$S \circledast [S \circledast (a \ Rep - P \ m)] \tag{3b}.$$

Neither the first-level nor the second-level attitude is a critical attitude in the sense in which an art critic – whether or not he be a professional – claims universal acceptance or validity. But the second-level attitude is – as in the case of practical attitudes – capable of universalization. In other words, a person may have a second-level pure attitude towards everybody's having a pure first-level attitude, schematically,

$$S \circledast [U \circledast (a \ Rep - P \ m)] \tag{3c}.$$

Again, as in the case of practical attitudes, the higher and personally universal attitude may or may not be dominated. In the latter case it will be called a "supreme critical attitude". An example of a higher-level aesthetic attitude which is personally universal but *not supreme* would be a person's pro-attitude towards everybody's having a pro-attitude towards a certain pornographic picture or political pamphlet, if the second-level attitude were itself dominated by an anti-attitude towards certain kinds of commercial exploitation or political manipulation.

  If a person's first-level attitude towards the representation of an aesthetic meaning by an aesthetic object or his preferential ranking of this representation in comparison with other representations of the same aesthetic meaning by other aesthetic objects is, as has been noted, of great complexity, then a person's supreme aesthetic attitude or ranking is still much more complex. For this attitude or ranking involves in addition the claim to speak for all human beings and, hence, a conception of them in their separateness and interrelation. While the schematic indication of these first- and higher-level attitudes clearly emphasizes the often-neglected rôle played by stratification and personal, as opposed to circumstantial, universalization, it obviously is neither intended to express, nor capable of expressing, the complex, rich and specific content of aesthetic – especially of supreme critical – attitudes.

The artist differs from the pure critic in *at least* the following three respects. He is, first of all, capable of grasping aesthetic meanings, i.e., grounded, concrete and complete feelings, independently of the fully realized aesthetic objects representing them. Second, he is capable of creating aesthetic objects which represent their aesthetic meanings and which in doing so conform more or less perfectly to his supreme critical attitudes. Last, he is capable of experiencing an interaction between aesthetic object and aesthetic meaning and to adjust them to each other in the light of a sense of proportion which demands *ad hoc* decisions and their *ad hoc* implementations. This aesthetic equity, as it might be called by analogy to legal and moral equity, is a most elusive and most important feature of artistic creation. It seems to reveal itself more readily in even the most amateurish attempt at writing a poem or creating a work of art of another kind than in the serious contemplation of works of art which have been created by others.

The little that has been and, for the purpose of this inquiry, had to be said about aesthetic criticism and creation in the arts implies at least a partial answer to the problem of the relation between art and morality. It follows mainly from comparing the form of a person's moral attitudes, namely,

$$S * [U * f],$$

with the form of his supreme critical attitudes, namely,

$$S \circledast [U \circledast (a \ Rep - P \ m)].$$

For if, as seems reasonable, we assume that all human beings (all members of the class U) to some extent are, or might become, artists and thus capable of turning their critical into practical attitudes, then some of any person's supreme critical attitudes coincide with some of his moral attitudes. In this sense "any true or genuine work of art" (any representation which is the object of a person's supreme critical attitude) is never immoral but is "either moral or else morally neutral" (*either* a deed which is dominated by a sequence of the person's practical attitudes, of which the first member is directed towards the deed itself, of which every subsequent member is directed towards the practical attitude preceding it in the sequence, and of which the penultimate practical attitude is personally universal, *or else* a deed which is not so dominated).

IMMANENT AND TRANSCENDENT PHILOSOPHY

The purpose of the preceding analyses was to draw attention to the way in which, as a matter of anthropological fact, a person's beliefs, his practical and his pure attitudes are organized. To say correctly that the manner of this organization leaves room for a great variety of internally consistent, but mutually inconsistent, systems of beliefs and attitudes is to emphasize the plurality of these systems and the relativity of beliefs and attitudes with respect to them. To say with equal correctness that the common manner in which beliefs and attitudes are organized by different persons or groups of persons limits the variety of these internally consistent, but mutually inconsistent, systems is to emphasize the limits of cognitive and evaluative pluralism and relativity. It is one of the aims of this essay to strike the proper balance between cognitive and evaluative pluralism on the one hand and cognitive and evaluative absolutism on the other.

The main purpose of this chapter is to show that, and how, the need to strike such a balance gives rise to, among other things, the distinction between immanent and transcendent philosophy. The chapter begins by indicating the manner in which a person's supreme cognitive and practical principles and, hence, his categorial framework and general morality function as standards of what is cognitively and practically rational (1). There follows a discussion of the relative character of cognitive and practical rationality and of the limits of this relativity (2). The chapter ends with a preliminary distinction between immanent and transcendent philosophy (3).

1 On cognitive and practical rationality

The supreme cognitive principles, which together constitute a person's categorial framework, are, as has been argued (chapter 1), cognitively supreme, intersubjective, personally universal and circumstantially general. Since the principle of the conservation of substance is widely –

though by no means generally – accepted, it may serve as an example. For the person for whom it is a supreme cognitive principle, it is necessary in the sense of belonging to the class of his supreme beliefs. It is intersubjective in the sense that in asserting the principle the person is applying an intersubjectivity-concept (i.e., the concept 'x is a substance', the applicability of which logically implies 'x is intersubjective'). The principle is personally universal in, at least, the weak sense in which the person accepting it regards it and the set of supreme principles to which it belongs as acceptable not only by himself but by everybody. The principle is circumstantially general in the sense of being applicable to a kind of case and not to either a singular case or even a strictly singular case (which cannot be characterized by a finite conjunction of general attributes).

In a similar manner a person's supreme practical principles or moral principles, which constitute his general morality, are, as has been argued (chapter 2), practically supreme, intersubjective, personally universal and circumstantially general. Since the moral principle of keeping one's promises in all circumstances is widely – though not generally – accepted, it may serve as an example. For the person for whom it is a moral principle, it is practically necessary in the sense of belonging to the class of his supreme practical attitudes. It is Intersubjective in the sense that in applying the principle one is applying it to intersubjective practicabilities, i.e., to practicabilities to which an intersubjectivity-concept is applicable. It is personally universal in the strong sense of being a pro-attitude towards everybody's having a pro-attitude towards keeping a promise. And it is circumstantially general in the sense that the first-level attitude involved is directed towards a kind of practicability rather than a singular or a strictly singular one.

Cognitive or practical necessity, intersubjectivity, personal universality and circumstantial generality are necessary conditions which a person's supreme cognitive principles and, thus, his categorial framework and a person's supreme practical principles and, thus, his general morality have to fulfil. What distinguishes his categorial framework or morality from any other is that he accepts it as true, correct or adequate. Accepting a principle as true is, of course, not to make it true. Nor does any definition of truth by itself provide a criterion of truth. Yet even if no criterion should be, or become, available by means of which one could decide between sets of internally consistent and mutually inconsistent sets of supreme cognitive or practical principles, it does not follow that a decision between them is beyond the reach of arguments. A discussion of the notion of accepting a categorial framework and of metaphysical arguments must be postponed until the nature of their subject matter has been discussed in more detail (see chapter 10, section 1, and chapter 15).

In the meantime it is important to distinguish between three different types of question which are all too often conflated – namely, first, 'What is *a* system of supreme (cognitive or practical) principles?'; second, 'What is *my* system of supreme principles?'; and third, 'What, if any, is *the true* system of supreme principles?' A partial answer to the first question has been given by some of the preceding analyses, resulting in the definition of *a* categorial framework and *a* general morality. It enables one to exhibit the general function of these systems in a person's factual and practical thinking independently of its specific content.

The principles which determine a person's conception of logical consistency, i.e., the principles of his logic, and the cognitively supreme principles which determine his categorial framework, including his logic, are his standards of cognitive rationality. If one expresses the conjunction of his logical principles by L and the conjunction of his cognitively supreme principles by F – whatever the precise demarcation of L within F may be – then a person's conception of what is logically irrational (irrational with respect to L, briefly, $\neg \Diamond_L$) and his conception of what is cognitively irrational (irrational with respect to F, briefly, $\neg \Diamond_F$) can be characterized as follows:

$$(1) \quad \neg \Diamond_L f =_{Df} \neg \Diamond_L (L \wedge f)$$

$$(2) \quad \neg \Diamond_F f =_{Df} \neg \Diamond_L (F \wedge f).$$

In words, a proposition f is logically irrational (logically impossible) if, and only if, the conjunction consisting of f and L is by the principles of L logically inconsistent. And f is cognitively irrational if, and only if, the conjunction consisting of F and f is by the principles of L logically inconsistent.

The principles which determine a person's conception of practical inconsistency and the moral principles, if any, which determine his general morality are his standards of practical rationality. If one expresses the person's conception of practical inconsistency – i.e., of opposition, discordance or incongruity – by $\neg \Diamond$ (more precisely by $\neg \Diamond_L$, since opposition and incongruity depend on logical inconsistency) and the conjunction of his moral principles (as opposed to singular moral attitudes) by Φ, then a person's conception of what is practically irrational and his conception of what is morally irrational or irrational with respect to Φ, briefly, $\neg \Diamond_\Phi$, can be characterized as follows:

(3) $\neg \Diamond a \overset{=}{Df} a$ is a conjunction of at least two practical attitudes, a_1 and a_2 and $\neg \Diamond (a_1 \wedge a_2)$; and

(4) $\neg \Diamond_\Phi a \overset{=}{Df} \neg \Diamond (\Phi \wedge a)$.

Thus a person's practical attitude is practically irrational if, and only if, it is composed of at least two practical attitudes which are practically inconsistent with one other. And it is morally irrational if, and only if, it is inconsistent with one of his moral principles, i.e., not merely with a moral attitude which lacks circumstantial generality.

In terms of the various notions of irrationality ($\neg \Diamond_L f$, $\neg \Diamond_\Phi a$, etc.), other notions can be defined. In doing so it is important to distinguish rationality in the sense of nonirrationality ($\Diamond_L f$, $\Diamond_\Phi a$, etc.) from rationality in the strong sense of rational necessity ($\neg \Diamond_L \neg f$, $\neg \Diamond_\Phi \neg a$, etc.). There is no need to go into further details, except for recalling (see chapter 2, section 3) that $\neg a$, or the 'negation of the practical attitude a', does not merely mean the absence of a (e.g., the absence of a practical pro-attitude towards a certain practicability), but the disjunction of the practical attitudes to which it is opposed (the presence of either a practical anti-attitude or of the practical attitude of indifference towards the practicability).

Two further comments may help to avoid misunderstandings. First, just as a person may be more or less clearly aware of the logical irrationality of a proposition without being aware of the principles which are the grounds of this irrationality, so he may be more or less clearly aware of the cognitive irrationality of a proposition and the practical or moral irrationality of a practical attitude without being aware of the principles on the violation of which these kinds of irrationality are based. Second, all the types of irrationality considered are "circular" or relative (to L, F, Φ) in the sense that the principles determining them are supreme and thus themselves not subject to higher principles by which their rationality is tested. This relativity is not a shortcoming of the definitions since one of their main points is to exhibit it clearly.

2 On the relative character of cognitive and practical rationality and on the limits of this relativity

In accepting a cognitive principle – such as the principle of the conservation of substance or a principle inconsistent with it – a person accepts a test of rationality towards whose universal acceptance he at least has no practical anti-attitude. In accepting a practical principle – such as Bentham's principle of utilitarianism or a principle inconsistent with it – a person accepts a test of rationality towards whose universal acceptance he has an undominated pro-attitude. Yet there are cognitive principles, and, hence, categorial frameworks, and practical principles, and, hence, general moralities, which *as a matter of empirical fact* are not universally accepted so that what is cognitively or practically rational for one person (i.e., rational with respect to his categorial framework or general morality) may not be so for another person.

The empirical thesis of a plurality of categorial frameworks and general moralities is supported by a study of the intellectual and social history of mankind, as well as by attempts at understanding one's own and one's contemporaries' conceptions of rationality. It is compatible with the admission of mistakes about one's own or other people's acceptance or rejection of certain supreme cognitive or practical principles. In this connection it seems appropriate to mention the important phenomenon of metaphysical or moral wavering, which is characteristic of periods of fundamental intellectual or social change, and consists in a person's inability to decide between the acceptance or rejection of one or more supreme cognitive or practical principles. Such wavering between categorial frameworks or general moralities is analogous to the wavering between obsolescent and newly emerging scientific beliefs, legal rules and to similar oscillations which occur within a categorial framework or a general morality.

To acknowledge a plurality of categorial frameworks and of general moralities is to acknowledge that the concepts of cognitive and practical rationality are relative. To draw attention to features of these systems which limit their possible differences is to exhibit the limitations of this relativity. Although some of these limitations have already been outlined and will together with others receive more detailed attention later, it seems appropriate and important to list the respects in which the relative character of cognitive and practical rationality – like every other kind of relativity – is relative to something which is not in the same sense relative.

One feature which is common to all categorial frameworks and general moralities is their structure, resulting, as has been shown (in chapters 2 and 3), from the logical organization of beliefs, which is to protect them against logical inconsistency; from the logical organization of practical attitudes, which is to protect them against practical opposition; from the interpretative stratification of beliefs; from the epistemic stratification of beliefs; and from the practical stratification of attitudes. A second feature which is common to all categorial frameworks and general moralities is the kind of material on which the common structure is imposed, namely, beliefs of various levels of epistemic and interpretative stratification and practical attitudes of various levels of practical stratification. In considering these levels it appears to be an empirical fact that the lower the levels, the greater the agreement between the different systems. To put it differently, whereas ascending levels of beliefs or practical attitudes involve a greater possibility of divergence between different categorial frameworks and general moralities, descending levels suggest a convergence to the same basic beliefs or practical attitudes.

A third feature which is common to all categorial frameworks and general moralities is the personal universality of their defining supreme principles, which, more than anything else, reveals their social basis and function. In assuming that an accepted supreme principle of cognitive or practical rationality is addressed *to every human being*, its acceptor makes certain assumptions about a common human nature of which he is aware in himself and which he finds in those with whom he has been in more or less direct contact and interaction. He assumes in particular that human beings can understand each other's beliefs and practical attitudes, even if they do not share them all, and that this mutual understanding extends also to the principles of rationality. That there is such an understanding – whatever its proper analysis (see chapter 9, section 2) – is a social fact which limits the plurality of categorial frameworks and general moralities to such as are accessible to each other.

The possibility of understanding an alien categorial framework or general morality is a precondition of a fourth feature which may limit the actual variety of such systems. This is the frequently realized possibility of arguments which may lead to the abandonment of one system in favour of another or at least to some assimilation between them (see chapter 15). Last, there are many agreements in the content of different categorial frameworks and general moralities, the discovery and explanation of which is a task for anthropology.

3 On immanent and transcendent philosophy

The term "immanent philosophy" is here, in accordance with traditional terminology, understood as referring to inquiries into the supreme principles governing one's own and other people's beliefs about the world of intersubjectively interpreted experience, as well as one's own or other people's attitudes towards this world. These inquiries can proceed independently of any assumption about transcendent reality, i.e., reality as it exists independently of human experience and existence. The term "transcendent philosophy", on the other hand, refers to attempts at grasping the nature of this reality and at answering questions which cannot be answered without a grasp of it.

It is possible to be aware of a plurality of categorial frameworks and moralities without distinguishing between the world of intersubjective experience and transcendent reality and, hence, between immanent and transcendent philosophy. Yet when one considers the justifications, if any, given for accepting particular categorial frameworks and moralities in preference over others, a desire to compare them, if at all possible, with a reality transcending all of them is likely to arise. A strong reason for the emergence of this desire is a person's experience of an intellectual and moral change affecting his own supreme cognitive or practical principles. Examples are a change from the conviction that *natura non facit saltus* to the conviction that it makes *quantum jumps* or a change from a morality which demands that some people be the slaves of others to a morality which considers every kind of slavery immoral. A somewhat weaker reason is the study of historical documents which describe that, and how, such changes happened in the past, especially when they affected whole societies or large sections of them.

The characterization of immanent philosophy implies its tasks. These include in the first place the exhibition of the categorial framework and the general morality of the person or persons whose systems of beliefs and practical attitudes are being examined. It may, of course, be that a person's system of beliefs and practical attitudes is too indefinite to involve a definite categorial framework or general morality or that he is living through an intellectual or moral crisis which manifests itself in his wavering between two or more competing systems of supreme cognitive or moral principles. Again, it may happen and – if we can trust certain intuitionist moral philosophers describing their morality – often does happen that a person's supreme moral attitudes lack circumstantial generality, i.e., that his morality is not general. It is then the task of immanent philosophy to exhibit that this is the case.

Although supreme cognitive and practical principles dominate all beliefs and practical attitudes of a person or group of persons, different sets of these principles may become the special concern of certain theoretical or practical disciplines, e.g., logic, the natural sciences, the social sciences, jurisprudence, etc. Such a special concern of a certain discipline with a certain set of supreme principles may express itself within the discipline on the one hand by attempts at formulating the principles clearly and on the other by systematic appeals to them as standards of rationality. Thus the acceptance or rejection of the principle of excluded middle is a special concern of logic; the acceptance or rejection of the principle of continuity, a special concern of the natural sciences; the acceptance or rejection of the principle of Benthamian utilitarianism, a special concern of welfare economics; etc. And to the extent to which various special disciplines hold some of their principles to be supreme, immanent metaphysics is concerned with these disciplines.

Apart from the exhibition of a thinker's supreme cognitive and practical principles, immanent philosophy may also undertake the task of replacing some of the assumptions which it finds within the special disciplines and which by its standards are irrational by rational assumptions which retain the suitability of the replaced assumptions for their original purpose.[1] Another task of immanent metaphysics is the defence of the exhibited supreme principles against the principles defining competing categorial frameworks and general moralities.

It is the task of transcendent philosophy to exhibit or to propose a conception of reality which exists independently of a person's world of appearance. Transcendent reality need not – or need not only – contain a person's subjectively given particulars or his intersubjectivity-concepts whose application creates intersubjectively given situations and possibilities, especially practical possibilities for evaluation and action. And the adequacy of a conception of transcendent reality to a person need not be defined by a set of principles, as can the immanent rationality of his beliefs about his world of intersubjective experience. The statement that a person's conception of transcendent reality need not contain his subjectively given and intersubjectively interpreted particulars and the other features of the world of his intersubjective experience, especially his categorial framework or general morality, does not imply that transcendent reality bears no relation to that world. On the contrary, a person's conception of transcendent reality must make it more or less intelligible why his intersubjective experience is what it is. Thus, although a person's conception of transcendent reality transcends his intersubjective beliefs and practical attitudes and, hence, his supreme cognitive and practical principles, it must not be (logically or practically) inconsistent with them.

A philosopher who holds that his insight into transcendent reality *logically* implies the *logical* inconsistency of his or anybody's beliefs about the world of his intersubjective experience contradicts or deceives himself.

---

[1] For a more detailed discussion and comparison of exhibition and replacement analysis, see *Fundamental Questions of Philosophy* (London, 1969), chapter 2.

The same applies to a philosopher who holds on the one hand that a certain supreme cognitive or practical principle – such as the principle of continuity or the principle that promises ought never to be broken – is in the world of intersubjective experience valid without exception and on the other that a transcendent deity may legitimize such an exception. However, the demand that transcendent metaphysics should be consistent with the requirements of immanent – cognitive and practical – rationality does not prejudge the possibility of apprehending transcendent reality through mystical experience. For such experience, if it exists, is not expressible by judgments or practical attitudes and thus not subject to any principle of immanent rationality (see chapters 11 and 12).

The following chapters will not discuss all aspects of immanent and transcendent philosophy. They will on the whole be devoted to immanent and transcendent *metaphysics*, the topics of which are the structure of the intersubjective world and the nature of mind-independent reality, rather than the organization of our moral and other attitudes towards them.

PART II

ON IMMANENT AND
TRANSCENDENT METAPHYSICS

THE PRINCIPLES OF LOGIC
AS SUPREME COGNITIVE PRINCIPLES

The principles of logic are supreme cognitive principles which determine the internal consistency or inconsistency of any belief and – because logical implication is defined as inconsistency between its antecedent and the negation of its consequent – the validity or invalidity of any deductive inference. The principles of logic thus embody necessary conditions for the rationality of all beliefs – immanent as well as transcendent. The purpose of this chapter is to outline and to exemplify the structure and function of deductive logic by elaborating what has been said (in chapter 1) about the core of a person's logic and its possible extensions. The chapter begins with an examination of logical validity by distinguishing a logical principle from the empirical fact of its being accepted (1). It then considers some extensions of the logical core which result from various ways of dealing with neutral, indeterminate and undecidable statements (2) and gives examples of a logic admitting exact and inexact attributes (3), as well as of a constructivistic logic (4). It then considers the problem of infinite domains of particulars (5). The chapter ends with some brief remarks on logic and existence (6).

1 On the validity of the weak principle of noncontradiction and other logical principles

As has been emphasized (in chapter 1, section 2), there would be no point in differentiating between attributes and particulars without accepting the weak principle of noncontradiction. In order to understand the sense in which this principle is a valid principle of every logic, it will be useful to compare it with a principle which is valid in some logical systems only, e.g., the principle of excluded middle in systems of logic assuming nonfinite domains of individuals. In the case of such a principle one must distinguish between the *empirical* thesis that somebody has accepted the principle as a (partial) characterization of the consistency or inconsistency of beliefs and, hence, of the validity or invalidity of deductive inferences, and the *logical* thesis which is this characterization itself. If the empirical thesis is true of a certain person, then he explicitly or implicitly accepts the logical thesis which is thus logically necessary for him. But the empirical thesis may be true of one person and not true of another so that a logical principle, such as the principle of excluded middle, may be logically necessary for one person, e.g., Frege, and not for another, e.g., Brouwer.

The weak principle of noncontradiction differs from the principle of excluded middle in being implicit in the very differentiation of experience into particulars and attributes and thus in all thinking within any categorial framework. However, its being accepted by all thinkers whose thinking involves the application of attributes to particulars does not make its acceptance by them any less empirical. For that all normal human beings think in this manner is itself an empirical fact about human beings, as opposed, for example, to butterflies or, perhaps, to some posthuman species of the future whose members will apprehend the world quite differently. The weak principle of noncontradiction and the principle of excluded middle are thus logically necessary for everybody who as a matter of empirical fact accepts them, in the case of the former principle all normal human beings, in the case of the latter only some of them.

The important difference between logically necessary statements and empirical statements about them is merely one example of the different relations between statements and metastatements, which may or may not share their logical status. Just as the metastatements considered are examples of empirical statements about logically necessary statements, so it is easy to think of examples of empirical statements about empirical statements (e.g., that a certain empirical statement has been found interesting by somebody); of logically necessary statements about empirical ones (e.g., that a certain empirical statement has certain logical consequences) and of logically necessary statements about logically necessary statements (e.g., that a certain logically necessary statement logically implies another such statement).

2 Truth-values, neutrality and indeterminacy

If – as the weak principle of noncontradiction guarantees for some attributes and some particulars – a certain attribute is correctly applied but not correctly refusable to a certain particular (or ordered set of particulars), the resulting statement is true. But the principle allows for the possibility of four kinds of (atomic) statements, namely, (i) true statements, i.e., statements in which a certain attribute is correctly applied and not correctly refusable to a particular; (ii) false or, more generally, untrue statements, with a truth-value other than truth, in which an attribute is correctly refused and not correctly applicable to a particular; (iii) neutral statements, in which an attribute, whether applied or refused to a particular, is both correctly applicable and correctly refusable to it; (iv) indeterminate statements, in which an attribute, whether applied or refused to a particular, is both incorrectly applicable and incorrectly refusable to it. (The meaning of "accepting a proposition as true" will be discussed in chapter 10, section 1.)

Of these four classes of statements the class of true and the class of untrue statements (statements with a truth-value other than truth) cannot be empty. This is so on the one hand because the weak principle of noncontradiction guarantees that there is at least one attribute P and one particular (or ordered set of particulars) o such that 'o has P' is true and on the other hand because, if $\bar{P}$ is defined as the attribute which is correctly refusable (applicable) to o just in case P is correctly applicable (refusable) to it, then there is at least one attribute, namely, $\bar{P}$, such that 'o has $\bar{P}$' is untrue.

With regard to the class of neutral and the class of indeterminate statements one may, by accepting further logical principles, enforce their emptiness. Thus the classical logic which underlies the classical theory of real numbers and, therefore, a large part of the natural sciences excludes by virtue of Frege's principle of exactness (see chapter 1, section 2) the possibility of neutral statements. Certain subsystems of this logic – e.g., the finite predicate logic of first order – exclude the possibility of indeterminate ones. However, a person who accepts either of these restrictions as logically necessary, not only for himself but also for everybody else, would have to justify this position – either by showing that, contrary to appearances, everybody's immanent logic implied the impossibility of neutral or in-determinate statements or else by adducing speculative considerations about the nature of transcendent reality in favour of a logic implying this impossibility.

The further determination of untrue statements, as distinguished from true, neutral and indeterminate ones, leads either to a two-valued logic in which every statement can have only two truth-values, i.e., truth or falsehood, or to an n-valued logic in which every statement has either the truth-value truth or one of n-1 truth-values other than truth. In what follows, we shall be concerned only with two-valued systems of logic since systems of more than two truth-values are rarely used and since what will be said about two-valued systems can without difficulty be extended to systems with more than two truth-values. In this connection it may be worth emphasizing that a logic which has only two (definite) truth-values but admits neutral statements, in the sense explained earlier, must not be confused with a (definite) three-valued logic, which may or may not admit of neutral statements with respect to two or all three of its truth-values. Many, if not all, perceptual attributes and some others are inexact in the sense that they admit of borderline cases. The inexactness of perceptual attributes is closely related to perceptual continuity or the continuous connectedness of inexact attributes with each other. For example, the attribute 'green' has such borderline cases and is in virtue of having common borderline cases with its complement 'nongreen' continuously connected with it (see chapter 6, section 4). The inexactness and continuous connectedness of perceptual attributes, i.e., attributes employed by (almost) all human beings, give rise to two tasks of immanent metaphysics.

The first is simply to exhibit the logical principles which govern the application of exact and inexact attributes, the consistency or inconsistency of the resulting exact and neutral statements and the validity or invalidity of deductive inferences involving these statements as premises and conclusions. The second task is to determine the relation between such a logic (of exactness and inexactness) and a logic which does not admit inexact attributes or neutral statements. It is, in other words, to determine whether, and if so in what sense, exact logic is fundamental or primary and inexact logic merely auxiliary or secondary; whether the converse is the case; or whether there can be both thinkers for whom exact logic is primary and inexact logic secondary and thinkers for whom inexact logic is primary and exact secondary. The question of primacy arises whenever the possibility of more than one logic is admitted.

3 On a simple example of a logic admitting exact and inexact attributes

In order to characterize the structure of a logic admitting both exact and inexact attributes, it is useful to consider it as a *formal* extension of a logic admitting exact attributes only. This approach does not prejudge the problem of primacy since it is compatible with both the metaphysical thesis that the extension is merely provisional and the metaphysical thesis that it is ultimate and in no way reversible. A very simple, yet sufficiently clear, example of a simple "logic of exactness" which can be extended into a correspondingly simple "logic of inexactness" is finite predicate logic. (For more detailed discussions see *Experience and Theory*, chapter 3.) Finite predicate logic differs from predicate logic in assuming only a finite domain of individuals and – since in this logic a predicate is defined as a subclass of individuals or ordered

n-tuples of them – only a finite number of predicates. If the individuals are $a_1, a_2, \ldots, a_n$ and the predicates $f_1(x), f_2(x), \ldots, g_1(x, y), g_2(x, y), \ldots,$ $h_1(x, y, z), h_2(x, y, z)$, etc., then true or false atomic statements result from substituting individual constants in the place of the individual variables of the predicates – e.g., $f_3(a_4)$ or $h_3(a_1, a_5, a_6)$. Molecular statements are formed by means of the sentential connectives $\wedge$ (and), $\vee$ (or), $\neg$ (not), etc., in such a manner that the truth-value of a compound statement depends on the value of the components as defined (e.g.), by truth-tables. In finite predicate logic statements involving quantifiers are merely abbreviations of molecular statements – e.g., $(\forall x) f_1(x)$ (for all x, x is f) being an abbreviation of the conjunction $f_1(a_1) \wedge f_1(a_2) \wedge \ldots \wedge f_1(a_n)$ and $(\exists x) f_1(x)$ (there is an x such that x is f) being an abbreviation of the disjunction $f_1(a_1) \vee f_1(a_2) \vee \ldots \vee f_1(a_n)$.

If only exact predicates and definite statements are admitted, then a negated statement, $\neg f$, is true if f is false and false if f is true; a conjunction $f_1 \wedge \ldots \wedge f_n$ is true if all conjuncts are true and false if at least one of them is false; a disjunction $f_1 \vee \ldots \vee f_n$ is false if all disjuncts are false, and true if at least one of them is true. The rules governing conjunction and negation or else disjunction and negation are sufficient to define every other truth-functional compound and, in view of the finiteness of the domain of individuals, also every compound involving quantified expressions. The extension of the finite logic of exactness, which has just been sketched, into the corresponding logic of inexactness follows from the nature of inexact predicates, borderline cases and neutral statements.

Calling the finite logic of exactness L_0 and its extension by admitting inexact predicates and neutral statements $L_0{}^*$, it is then clear that the rules for the formation of the compound expressions of $L_0{}^*$ must satisfy the following conditions: (i) for compound statements of $L_0{}^*$ whose atomic components are all exact the rules of composition are the same as those of L_0, (ii) a compound statement of $L_0{}^*$ containing neutral statements is (a) neutral if at least one assignment of the definite truth-values of truth or falsehood to the neutral components makes the compound statement true and if at least one such assignment makes it false, (b) true if every such assignment makes the compound statement true, (c) false if every such assignment makes the compound statement false.

The two conditions, which can be easily generalized to other extensions of a logic of exactness to a logic of inexactness, lead to the following rules of $L_0{}^*$: a negation $\neg f$ is true if f is false: false if f is true, and neutral if f is neutral; a conjunction $f_1 \wedge \ldots \wedge f_n$ is true if all conjuncts are true, false if at least one conjunct is false, and neutral in all other cases; a disjunction $f_1 \vee \ldots \vee f_n$ is true if at least one disjunct is true, false if all disjuncts are false, and neutral in all other cases. As in L_0 all other truth-functional compounds are definable in terms of conjunction or disjunction and of negation so that, e.g., the definiens of $f \to g$ in L_0 and in L_0* is $\neg f \vee g$.

The two conditions for the extension of L_0 into L_0* do not determine a unique definition of validity and deducibility in L_0*. The following definitions, among others, seem natural. A compound statement of L_0* is valid if, and only if, it is true and if every assignment of the definite truth-values to its atomic components yields a true statement. It seems correspondingly natural to define the deducibility of g from f as the validity of $f \to g$ or, which comes to the same, of $\neg f \vee g$. The extension of L_0 into L_0* is not only a simple, but also a characteristic, example of the way in which a logic of exactness can be extended to accommodate inexact attributes. This should become clear after some alternative logics of exactness have been considered.

4 On constructivistic logics

Among the possible relations between an attribute and a particular is the relation of indeterminacy, i.e., the case where a predicate is neither correctly applicable nor correctly refusable to a particular. An indeterminate statement thus differs from a neutral statement and a statement which has a definite truth-value, i.e., which, if one restricts oneself to two-valued logic, is true or false. In order to emphasize the difference between neutrality and indeterminacy, it is useful to note that although neither is compatible with the unrestricted principle of excluded middle, the grounds of this incompatibility differ in the two cases. If one has hitherto asserted that every statement is either (definitely) true or (definitely) false, then one must on admitting neutrality replace the principle of excluded middle by the principle that every statement is true, false or neutral. But in view of the nature of neutrality (the correctness of both the application and the refusal of an inexact attribute to a borderline case), one may permit the choice between regarding a neutral statement as true and regarding it as false. On the other hand, if one has hitherto asserted that every statement is either true or false, then one must on admitting indeterminacy replace the principle of excluded middle by the principle that every statement is true, false or indeterminate. Indeterminacy, unlike neutrality, excludes the possibility of choosing between truth or falsehood.

Indeterminacy must be distinguished from undecidability by an accepted decision procedure. If for some reason one rejects indeterminacy, but acknowledges undecidability, one may preserve the principle of excluded middle. For the distinction between true or false statements which are

decidable and true and false statements which are undecidable is compatible with the thesis that every statement is either true or false. If,
however, one rejects the notion of an undecidable true or false statement as
meaningless or otherwise illegitimate, then one identifies truth or falsehood
with decidability. The result, whatever its reason, is a constructivistic logic
– with its characteristic principles governing the determination of consistent or inconsistent beliefs and, hence, of valid or invalid inferences. The
general nature of constructivistic logic is easily indicated.

Briefly, two-valued constructivistic logic differs from a two-valued
classical logic by identifying truth or falsehood with decidable truth or
falsehood and, consequently, by rejecting the principle of excluded middle
for any class of statements which includes undecidable ones. If truth
coincides with decidable truth and falsehood with decidable falsehood and if
some statements are undecidable, then one must reject the principle that
every statement is either (decidably) true or (decidably) false and, hence, the
validity of the inference from a statement's not being (decidably) true to its
being (decidably) false or from a statement's not being (decidably) false to its
being (decidably) true. The rejection of the principle of excluded middle
implies, of course, the rejection of all those logical principles which alone or
jointly allow its being deduced. Thus, if one considers a formalization of the
finitist logic discussed in the preceding section, one arrives at a constructivistic variant of it by simply eliminating the principle of excluded
middle and its deductive equivalents.[1]

A strong motive for the adoption of a constructivistic logic is the rejection
of nonconstructive proofs by some mathematicians. If one, for example,
regards the assertion that there exists a number possessing a certain
attribute as meaningful only if such a number can actually be exhibited,
then the principle of excluded middle breaks down for any class of numbers
and any class of numerical attributes which allow for undecidable cases of
the applicability of an attribute to a number. There are other regions of
thinking, especially practical thinking, which suggest the adoption of a
constructivistic logic. The possibility of adopting such a logic for all or some
parts of mathematical or practical thinking does not mean that constructivistic logic is fundamental and nonconstructivistic logic auxiliary.
Not does it mean that the converse relation holds. At the moment, however,
we are not concerned with justifying the adoption of either alternative or
with analysing the nature of such a justification, but with explaining the
meaning of the alternatives.

Just as exact, finitist, nonconstructivistic logic can be extended into a
corresponding logic of inexactness, so can the exact constructivistic logic be

---

[1] For details see *The Philosophy of Mathematics* (London, 1960), chapter 6.

extended into a constructivistic logic admitting exact and inexact attributes and definite and neutral statements. In doing so, one would – as in the case of the former logic – have to satisfy the conditions for forming compound statements from exact and neutral atomic statements and to provide a corresponding definition of validity and deducibility.[2]

5 On nonfinite domains of particulars

As has been argued, a person's explicit or implicit way of dealing with the fact or appearance of neutral, indeterminate and undecidable statements and of corresponding features of attributes and particulars expresses features of his deductive logic, i.e., principles determining the consistency or the inconsistency of beliefs and, hence, the validity or invalidity of deductive inference. They may also serve as indications of his "transcendent logic", his conception of transcendent reality as revealed or obscured by his deductive logic. The same holds for a person's explicit or implicit way of dealing with the problem whether and, if so, in what sense there is an infinity of particulars; and with the problem whether and, if so, in what sense some attributes are irreducibly relational. Although these problems were considered already by Aristotle and after him by many others, their relevance to a person's deductive, as opposed to his transcendent, logic has become clear only after they became topics of the theory of sets and of mathematical logic (see chapter 11).

A discussion of various assumptions to the effect that a domain of individuals is not finite might conveniently start by recalling that in the finitistic subsystem of two-valued predicate logic, the existential and universal quantifiers are respectively mere abbreviative devices for the expression of disjunctions and conjunctions, so that this subsystem is a version of the two-valued propositional logic in which every statement is decidable in a finite number of steps. "In principle" it does not matter how large the finite domain is, although a finite domain may be so large that the number of deciding steps could not in practice be taken by any single human being or any group of human beings working together (with or without computers) until the end of human history. Some philosophers, e.g., Brentano, mean by "potential infinity" no more than the permission to assume that a finite domain may be as large as is needed for the purpose in hand.

Decidability – in fact and in principle – is lost if a domain of particulars is considered *actually* infinite, as is the totality of all integers or the (greater) totality of all real numbers, which is somehow supposed to be completely given. Without going into further detail, it is clear that if decidability is lost and if 'truth' and 'falsehood' respectively are identified with 'decidable truth' and 'decidable falsehood', then the principle of excluded middle has to be relinquished. In other words, the adoption or rejection by a person of actually infinite domains of individuals is relevant to the determination of the consistency of beliefs and the validity of deductive inferences. It is possible to adopt a concept of potential infinity which allows the assumption of infinitely proceeding sequences and which differs both from the assumption of arbitarily large and of actually infinite domains. Such a conception, as has been shown by Brouwer and his intuitionist school, still fits into a constructive logic. If, as these sketchy remarks must suffice to show, a person's conception of infinity affects his logic, it *ipso facto* affects all his thinking. Beyond this it will, of course, more specifically affect his mathematical thinking, as will be shown by means of some philosophically important examples (in chapter 6).

6 Logic and existence

The question of the relation between alternative logics and of the possible primacy of one of them over its alternatives, which first arose in considering the contrast between a finite logic admitting exact and inexact predicates and a finite logic admitting only exact predicates, becomes even more urgent when one considers various other logical systems resulting from explicit or implicit assumptions about (at least) apparently indeterminate and undecidable statements or infinite domains of individuals. If, for one reason or another, one accepts one of the logics considered as fundamental or primary, it is possible to understand the others either by interpreting them as subsystems of the primary logic or else as more or less useful fictitious extensions of the primary logic. This manner of understanding an unaccepted secondary logic is a special case of understanding an unaccepted categorial framework and will be examined as such (see chapter 9, section 2).

Since a person's primary logic constrains all his beliefs, it also constrains his beliefs about what exists. Thus, in so far as every such logic includes the weak principle of noncontradiction, every logic implies the existence of at least one particular. In other words, the weak principle of noncontradiction, the acceptance of which is implied by the differentiation of experience into particulars and attributes, implies in turn that the domain of particulars is not empty.

Again, since a person's primary logic determines the consistency or inconsistency of all his beliefs, it determines in part what does not exist and thus cannot belong to a maximal kind of his categorial framework. For an allegedly existing particular cannot exist if the belief that it exists is logically impossible or internally inconsistent. (This, of course, does not mean that an object which one cannot describe consistently therefore cannot exist. It only means that an inconsistently described object cannot exist as described.)

In this connection it may be worthwhile to consider the rôle of the existential quantifier $(\exists x)\ P(x)$, where the variable x ranges over particulars. In a finitist logic in which the quantifier merely serves the abbreviation of a disjunction, it makes no difference to a person's ontology, especially as the nonemptiness of the domain of particulars is guaranteed by the weak law of noncontradiction. In an infinitist logic its nonabbreviative use implies that the domain of particulars is not finite. If, following Lesniewski, one uses an existential quantifier $(\exists x)\ P(x)$, where the variable x ranges over names which may or may not designate existing particulars, then the introduction of this quantifier into a logic obviously does not increase its ontological implications. But it also does not decrease them.[3]

---

[3] See, for example, S. Lesniewski, "Grundzüge eines neuen Systems der Grundlagen der Mathematik", in *Fundamenta Mathematicae*, 14 (1929), 1–81.

CHAPTER 6

ON MATHEMATICAL THINKING
AS A POSSIBLE SOURCE OF
IMMANENT METAPHYSICS

Mathematical thinking is thinking about structures, i.e., sets of particulars standing in certain relations to each other. What distinguishes mathematical from nonmathematical structures is their abstractness and high degree of generality and idealization. An abstract structure consists of a set of particulars and a set of relations holding between them, such that the particulars are considered only in so far as they stand in these relations, that is to say, in abstraction from any other attributes which they may possess. If the set of particulars consists of entities – sentences, predicates, etc. – which may stand in *logical* relations to each other and if the set of relations consists of logical relations, then the abstract structure is a logical structure, which may be distinguished from mathematical structures in a narrower sense of the term.

The degree of generality and idealization of an abstract structure depends on its constitutive relations. Roughly speaking, a relation is general if it admits of specifications, i.e., divisions into species of decreasing membership. Thus 'x is more powerful than y' is less general than 'x is in some respect greater than y' which in turn is less general than 'x stands in a transitive relation to y.' Again, in so far as an ideal relation can be regarded as resulting from a sequence of steps removing it ever further from a perceivable relation, the relation resulting from a subsequence of modifying steps will be less idealized than the relation resulting from a sequence containing the subsequence.

Our characterization of mathematical structures could be sharpened in a number of ways – e.g., by requiring their definability in (some standard system of) set theory. This, however, is not necessary for our purpose, which is to exhibit metaphysical assumptions implicit in mathematical idealizations of perceptual phenomena and in the application of mathematics. The chapter begins with some remarks on what might be called the "empirical arithmetic of countable aggregates" (1). Next an indication is given how this empirical arithmetic is idealized into a pure arithmetic of natural numbers and integers (2) and, beyond, into a pure-mathematical theory of rational and real numbers (3). There follows a brief characterization of empirical continua (4); a discussion of the application of pure numerical mathematics to empirically discontinuous and empirically continuous phenomena; and some remarks on the application of mathematics in general (5). The chapter ends by drawing attention to pure and applied mathematics as possible sources of immanent metaphysics (6).

1 On the empirical arithmetic of countable aggregates

Whether or not Frege's analysis of the number-concept is sufficient as a foundation of (pure) arithmetic – an assumption which he himself rejected towards the end of his life – it clearly draws attention to what is involved in counting empirical objects. In order to do so, one must be able to identify the objects which are to be counted as particulars; to collect them into aggregates; to determine the equinumerousness or otherwise of different aggregates; and to produce or reproduce a fundamental sequence by reference to the subsequences of which the number of any empirical aggregate can be determined (as equinumerous with a particular subsequence). The mentioned empirical concepts of the identification and aggregation of particulars, of equinumerousness and of a fundamental sequence lack the precision and exactness of the corresponding Fregean notions.

Thus the identification of an empirical object need not be achieved by determining its membership in a class and by distinguishing it from the other members, if any, of this class by an attribute which it does not share with them. For an empirical particular may be successfully identified by being incorrectly classified – e.g., when the dog in the corner, which is to be counted as belonging to a given aggregate, is misclassified as a cat. Again, when collecting particulars into an aggregate for the purpose of counting, it is not necessary that the aggregate is a class, whose members are counted, a complex particular, whose parts are counted, or ambiguously either a class or a complex particular.

The determination of the equinumerousness or otherwise of two aggregates both of which are perceptually present is particularly easy. The same applies to counting the elements of a perceptually present aggregate by comparing it with a subsequence of a perceptually present fundamental sequence – e.g., an aggregate of horses which turn out to be three in number when matched with the corresponding subsequence of the fundamental sequence consisting of, say, the fingers on the two hands of a primitive tribesman, taken in an agreed succession. If this finite sequence is not sufficient for the counting of empirical objects, it can be either prolonged or stopped by calling the number of any aggregate which is larger than the fundamental sequence "larger than the last number", "many" or by another name which indicates an inability to count beyond a certain number, the lack of interest in doing so or both. Here one may without loss ignore this possibility and assume that a fundamental sequence excluding it always is – or can be made – available.

A fundamental empirical sequence is in an obvious manner ordered by the relation of succession: it contains a member which has no predecessor. It also contains a member which has no successor. Every other member has a unique predecessor and a unique successor. On the basis of this observation one can define the empirical number *one* as the number of the subsequence containing the predecessorless member and of any aggregate equinumerous with this subsequence; the empirical number *two* as the number of the subsequence containing the predecessorless member and its successor and of any aggregate equinumerous with this subsequence, etc., until one arrives at the successorless subsequence. The successor relation within the subsequences manifests itself also in their numbers, so that if two empirical numbers are the same, their predecessors and their successors (if any) are also the same. There is no need to show how 'addition', the relation 'less than' and 'multiplication' can be defined in our empirical arithmetic. Nor is it necessary to show that the resulting arithmetic will be affected with certain imprecisions and that, because of the inexactness of the empirical concepts used in developing it, the number-concepts admit borderline cases.

2 On the pure arithmetic of natural numbers and integers

The most important step by which pure arithmetic achieves the exactness of its concepts and operation, as well as the ability to overcome the limitations based on the finiteness of all empirical aggregates, is the replacement of an empirical by an ideal fundamental sequence. Of the various possible ones the sequence due to von Neumann is particularly well suited for our purpose, since it can transparently be constructed in a succession of steps such that if a step is taken the next step may, but need not, be taken. The construction is based on the concept of an exact class, including that of the empty class (e.g., as defined by the requirement that it contain all square circles), and the concept of one class including another.

In order to take the first step in constructing the von Neumann fundamental sequence one postulates (i) that the sequence has one and only one member which has no predecessor and at most one member which has no successor; (ii) that the empty class, briefly, Λ, is the predecessorless member; and (iii) that the successor of a member of the sequence is the class containing the preceding members as its elements. So far the sequence has the following form:

$$\Lambda, \{\Lambda\}, \{\Lambda\{\Lambda\}\}, \{\Lambda\{\Lambda\}\{\Lambda\{\Lambda\}\}\} \ldots \qquad (1)$$

where the dots indicate the continuation of the sequence up to the successorless member, if its existence is postulated, or the endless continuation, if its nonexistence is postulated. In the former case our fundamental sequence and the arithmetic based on it is finitist. Clearly a finite von Neumann sequence may be "larger" than any empirical aggregate (in a sense of the term which presupposes the applicability of pure finite arithmetic to empirical aggregates).

Once in possession of the arbitrarily large von Neumann sequence, one may define the corresponding natural numbers

$$0, 1, 2, 3, \ldots \qquad (2)$$

as respectively equinumerous with the members of the sequence in the order of their occurrence in it. A possible further step which is taken by almost all mathematicians is to postulate (iv) that no member of the fundamental sequence and, thus, no natural number is without successor, i.e., that the sequence of natural numbers is in some sense "endless" or "infinitely proceeding". In order to indicate the difference between the structure of finite or arbitrarily large sequences on the one hand and of endless progressions on the other, one might express the incompleteness of the former by "*etc*" and the incompleteness of the latter by "*ETC*". The question of the manner in which the sequence

$$0, 1, 2, 3, ETC \qquad (3)$$

is given is either not raised at all or (rightly) considered philosophical rather than mathematical. The so-called constructivists admit the infinitely proceeding sequence of natural numbers and other infinitely proceeding sequences into mathematics, while rejecting the assumption that the members of such a sequence can in any sense be given in their totality. They consequently have to reject the infinite totalities which are used by most mathematicians in the arithmetic of natural numbers, integers, fractions and – most importantly – real numbers.

The constructivists thus do not take the further idealizing step, which is taken by the majority of mathematicians in their conception of natural numbers either independently or *via* their conception of a fundamental sequence. This is to postulate (v) that there is available a set

$$\{0, 1, 2, 3, ETC\}, \tag{4}$$

i.e., to postulate "as given a set, *i.e.* a totality of things called natural numbers".[1] In accordance with a widely accepted terminology one might call the sequence

$$0, 1, 2, 3, ETC, \tag{3}$$

which satisfies the first four postulates, the "constructivist" sequence of natural numbers; and the totality

$$\{0, 1, 2, 3, ETC\}, \tag{4}$$

which in addition satisfies the fifth postulate, the "classical", the "non-constructivist" or "platonist" totality of natural numbers. The constructivist sequence serves as a foundation of constructivist, the classical totality as a foundation of classical arithmetic.

Just as empirical arithmetic, involving the empirical relation 'less than' and the empirical operations of addition and multiplication, is founded upon the availability of a fundamental, empirical sequence, so constructive and classical arithmetic are respectively founded on the fundamental constructivist sequence or on the totality of natural numbers. And since both of them are idealizations of empirical fundamental sequences, both of them are idealizations of empirical arithmetic. Classical arithmetic, though a more radical idealization of empirical arithmetic than constructive arithmetic, is nevertheless more familiar than the former.

The axioms of the classical arithmetic of natural numbers are found in textbooks on the foundations of mathematics and include axioms governing addition, multiplication, the ordering relation 'less than', as well as an axiom connecting addition and multiplication, namely $x(y+z) = xy + xz$, axioms connecting addition and ordering, e.g., $(x < y)$ *implies* $x + z < y + z$, and axioms connecting multiplication and ordering, e.g., if $z > 0$ *then* $x < y$ *implies that* $xz < yz$. In the pure arithmetic of natural numbers not every equation of form $x + n = m$ has a solution. In order to close this gap one must extend the totality of natural numbers into the totality of (positive and negative) integers and show that the properties which characterize the

---

[1] The quoted words form part of the first sentence of the first chapter of a book by E. Landau explaining the calculation with whole, rational, irrational and complex numbers. See *Grundlagen der Analysis* (Leipzig, 1930).

addition, multiplication and ordering of the natural numbers also characterize the integers. There is no need to show this here except to compare the domain of natural numbers with the domain of integers: while the series of integers

$$\{\ldots, -3, -2, -1, 0, 1, 2, 3, \ldots\} \tag{5}$$

obviously differs in structure from the sequence of natural numbers by having no first member, the two series are equinumerous, which can be seen, for example, by matching the odd natural numbers with the positive integers and the even natural numbers with the negative integers. Calling the cardinal number of the infinite totality of all natural numbers and of every equinumerous set $\aleph_0$ (aleph-zero), one may also say that the set of all integers is of the same size or has the same cardinal number as the set of all natural numbers. Just as constructivists reject any infinite totality, so some mathematicians reject any infinity greater than $\aleph_0$.

3 On the pure mathematics of rational and of real numbers

Neither the pure arithmetic of natural numbers nor the arithmetic of integers contains a solution for every equation of the form $x \cdot n = m$. In order to achieve this, it is necessary to extend the totality of natural numbers or the wider totality of integers into the totality of rational numbers or of positive and negative rational numbers and to show that the properties of addition, multiplication and ordering which are characteristic of the original system are also characteristic of the extended one. While there is again no need to show in detail how this programme is implemented, it will be useful for our philosophical purpose to compare the pure arithmetic of rational numbers with the pure arithmetic of integers in two respects – one in which they resemble each other and one in which they differ.

They resemble each other in that the cardinal number of the set of all integers and of the set of rational numbers is the same, namely, $\aleph_0$. It is sufficient to outline the well-known demonstration of this theorem for positive integers and positive rational numbers. All rational numbers can be represented by:

$$\frac{1}{1}, \quad \frac{1}{2}, \quad \frac{1}{3}, \quad \frac{1}{4}, \quad ETC$$

$$\frac{2}{1}, \quad \frac{2}{2}, \quad \frac{2}{3}, \quad \frac{2}{4}, \quad ETC$$

$$\frac{3}{1}, \quad \frac{3}{2}, \quad \frac{3}{3}, \quad \frac{3}{4}, \quad ETC$$

. . . .

where the denominator of each fraction indicates the row and its denumerator indicates the column in which it occurs. The fractions can then be matched with 1, 2, 3, *ETC*, if taken in the order 1/1, 1/2, 2/1, 1/3, 2/2, 3/1, *ETC*, i.e., by starting with the first member of the first row, taking the second member and going down the diagonal (1/2 to 2/1), then taking the third member and going down the diagonal (from 1/3 to 3/1) . . . taking the nth member and going down the diagonal (from $1/n$ to $n/1$), *ETC*. Since this sequence of cardinal number $\aleph_0$ contains fractions expressing the same rational (e.g., 1/1, 2/2, 3/3, . . .), the superfluous fractions can be eliminated without, of course, reducing the cardinal number $\aleph_0$ of the sequence.

The pure arithmetic of integers and the pure mathematical theory of rational numbers differ radically in that the totality of all rational numbers is dense, i.e., that between any two rational numbers there lies another rational number and that consequently between any two rational numbers – however small the difference between them – there lies an infinity of rational numbers, more precisely, a set of rational numbers of cardinal number $\aleph_0$. The density of the mathematical interval between *0* and *1* is thus very far removed from the divisibility of the unit length of a physical measuring rod.

Still further removed from this divisibility is the pure arithmetic of real numbers according to which the interval between any two whole numbers contains not only fractions but irrational numbers. That, for example, $\sqrt{2}$ – the length of the hypotenuse of a right-angled triangle whose two other sides each have length 1 – is not a rational number was known to the Greeks and had a profound influence on the development of Greek mathematics. There are a number of different ways for extending the domain of rational numbers into the domain of real numbers. One such way is to introduce the notion of a "cut" of the totality of rational numbers and by defining the arithmetical operations of addition and multiplication as well as the relation 'less than' for cuts. A cut is a set of rational numbers with the following properties: (i) it contains some but not all rational numbers; (ii) every member of the set is smaller than any rational number which is not a member of the set; and (iii) the set contains no rational number greater than every other rational number belonging to the set. A set of rational numbers smaller than a given rational number is defined as a rational cut. Rational cuts, which are shown to "behave" like rational numbers, do not exhaust all cuts. In terms of the rational and the nonrational cuts the totality of all real numbers is defined and the pure arithmetic of real numbers developed.

For our purpose it is important and sufficient to note that the totality of real numbers, if its existence is postulated, is greater than the totality of natural numbers or of rational numbers, i.e., that its cardinal number is greater than $\aleph_0$. In standard set theory this is shown in the following steps. First one defines the powerset of a set as the set of all its subsets, including the empty set and the set itself. One proves, second, that both in the case of finite *and of* infinite totalities the cardinal number of a set is smaller than the cardinal number of its powerset. (In the finite case this is obvious since the powerset of a set with cardinal number n is a set with cardinal number 2^n – since, e.g., the powerset of the set with three members, $\{a, b, c\}$, is the set with $2^3 = 8$ members, $\{\Lambda, (a), (b), (c), (a, b), (a, c), (b, c), (a, b, c)\}$.) Having shown that the cardinal number $2^{\aleph_0}$ of the powerset of the set of natural numbers is greater than the cardinal number $\aleph_0$ of the set of all natural numbers, one proves, third, that the set of all real numbers is equinumerous with the powerset of all natural numbers, i.e., that it has the cardinal number $2^{\aleph_0}$.

If after the fashion of analytical geometry one considers an ideal line-segment of unit length as consisting of dimensionless points and establishes the usual correspondence between the proper fractions and points of the line, then the set of all points numbered in this way will be mathematically infinite and *dense* in the sense that between any two numbered points there will be one and, hence, an infinity of numbered points (of cardinal number $\aleph_0$). But the set will *not* be mathematically *continuous* since it – and the interval between any two rational numbers – will contain an infinity of unnumbered irrational points (of cardinal number $2^{\aleph_0}$). Since an infinity of *distinct* points or other objects is not perceptually accessible, a perceptual continuum is neither mathematically continuous nor mathematically dense.

4 On empirical continua

Empirical or perceptual continua are not infinitely divisible but only finitely divisible. What, moreover, characterizes such a continuum – be it a drawn line, a time interval, a painted colour spectrum, a continuous movement – is that it can be divided into two gapless subcontinua in such a manner that their common border exists only *qua* border of the subcontinua, and that this process can be continued a finite number of times depending on the percipient's (finite) powers. The distinction between two kinds of parts of a continuum, namely, subcontinua and common borders of subcontinua, was emphasized by Aristotle and, in a more precise way, by Brentano.[2] Yet, even Brentano's notion of a common border of two subcontinua which, unlike these, has no independent existence stands in need of further analysis.

Such an analysis can be given by means of a logic admitting not only exact predicates, i.e., predicates with positive and negative instances only, but also inexact predicates, i.e., predicates with positive, negative and neutral instances. When (in chapter 5) these predicates were considered, it was pointed out that two such predicates may have some or all of their neutral instances in common. Thus every inexact predicate and its complement – e.g., 'x is green' and 'x is not green' – share all their neutral cases, whereas, e.g., 'x is green and heavy' and 'x is green' share only some of them.

By combining inexact predicates one can form new predicates, including "degenerate" ones which have no positive, no negative or no neutral instances. Among them the border-predicates, as one might call them, are here of special interest. A predicate $B(F, G)$ is a border-predicate for F and G (characterizes the common border between F and G) if, and only if, its positive instances are the common neutral instances of F and G and its negative instances all other objects. A border-predicate – e.g., $B(green, not green)$, $B(x$ lies on the left side of a certain dividing line of a perceived line segment, x lies on the right side of this dividing line$)$ – has no neutral cases. It does not characterize a subcontinuum, but the common border which connects two subcontinua, and it is defined only as their common border. Brentano's characterization of continua as containing two kinds of parts, namely, parts which can exist independently of the continuum of which they are parts and parts which exist only as borders, is thus made more precise by distinguishing between inexact predicates applying to the former and (exact) border-predicates applying to the latter. The latter distinction does not imply that a continuum has an infinite number of parts or is divisible *ad infinitum*.[3]

A more elaborate analysis of empirical continua might, among other things, involve a distinction between continua of one or more dimensions. Thus one might define an empirical continuum as one-dimensional if, and only if, no border between any of its subcontinua is itself a continuum; an empirical continuum as two-dimensional if, and only if, at least one border between two of its subcontinua is one-dimensional and every other border is

---

[2] See Aristotle, *Physics*, book VI, and Brentano, *Raum, Zeit und Kontinuum* (Hamburg, 1976).

[3] For a more detailed discussion of empirical continuity see chapter 4 of *Experience and Theory*. For a formal analysis, see J. P. Cleave, "QuasiBoolean algebras, empirical continuity and three-valued logic", in *Zeitschr. für Math. Logik und Grundlagen d. Mathematik*, 22 (1978), 481–500.

either one-dimensional or no continuum; and as n-dimensional if, and only if, at least one border between two of its subcontinua is $(n-1)$-dimensional, and every other border is less than $(n-1)$-dimensional or no continuum. Examples of one-, two- and three-dimensional continua are respectively empirical line-segments, planes and bodies. Continua of higher dimensionality might be produced by combining spatially continuous phenomena with such as exhibit continuous gradations of colour, weight, motion, etc. And one might point to other parallels between mathematical and empirical continua.

But, it may be asked, are not the continuous structures which can be formally characterized by means of a finite logic of exact and inexact predicates themselves ideal rather than perceptual structures? I prefer to leave this question open. Yet, whatever the answer, it will be sufficient to agree that mathematically dense or continuous structures are radically different from empirical continua; and that the structures characterized in terms of a finite number of subcontinua and borders or a finite number of exact and inexact border-predicates at the very least preserve, and draw attention to, *some* features of empirical continua which are no longer present in mathematically dense or continuous sets.

5 On the application of pure numerical mathematics to empirically discrete and continuous phenomena and the application of mathematics in general

The application of the pure arithmetic of natural numbers and integers to empirically given particulars and aggregates is a species of idealizing representation (see chapter 3). It consists mainly in identifying an ideal fundamental sequence with an empirical one, even though the former may be larger than any finite, empirical sequence, may be infinitely proceeding or may be infinitely proceeding and "given" as a complete totality; and in similarly identifying the empirical less-than relation, sum and product with the corresponding ideal relations and operations. This identification is, like any other representation, justified by its purpose and context. The application of the pure mathematics of rational and irrational numbers to empirical continua consists in identifying even more disparate entities, since empirical continua are not sets of distinct elements whose cardinal number is $\aleph_0$ or even $2^{\aleph_0}$.

The preceding account of the application of pure arithmetic and the mathematical theories of rational and real numbers can be extended to other mathematical theories and their application to empirical phenomena. It fits in well with the manner in which empirical inquiries may inspire the creation of new mathematical theories. For these inquiries frequently involve the search for a representation of empirical phenomena such that, on the one hand, the *representans* is simpler or in other respects structurally different from the *representandum* and such that, on the other hand, the structural differences between *representans* and *representandum* are for the purposes of the representation wholly irrelevant or, at least, negligible.

It is worth noting that the dominant, modern philosophies of mathematics give altogether different accounts of the application of mathematics to experience. According to Leibniz, Frege and recent logicists, mathematics is logic and is, thus, like logic, implicit in all consistent thinking so that the problem of the application of mathematics is no more and no less a problem than that of the application of logic. According to Kant, Brouwer and his intuitionist school, pure mathematics *describes* perceptual structures and constructibilities so that there is no difference between pure and applied mathematics. Similarly according to Hilbert and his school, finite mathematics is the description of some aspects of perception while infinite mathematics is strictly meaningless. None of these views thus takes any notice of the gap between the description and mathematical idealization of empirical structures and the manner in which the gap is bridged in the application of mathematics.[4]

The gap between mathematical and perceptual structures and the manner of its being bridged by *as-if* identification, for which he uses the terms "participation" ($\mu\acute{\epsilon}\theta\epsilon\xi\iota\varsigma$), "approximation" and cognate expressions is clearly seen and explained by Plato. His analysis of the relation between mathematics and perception is, however, combined with some of the most characteristic theses of his transcendent metaphysics. Among them is the thesis that while perceptual judgments do not describe Reality, mathematics does describe Reality. It follows that in so far as arithmetic, Euclidean geometry or any other mathematical theory describes Reality, it is not a "mere idealization" of perception or an idealization admitting of alternatives which, depending on the context and purpose of their use, may be more or less adequate.

6 *On some immanent metaphysical constraints on the content, the logical form and the ontological status of mathematical theories*

The preceding analyses imply that mathematical thinking involves the acceptance of immanent metaphysical principles, i.e., of principles which are epistemically supreme, intersubjective, personally universal and

---

[4] From Hilbert's formalism one should distinguish the formalism of A. Robinson, whose view on the application of mathematics is similar to the view which has been taken here. See his "Formalism 64" and "Concerning progress in the philosophy of mathematics", in *Selected Papers* (New Haven and London, 1979), vol. 2.

circumstantially general and thus partially determine their acceptor's categorial framework. They imply in particular that there is in mathematical thinking room for alternative mathematical theories, the content of which depends on metaphysical principles. Thus, if a person considers two axiomatized mathematical theories the theorems (and axioms) of which overlap and if he notices that one of these theories is inconsistent with his metaphysical principles, then he will reject it on metaphysical grounds. A well-known example is the rejection by Kantians of non-Euclidean geometry as metaphysically incorrect, because it is inconsistent with the nature of space as determined by their metaphysical principles. In this connection it does not matter whether they regard the parallel postulate (or one of its deductive equivalents) as belonging to metaphysics, geometry or both. Similar remarks apply to alternative mathematical theories of natural numbers, integers, rational and irrational numbers, to which a person's metaphysics is relevant in so far as it includes principles about the nature of a fundamental sequence as finite, as infinitely proceeding, as infinitely proceeding and completely given, as being completely given with or without its powersets also being completely given, etc.

A second metaphysical issue about mathematics concerns the logical status of the ideal structures which are its subject matter. That is to say, one may ask and in different ways answer the metaphysical question, whether mathematics is about particulars which are structures; about structural attributes of particulars having structures; or indifferently about either. Thus Plato held that all mathematics is about particulars, namely, the Ideas or Forms; Kant that (Euclidean) geometry is about a particular entity, namely, the pure intuition of space, and that arithmetic (as based on a merely potentially infinite, fundamental sequence) is about another such entity, namely, the pure intuition of time; Leibniz that arithmetic and geometry are about structural attributes, namely, temporal and spatial relations between particulars. Modern set theory (from which our concept of structure is taken) conceives mathematical structures as sets of individuals standing in certain relations. It is nevertheless compatible with both positions, since the individuals can be conceived both as real individuals or as dummies whose only function is to characterize relations.

The applicability of at least some mathematical theories, i.e., the identifiability of empirical with mathematical structures in certain contexts and for certain purposes, raises a third metaphysical issue about mathematics. It concerns its ontological status, i.e., the answer to the questions, whether mathematical structures exist independently of empirical structures or whether they exist only or mainly as their idealizations, i.e., only or mainly in so far as they are identifiable with the empirical structures of which they are idealizations. The answers to these questions cover a wide spectrum. At one extreme lies the radical empiricist answer (of, e.g., Berkeley) that in so far as mathematical structures differ from perceptual ones, they are at best fictions. At the other lies the radical rationalist answer (of, e.g., Plato) that only mathematical structures are genuinely "real" and that empirical phenomena can only be conceived as imperfect approximations to them. Between these extremes lie views which regard some mathematical structures as independently existing particulars or as characterizing such particulars and others as fictions. An example is Hilbert's formalism, according to which finite arithmetic and combinatorics is true of the empirical world (or a negligibly idealized version of it), while infinitistic mathematics is fictitious. The nature of assumptions to the effect that mathematical and certain other particulars or attributes exist merely in the mind is best discussed as part of the general problem of mental phenomena (see chapter 8).

CHAPTER 7

ON PREDICTIVE AND
INSTRUMENTAL THINKING ABOUT NATURE
AS A POSSIBLE SOURCE OF
IMMANENT METAPHYSICS

All beliefs of a person are subject to his supreme logical principles. These principles, which determine the difference between consistent and inconsistent beliefs, include at least the weak principle of noncontradiction. Again, all his beliefs about complex particulars and aggregates are subject to his supreme mathematical principles. These principles, which impose constraints on his conception of empirical and ideal structures, normally include – apart from an empirical arithmetic and some beliefs about the structure of empirical continua – at least a rudimentary pure arithmetic of natural numbers. Yet, however developed his logic or mathematics, a person's immanent metaphysics is not exhausted by his supreme logical and mathematical principles. Thus his predictive and instrumental thinking about the course of nature and about possible human interventions in it is subject not only to "formal" principles of logic and mathematics, but also to supreme "substantive" principles. Among them are constitutive and individuating principles, associated with kinds of entities – e.g., material objects, human beings, social groups – which, though undergoing changes, yet retain their individuality.

The present chapter begins with some remarks on the persistence of material objects through change (1) and on their individuation (2). There follows a discussion of the classification of material objects and of the manner in which it serves the need to discover and to express regularities in nature (3). Next – as was done in discussing empirical and mathematical structures – the gap between unidealized experience and idealizing theory is exhibited, as well as the application of theories to experience (4). The chapter ends with some remarks on commonsense and scientific thinking as possible sources of metaphysical principles (5).

1 On the persistence of material objects

It is an empirical fact that the world in which we live appears to contain material objects and that we use material-object concepts. The general or –

to be more carefully anthropological – the widespread use of such concepts does not imply that anybody who uses them therefore regards the class of material objects as a maximal kind of independent particulars. For it may well be that a person using material-object concepts regards material objects as merely dependent particulars, which are analysable in terms of independent particulars belonging to very different maximal kinds – be they Humean impressions, unperceivable physical atoms, Leibnizian monads, fields of force, etc. However, a person who uses material-object concepts and at the same time regards material objects as merely dependent particulars is faced with the task of accounting for his independent particulars in such a manner that what he judges to be true of them is compatible with what appears to be true of material objects. This task of "saving the phenomena" has in fact been undertaken by philosophers, scientists and others who regard material-object concepts as merely auxiliary or who have dispensed with them and wish to persuade others to do likewise.

The importance of material-object concepts to predictive and instrumental thinking derives from their applicability to objects which may change and yet persist. In order to understand this persistence through change of material objects, it is necessary to make two distinctions. The first, which is rather obvious and customary, is between two senses of "sameness and difference". There is one sense of the terms in which any two objects which differ in one of their attributes are necessarily different and in which, consequently, any change of an object results in a different object. And there is a sense of "sameness" and "difference" in which an object may remain the same in spite of losing or acquiring an attribute.

The second distinction, which is perhaps equally obvious but less customary, is based on the difference between particular material objects which consist of (can be segmented into) distinct, temporally ordered, phases (slices, segments) and these material-object-phases themselves. For example, a particular material object, say, a table, consists of distinct, temporally ordered material-object-phases, say, table-phases, which make up, or are unified into, the particular material object. One must, consequently, distinguish between (i) the *unification* of material-object-phases into particular material objects and (ii) the *classification* of material-object-phases into classes of material-object-phases, such as a class of table-phases, elephant-phases, etc. This classification differs, strictly speaking, from (iii) the classification of material objects. Since, however, to characterize an object as a material-object-phase of a certain kind is *ipso facto* to characterize it as belonging to some particular material object of a corresponding kind (since, e.g., to characterize an object as a table-phase is *ipso facto* to characterize it as belonging to some table), one may take the relation between the two types of classification as understood.

Before inquiring into the nature of the unification and the classification of material-object-phases and the interrelation between unification and classification, one must consider the constitution of a material-object-phase. Although there are many different and mutually incompatible concepts of material object and, hence, of material-object-phase, it seems possible to define the common or minimal meaning of material-object-phase as follows: 'x is a material-object-phase' logically implies (i) 'x is perceptually uniform' in the sense of not being divisible into two temporally distinct phases which are perceptually different; (ii) 'x is intersubjectively perceivable'; (iii) 'x consists of some material' and (iv) 'x has a certain structure.'

Some comments are in order. The perceptual uniformity of a material-object-phase does not imply that it is perceivable only for a short time or that it is immobile. (One can even in the so-called specious present be aware of a moving object.) To assert that an object is intersubjectively perceivable is to apply an intersubjectivity-concept to it, i.e., a species of interpretative concept which has many subspecies, of which Kant's Categories, in particular his Categories of substance and causality, are an example (see chapter 1, section 3). The material of which material-object-phases consists may be of one kind or of different kinds and is normally not clearly determined. However, material objects consist of material in a sense in which illusions do not. The distinction between 'consisting of material' and 'not consisting of material' is not sharp, but admits of common borderline cases. Last, the structure of material objects is not only mereological (part–whole) but also subject to further conditions. In this connection it is worth remembering that mass-terms like 'butter' or 'wood' do not refer to material objects, but to their material. As opposed to this, e.g., 'a piece of butter' or 'a piece of wood' refers to a material object which has some shape and, thus, more than mereological structure.

2 On the unification of material-object-phases into particular material objects

In trying to characterize the unification of material-object-phases into particular material objects, it seems best to distinguish the general conditions, which every such unification has to satisfy, from the variable, special conditions which account for the distinctness of particular material objects. To start with the former, one must explain the sense in which the material-object-phases of a particular material object "belong" to it. Clearly, every material-object-phase represents this object in all contexts involving it (such as being aware of it, pushing it, selling it, etc.); and in representing the particular material object it also represents every other material-object-phase representing the material object. This relation between material-object-phases may be called the "relation of interrepresentability with respect to their unification into a particular" and may be schematically represented by x $Interrep - U$ y. It is an equivalence-relation. That is to say, for all x, y, z ranging over material-object-phases: (a) x $Interrep - U$ x (relexivity); (b) if x $Interrep - U$ y then y $Interrep - U$ x (symmetry); (c) if x $Interrep - U$ y and y $Interrep - U$ z then x $Interrep - U$ z (transitivity).

The variable, special conditions or requirements which every unifying relation of interrepresentability has to satisfy may be characterized as (i) requirements of resemblance; (ii) requirements of continuity and (iii) pragmatic requirements. The customary use of material-object concepts leaves little doubt that these requirements play an important rôle in identifying particular material objects and in distinguishing them from others. It equally shows that the observance of these requirements allows for considerable latitude and flexibility. This is so not only because of the frequent need for dealing with borderline cases of perceptual concepts, but also because of occasional conflicts arising from competing requirements.

The resemblance-requirements select one or more respects or dimensions of similarity as relevant to the unification and determine a range of similarity within each relevant dimension. In order to indicate a selected dimension of resemblance (e.g., colour) and to indicate a rejected dimension (e.g., hardness) one may produce a set of material-object-phases which form an empirical continuum in the selected, but not also in the rejected dimension. (It should be noted that this way of indicating a selected dimension presupposes the concept of an empirical continuum.) In order to indicate a selected range within a dimension, one may produce standard positive examples of objects falling within the range, standard negative examples of objects falling outside the range and – sometimes – also neutral examples. (To select a range of resemblance does not imply that the objects falling within it should form an empirical continuum.)

With regard to multidimensional resemblance-requirements, which demand that the unified material-object-phases resemble each other in more than one dimension and within each dimension in more than one range, it seems realistic to distinguish between strong and weak requirements. A multidimensional requirement is strong if, and only if, its not being satisfied in every selected dimension and range means that it is not satisfied. A multidimensional resemblance-requirement is weak if, and only if, it permits, under certain circumstances determined by the purpose of the unification, a candidate for unification to fall outside a certain dimension or range of resemblance. The permission may in particular depend on an *ad hoc* decision that in certain concrete situations the importance of one of the components of the multidimensional requirement is outweighed by the others. Under certain circumstances one may discount that a certain material-object-phase (e.g. of the writing desk which I inherited from a friend) has ceased to resemble its temporal predecessors (e.g., through destruction of its top in a manner which would normally have meant that it no longer existed). Analogous exceptions and *ad hoc* decisions are familiar from the administration of the law and moral experience.

The continuity-requirements strengthen – again with some more or less clearly specified exceptions – the resemblance-requirements in one or more of the selected dimensions. They demand that material-object-phases, which in these dimensions are perceptually distinguishable, be continuously connected, i.e., form empirical continua, in these dimensions. Thus one might require of a table which has changed in structure that the structurally different phases be continuously connected. The requirement might in some cases be qualified by the admission of exceptional discontinuities such as an occasional division of the table into separate and separately stored parts. Indeed the distinction between strong and weak continuity-requirements and the making of *ad hoc* decisions in the light of the purposes of the unification is no less justified for the continuity- as it is for the resemblance-requirements.

The pragmatic requirements for the unification of material-object-phases into particular material objects depend on the purposes which they serve in the personal and social contexts of their uses. They may be very general, as are the requirements which are based on the use of material objects as tools and products of personal or cooperative labour, and often find expression in legal institutions (e.g., the *usufruct* of Roman law, which consisted in the right to use a thing owned by another *salva rei substantia*). They may be special, as are the requirements based on the use of material objects in special arts and crafts. And they may be idiosyncratic, as are the requirements based on the desire that certain material objects serving as memorials do not change at all.

The preceding characterization of the manner in which material-object-phases are unified into particular material objects is compatible with the assumption that a material object's *possible* features can differ from its actual features, without the object's ceasing to be the same particular object. For the assumption amounts to no more than a distinction between a "central core" of requirements for unification and a number of "outer shells" of such requirements: the actual particular material object satisfies the central core of requirements and one outer shell of them, which may be called the "actual shell". Each merely possible version of the material object satisfies the central core and one outer shell (other than the actual shell). The merely possible versions of a material object are *logically* possible if, and only if, their description is logically possible. They are *physically* possible if, and only if, their description is logically consistent with what are believed to be the laws of nature: *legally* possible if, and only if, they are logically consistent with the law of the land; etc.

3 On the classification of material-object-phases

A changing material object of a certain kind may remain the same particular material object while ceasing to be the same kind of material object (e.g., when a particular table gradually loses its legs). And it may remain the same kind of material object while ceasing to be the same particular material object (e.g., when two wooden tables of similar structure are sawn into halves, a half of one table is glued to the corresponding half of the other and the remaining two halves are burned). The appearance of paradox in this remark vanishes if one recalls the distinction between material-object-phases and material objects and notes the difference between the relation which a material-object-phase bears to the particular material object into which, together with other material-object-phases, it is unified; and the relation which a material-object-phase bears to the kind of material object as which, together with other material-object-phases, it is classified.

That the unity of a material-object-phase with other such phases and its membership in various kinds of material-object classes do not coincide and may change independently of each other calls for an explicit comparison between the unification and the classification of material-object-phases. If one regards the material-object-phases which belong to a certain kind as interrepresentable *qua* members of the kind, then the needed comparison can be conceived as comparing the requirements of two types of inter-representability, namely, unifying and classifying interrepresentability. Perhaps the most obvious difference between them is that, whereas the former is characterized by specific requirements of resemblance and continuity and by pragmatic requirements, the latter is free from specific requirements of continuity. This is so because two material-object-phases of the same kind need not belong to the same relevant, multidimensional continuum (e.g., two table-phases whose predecessors always occupied widely separate locations).

Classification, like unification, involves the observance of resemblance-requirements. However, the resemblance-requirements that a particular material-object-phase of a certain kind is a particular material object and that it belongs to this kind may diverge. They may diverge in dimension, e.g., when one requires that a material-object-phase belonging to a particular table resembles its other phases in colour but regards colour irrelevant in deciding whether or not an object is a table. They may diverge in range, e.g., when one allows smaller variations in size between a material-object-phase belonging to a particular table and the other material-object-phases belonging to it than one allows between material-object-phases which belong to some table or other. Last, there are divergences in the manner in which one allows for exceptions and in which one resolves conflicts arising on the one hand in the unification of a material-object-phase with others of the same kind and on the other hand in the classification of a material-object-phase as being of the same kind as others.

The reasons for all these divergences, in particular the last mentioned, lies in the divergence of the pragmatic requirements of unification and classification. For while classification does serve the purposes of unification, it also serves other purposes, especially the purpose of exhibiting regular connections between material-object-phases of different kinds. It may be more important to know that everything that is a P is a Q than to know whether a certain P is the *same particular* as another encountered earlier. Classifications of material-object-phases are normally based on the assumption that there is no difficulty in deciding to which particular material object a classified material-object-phase belongs. Where this assumption is justified and its limitations acknowledged, one may – as is commonly done and will be done in the remaining part of this chapter – ignore the difference between classifying material-object-phases and classifying material objects.

From the point of view of formal logic any classification of material objects is a partition of the universal class of material objects into a finite number of subclasses which are mutually exclusive and jointly exhaustive of the universal class – the partition being sometimes in an obvious manner followed by a finite sequence of subpartitions. The mutual exclusiveness between two "adjacent" classes of a partition may be strong or weak. It is weak if, and only if, they have common borderline cases; and strong if, and only if, they have none. A logic the principles of which admit only exact predicates obviously admits no weak exclusion. On the other hand a logic the principles of which admit exact and inexact predicates may admit both weak and strong mutual exclusiveness between two adjacent classes of a partition. For if two adjacent classes of a partition have common borderline cases in one or more dimensions of resemblance (e.g., colour and structure), they may or may not have common borderline cases in all of them.

It is easy to think of logically correct classifications which one would regard as wholly unnatural. That this is so raises the question of the difference between (more or less) natural and (more or less) artificial classifications and, thus, between so-called "natural kinds" and other classes of material objects. The nonlogical requirements which are satisfied by natural classifications are of two types which may, but need not, conflict with each other. Those of the first type are requirements of predictability to the effect that a classification of material objects which serves the prediction of their change or stability better than a competing classification be preferred to it as more natural. The requirements of the second type are requirements of explanation to the effect that a classification linked to a certain account of Reality or one of its aspects be preferred to a competing classification which is not so linked (or "less closely" linked) to it. Although the account of Reality at issue could be – and has often been – a myth or a religious system, the modern conception of a natural classification or a natural kind links it to scientific theories. The following remarks will be devoted to a brief examination of this link and of some other aspects of the relation between beliefs about material objects and scientific theories.

4 *From commonsense beliefs about material objects to scientific theories*

Commonsense classifications of material objects rest on a logic admitting exact and inexact predicates and require either that two adjacent classes of material objects be weakly exclusive or that they be strongly exclusive. The requirements for scientific classifications are usually less permissive. Thus all classifications within a scientific theory whose underlying logico-mathematical principles are those of classical logic and of the arithmetic of rational or real numbers obviously imply that mutually exclusive classes are strictly exclusive of each other. On the other hand a scientific theory may well require of some of its classifications that certain adjacent classes be weakly exclusive of each other, i.e., have common borderline cases. A case in point is the Darwinian theory of evolution – at least in the opinion of some of its prominent expositors. One of them argues explicitly that a "rigid definition of species is impossible" and that "a universally applicable static definition of species", i.e., one which would not allow common borderline cases between two species of which one is the evolutionary successor of the other, "would cast serious doubts on the theory of evolution".[1]

Although one classification of material objects may serve the prediction of change and stability in all or some domains of nature better than another, any such classification falls short of the ideal of distinguishing sharply between what is changing and what is permanent and of explaining what changes by what is permanent. This ideal, which is also found in myth, theology and speculative metaphysics, manifests itself in the form of supreme principles of invariance or conservation for scientific prediction and explanation. The reason why material objects do not satisfy such principles is, as was shown earlier, that (i) the conditions under which a changing material object continues to be the same particular material object and (ii) the conditions under which it continues to belong to the same kind allow not only for borderline cases and anticipated exceptions, but also for *ad hoc* resolutions of conflicts between competing resemblance-, continuity- and pragmatic requirements.

By reducing the number of subclasses of material objects, one decreases the likelihood of awkward decisions about class-membership, but also the variety of purposes which may be served by a classification. Thus people borrow and lend books *qua* books and not *qua* material objects. Yet even if one were to concern oneself only with material objects *qua* material objects, not only the conditions under which a changing object remains the same material object, but also the conditions under which it remains a material object at all remain imprecise. There are in particular no precise criteria by which one can determine whether or when after the division of a material object into parts one of them has inherited its particularity or whether the particular object has ceased to exist as a particular. The decision may depend on the nature of the process from which the parts emerged. Again, there are no precise criteria by which one can determine when a material object which has been destroyed in certain ways, e.g., by being turned into a containerless liquid or gas, has ceased to exist as a material object. Such occurrences give rise to the metaphysical or scientific conjecture that while something has ceased to exist something else has been conserved, e.g., atoms which are the ultimate parts of material objects or a plenum or field of which material objects are manifestations.

The transition from commonsense predictive and instrumental thinking by means of variously unified and classified material objects is most easily exemplified by considering classical particle mechanics, which idealizes the concept of a material object and of the relations between material objects in

---

[1] T. Dobzhansky, *Evolution, Genetics and Man* (New York, 1955) p. 183.

a transparent manner. Apart from the general modifications which are due to the logico-mathematical apparatus employed in classical particle physics, some special modifications are also involved, of which the following are of particular importance: (i) the idealization of the concept of a changeable and destructible material object consisting of changeable and destructible parts into the concept of a changeable and destructible compound structure consisting of unchangeable and indestructible particles; (ii) the idealization of resemblance-requirements allowing for exceptions and conflicts (e.g., heaviness, speed and change of speed) into measurable attributes (e.g., mass, force, velocity, acceleration); (iii) the idealization of the more or less qualified requirement that some changes be continuous into the requirement that all change be continuous and expressible by differentiable functions; (iv) the idealization of the requirement that the classification of material objects serve the purpose of predicting the regular copresence and succession of different attributes of one or more material objects into the requirement of deterministic laws.

This is not the place to discuss classical particle mechanics or other physical theories and to compare them with the predictive and instrumental beliefs of which they are idealizations. Nor is it necessary to do more than mention that the idealizations involved in the nonphysical natural sciences are on the whole less radical than those which are characteristic of physics – whether or not it is held that any natural science is, will be or should be reducible to physics. Yet, however slight the idealization, idealized concepts (unlike interpretative concepts and their *a priori* components) are *not* instantiated in perception, but linked to it by being identified with concepts which are instantiated in perception.

Whereas the interpretative concept '*x* is a material object' is instantiated by what I perceive and interpret as intersubjectively given, the idealizing concept of classical particle mechanics '*x* is a changeable and destructible compound consisting of unchangeable and indestructible particles' is not so instantiated. Yet the latter concept can *within certain contexts and for certain purposes* represent the former or be treated *as if* it were identical with it, so that within these contexts and for those purposes the instances of '*x* is a material object' which are *not* instances of '*x* is a changeable and destructible compound of unchangeable and indestructible particles' can be treated *as if* they were instances of that concept. Quite apart from their mathematical content, scientific theories contain nonmathematical ideal concepts. The so-called application of these ideal concepts is just like the so-called application of the mathematical concepts based on an *as-if* identification of ideal with empirical concepts and thus a special case of what has been called "idealizing representation" (see chapter 3, section 2).

5 Thinking about material objects as a possible source of immanent metaphysics

The preceding remarks do not imply the doubtful conjecture that common-sense predictive and intrumental thinking has always proceeded and will always proceed by the application of material-object concepts. Nor do they imply the false thesis that all scientific thinking rests in one way or another on classical mechanics. However, beliefs about material objects are clear examples of commonsense beliefs, expressed by means of more or less interpretative, empirical concepts while classical mechanics is an equally clear example of scientific beliefs expressed by means of more or less idealizing, ideal concepts. As such they give rise to a number of problems which are relevant to the understanding of a person's immanent metaphysics.

One of these problems has already been encountered in comparing beliefs about empirical structures with beliefs about mathematical structures. It concerns the relation between the use of material-object concepts on the one hand and the use of corresponding concepts of classical mechanics which, in conformity to established custom, may be called "rigid-body concepts". As in the mathematical case, the formal relation between the empirical and the ideal concepts does not prejudge the question as to which of them is primary or fundamental and which secondary or auxiliary. More precisely, that (i) the concept of a material object is perceptual, i.e., instantiated in perception, whereas the concept of a rigid body is ideal, so that the two concepts are logically exclusive of each other and that (ii) the latter is an idealization of the former so that the concepts are nevertheless in certain contexts and for certain purposes identifiable with each other leaves open the following logically possible answers to the question of primacy.

One possible answer is that material-object concepts are fundamental and that their representation – or "misrepresentation" – by rigid-body concepts is justifiable as a mere auxiliary device in our thinking about material objects and in our manipulation of them. Another possible answer is that rigid-body concepts are fundamental and that our use of material-object concepts is merely a manifestation of certain human limitations from which science – at least in some cases – is delivering us. A third possible answer is that material objects (empirical triangles, etc.) and rigid bodies (Euclidean triangles, etc.) exist in different ways (e.g., mentally and physically) or in different realms of being (e.g., in nature and in the mind), neither of which is more fundamental than the other. Each of these answers is consistent with material-object concepts being idealized, or represented, by rigid-body concepts. And each of them avoids the logically impossible conclusion that a certain particular is both a material object and a rigid body. (It might be helpful to compare the internally consistent statement that a material object may in certain circumstances be treated *as if* it were a rigid body with the internally consistent statement that a square handkerchief may in certain circumstances be treated *as if* it were round, and to compare the internally inconsistent statement that a certain object is both a material object and a rigid body with the internally inconsistent statement that a certain object is both a square handkerchief and a round handkerchief.)

Each of these answers may be – and often is – implied by a person's beliefs about the relation of epistemic precedence or domination between commonsense and scientific beliefs and, beyond this, by the epistemic stratification of *all* his beliefs. If, for example, a person's scientific beliefs dominate all his other beliefs, then his undominated scientific principles are at the same time supreme principles and part of his immanent metaphysics. This type of epistemic stratification is, as has been pointed out earlier, characteristic of Plato, Descartes and the rationalists. Again, if a person's commonsense beliefs dominate all his other beliefs, then his undominated commonsense principles are principles of his immanent metaphysics. This type of epistemic stratification is characteristic of Hume and some empiricist or, at least, antirationalist philosophers.

Some philosophers tend to neglect the contrast between perceptual and ideal concepts and, hence, between commonsense and scientific thinking and, consequently, regard their supreme principles as identical. Thus Aristotle's analysis of a commonsense concept of a material object leads to a metaphysical principle which is compatible with transsubstantiation, i.e., nonconservation of substance. On the other hand, Kant's analysis of the Newtonian concept of a rigid body leads to the metaphysical principle of the conservation of substance. More generally, since the supreme scientific principles of the science of his day contained certain specific laws of conservation and change, he acknowledged them also as supreme cognitive principles to which all thinking must conform.

In so far as a person's metaphysics rests on natural science – whether as a consequence of assuming the superiority of science over common sense or of ignoring their differences – it will contain principles of conservation and principles of change. For natural science, as we know it, aims at the prediction and explanation of change by means of that which is conserved. Yet there are different laws of change and conservation. For example, Kant's metaphysical principle of the conservation of substance, i.e., matter (see, for example, B 228), has in modern relativity physics been replaced by a law of the conservation of matter or energy. And his metaphysical principle of continuity, to the effect that all change is continuous – so that all laws of nature must be expressible as continuous functions – has in quantum physics been replaced by principles which allow for discontinuous change.

The assumption that the supreme principles of natural science coincide with metaphysical principles implies a close interconnection between the history of science and the history of metaphysics; between scientific progress, if any, and metaphysical progress, if any; and between scientific explanation – as opposed to mere description or prediction – and metaphysical explanation or metaphysics as explanation. Whereas the history of science and the history of metaphysics fall outside the scope of this inquiry, the problem of scientific and metaphysical progress and the problem of explanation fall within it and will in due course be discussed (see chapter 16, sections 4 and 5).

ON THINKING ABOUT PERSONS AND MENTAL PHENOMENA AS A POSSIBLE SOURCE OF IMMANENT METAPHYSICS

A person's factual judgments and evaluations frequently involve a reference to himself or to other persons. Thus his thinking about the external world involves the application of intersubjectivity-concepts, i.e., a reference to an object's perceivability by others (see chapter 1, section 4). His moral evaluations involve references both to himself and to others, since such an evaluation expresses an attitude of his towards everybody's having a practical attitude towards something that he believes to be a practicability (see chapter 2, section 4). If a serious or tentative solipsist tried to eliminate such reference to others, he could at most replace the unqualified reference to them by making it conditional on their existence and by declaring the condition to be counterfactual.

The purpose of this chapter is to consider thinking about oneself and others as persons, in particular in so far as such thinking and the concepts employed in it constitute sources of immanent metaphysics. The chapter begins with a characterization of a minimal concept of a person the main stages of which are the definitions of the concepts of a reflective subject (1), of an agent (2) and of having access to others, as well as being accessible to them (3). There follows first a characterization of mental attributes and of material attributes, minds and bodies (4), and then an examination of the problem of the relation between a person's mind and body, as it arises if one employs the minimal concept of a person or some idealization of it (5). The chapter concludes by considering thinking about persons as a source of metaphysical materialism, mentalism and dualism (6).

1 On being a reflective subject

In being aware of oneself, one is aware of a person. This, however, does not mean that everybody who is aware of himself has the same concept of a person. For what is given in self-perception is, like anything that is given in perception, capable of being interpreted by a variety of interpretative concepts which, in spite of their common perceptual content, differ in their *a priori* components (see chapter 1, section 3). One may nevertheless, as was done when discussing material-object concepts, attempt to characterize the common core of the concept of a person or – to be once again carefully anthropological – of widely used versions of it. Since people's beliefs as to what constitutes a person are more likely to be imbued with stronger feelings than are their beliefs as to what constitutes a material object, it seems advisable to proceed rather slowly towards a definition of the minimal concept of a person and to begin by defining the concept of a reflective subject – a concept which is more general. In other words, 'being a reflective subject' does not logically imply 'being a person' in any sense of the term, while 'being a person' in all its senses logically implies 'being a reflective subject' in accordance with the following definition.

x is a reflective subject if, and only if, (i) x consists of temporally distinct phases in each of which a subject is not only aware of something, but also aware of being aware of it. (The temporally distinct phases of x will, after the fashion of the terminology used when speaking of material objects, be called "reflective-subject-phases"); (ii) the awareness of being aware of something, or, briefly, the reflective awareness, may occur in a number of dimensions, namely, bodily, cognitive, evaluative and active, and may in each of them be retrospective, prospective or circumspective (i.e., retrospective and prospective); (iii) the reflective awareness must during the existence of the reflective subject occur at least once in the physical, cognitive, evaluative and active dimension; (iv) the reflective-subject-phases determining a particular reflective subject must fulfil the formal requirements of interrepresentability, i.e., constitute an equivalence class; (v) the interrepresentable subject-phases must fulfil (a) certain requirements of resemblance, (b) certain requirements of continuity and (c) certain pragmatic requirements. In commenting on these defining characteristics, little needs to be said about those which are clearly analogous to the characteristics defining the minimal concept of a material object.

With regard to (i), it seems worth emphasizing that although my being reflectively aware (my being aware of being aware) of something logically implies that I exist while being reflectively aware, it does not also logically imply that I exist during other periods of time. This point is frequently made in connection with Descartes's doctrine of indubitable knowledge, by distinguishing between the valid inference *cogito ergo sum*, when *cogito* and *sum* are interpreted as contemporary, and the invalid inference *cogito ergo sum res cogitans*, when *res cogitans* is understood as an entity which is capable of thinking and endures even when not thinking. With regards to (ii) and (iii), reflective bodily awareness includes the reflective awareness of bodily feelings, of bodily movements, as well as the distinction between chosen and unchosen bodily movements. Reflective cognitive awareness is the reflective awareness of particular objects, as well as of beliefs that they have certain attributes. As the awareness of particular objects, it includes bodily awareness. Reflective evaluative awareness is directed towards something that is believed to exist or capable of being brought about. Being directed towards a belief, it includes cognitive awareness. Reflective active awareness, or reflective awareness of an action, involves, as will be presently shown (in section 2), bodily, cognitive and evaluative awareness and thus possesses – since it occurs in all dimensions of reflective awareness – the highest reflective dimensionality. Unlike immediate reflective awareness, a merely recalled or expected reflective awareness may be rejected as mistaken.

With regard to (iv), the formal conditions for unifying reflective-subject-phases into an interrepresentability class determining a reflective subject, to which they belong, are the same as the formal conditions for the corresponding unification of material-object-phases. With regard to (v), the resemblance-, continuity- and pragmatic requirements, the possible conflicts between them, as well as the solutions of these conflicts, are analogous to the corresponding requirements, conflicts and solutions which are familiar from thinking about material objects. For our purposes it seems best to give some brief examples of conflicting requirements and to discuss special issues when they arise.

Let us then consider Franz Kafka's hero Gregor Samsa, who on waking up one morning "found himself transformed into an immense bed bug".[1] If Kafka were concerned only with reflective bodily awareness, he would not identify the bed bug with the man – except perhaps if the change had been gradual. However, Samsa's recalled cognitive and evaluative awareness resembles, and is on the whole continuously connected with, his present cognitive and evaluative awareness. And within the context of Samsa's awakening, satisfaction of the resemblance- and the continuity-requirements in the cognitive and evaluative dimension overrides their violation in the dimension of reflective bodily awareness. On the other hand, Samsa's doctor might regard the bodily dissimilarity and discontinuity as outweighing the satisfaction of the resemblance- and continuity-requirements in the cognitive and evaluative dimension.

Just as Kafka's story and some more plausible – if less well told – stories of brain transplants exemplify the violation of resemblance- and continuity-

[1] F. Kafka, "Die Verwandlung", in *Sämtliche Erzählungen* (ed. P. Raabe, Frankfurt am Main and Hamburg, 1970).

requirements in the dimension of reflective bodily awareness, so one can easily give or imagine examples of their violation in the other dimensions of reflective awareness. Thus two reflective-subject-phases may resemble each other closely and be continuously connected in the dimension of reflective bodily awareness while being wholly dissimilar and disconnected in the cognitive and evaluative dimension. The persisting body which extends over the two reflective-subject-phases may have committed a killing, even though in the cognitive and evaluative dimension of the subject-phases at the time of the killing and at subsequent times there is not enough resemblance or continuous connection to judge them as interrepresentable. This possibility is acknowledged by many legal systems, which in such cases demand that a person accused of murder be acquitted.

2 On being an agent

In being aware of one's awareness of an action one combines reflective awareness in the bodily, cognitive and evaluative dimension. What makes the reflective awareness of actions particularly relevant to metaphysics is that actions connect the reflective subject not only with the course of nature but also with the course of social life. For to act is not only to interact with what is incapable of reflective awareness, but also to interact with reflective subjects. In order to examine this latter kind of interation – and, through it, the nature of understanding other people, society and history – a few words must be said about the nature of actions and agents.[2]

To be reflectively aware of a (deliberate) action is (i) to be aware of *chosen* bodily conduct, i.e., a chosen movement or nonmovement of one's body; (ii) to have certain beliefs about the retrospective aspect or retrospect of the action, i.e., about what preceded the chosen bodily conduct; (iii) to have certain beliefs about the prospective aspect or prospect of the action, i.e., about what will or is likely to follow the chosen bodily conduct; (iv) to have a certain evaluative attitude towards the prospect, as compared with other options believed to be practicable; (v) to believe that the chosen bodily conduct is effective in bringing about the prospect, i.e., (a) to believe that the retrospect and the chosen bodily conduct together predetermine (with certainty or a reasonably high likelihood) the prospect, (b) to believe or, at least, to acknowledge the prima facie impression that the retrospect by itself or without the supervention of the chosen bodily conduct does not predetermine the prospect and (c) to believe or, at least, to acknowledge the

---

[2] For details see *Experience and Conduct*, chapters 5, 6 and 8.

prima facie impression that the retrospect does not predetermine the chosen bodily conduct.

Reflective awareness of a (deliberate) action or deed must be distinguished from reflective awareness of various types of doings which do not satisfy all the conditions satisfied by the reflective awareness of an action. The relation of predetermination, in terms of which the belief in the effectiveness of the chosen bodily conduct is defined, is meant to admit of a wide variety of specifications, which could be and have at one time or other been accepted, such as various kinds of magical, efficient, final or probabilistic predetermination. In a similar manner the distinction between the belief and the mere prima facie impression that the retrospect does not predetermine the prospect of chosen bodily conduct is meant to avoid prejudging the issue between various libertarian and necessitarian doctrines.

A reflective subject is a particular the unity and temporal extension of which is determined by a class of reflective-subject-phases satisfying the formal conditions of interrepresentability, as well as certain resemblance-, continuity- and pragmatic requirements. If one of the so-unified phases is an immediate or recalled reflective awareness of an action, then this action is an action of the reflective subject or an action for which the reflective subject is responsible. The judge who thus ascribes responsibility to the reflective subject may either be the reflective subject itself or somebody else. The internal and an external ascription of responsibility for an action need not coincide. Yet social interaction demands a considerable convergence of the internal and external ascription of responsibility of actions to agents and, more generally, of the internal and the external aspects of actions.

It is largely in the light of this demand that natural classifications of actions within and outside the law are distinguished from unnatural ones. Thus the law acknowledges as natural the subclassification of robbery into robbery with and without violence, but not into robbery before and after lunch. Natural classifications of actions by demarcating ranges within the bodily, cognitive and evaluative dimension may – as do natural classifications of material objects – leave room for conflicts between competing criteria of class membership and for *ad hoc* resolutions of these conflicts. The needs of social life give rise to a great variety of further classificatory devices of which the following two examples must here suffice. One consists in distinguishing certain actions as attempts from complete actions of which they are the attempts and in treating attempts under certain conditions as if they were complete actions. The other consists in distinguishing certain actions which (as actions of a reflective subject) involve reflective awareness from the corresponding doings which do not involve such awareness and in treating the doings under certain conditions as if they were actions.

3 On being a person among persons

Being a person implies not only being a reflective subject, consisting of, and being determined by, reflective-subject-phases, but also being a subject consisting of nonreflective-subject-phases and of phases of unconscious awareness. Nonreflective awareness may under certain conditions be turned into a retrospective, reflective awareness whereas unconscious awareness can only be inferred from reflective awareness by means of some theory which conceives of a person as the unification of interrepresentable phases of reflective, nonreflective and unconscious awareness – a unification which, as in the cases of a changing but more or less enduring physical object or of a reflective subject, satisfies certain formal conditions as well as certain resemblance-, continuity- and pragmatic requirements. The interpolation of nonreflective and unconscious phases of awareness between the temporally separated reflective-subject-phases accounts for the high degree of continuous connectedness in the unified phases of a person as compared with the unified phases of a reflective subject.

Two further points concerning this interpolation, which may take different forms, are worth noting. First, it amounts to an interpretation of the concept of a reflective phase and, hence, indirectly of the concept of a reflective subject. More precisely, to judge that the awareness of which I am aware is more or less continuously connected with an awareness of which I am not aware is to interpret the reflective awareness by applying a nonperceptual or *a priori* attribute to it. Second, this interpretation does not make a person's reflective awareness intersubjective, i.e., accessible to other reflective subjects. That it is accessible to them has to be – and will be – separately assumed and stands in need of some explanation.

My access to the beliefs and evaluations of others depends on my interpreting their bodily conduct, either directly or from its results. This is most clearly so when I am confronted with bodily conduct which I interpret as a person's action. The interpretation, which will be considered more fully (in chapter 9, section 2), may be described as a step-by-step application of ever more specific intersubjectivity-concepts – provided that the order of increasing specificity is not confused with a temporal sequence. The first step is to judge something subjectively given as (intersubjectively given) bodily conduct. The bodily conduct is then interpreted as chosen bodily conduct, where 'x is being chosen by somebody other than myself' is no less *a priori* or nonperceptual than 'x is perceived by somebody other than myself.' The chosen bodily conduct is further interpreted as an action, i.e., as being believed to have a retrospect, together with which it predetermines a prospect – the retrospect and prospect being demarcated by certain more or less specific beliefs and evaluations which are ascribed to the agent to whom the action is ascribed. Although my access to my own beliefs and evaluations is independent of my doing anything, my trying to make them accessible to others involves me in applying to my bodily conduct the same intersubjectivity-concepts (e.g., 'x is chosen bodily conduct' in a sense in which a person's bodily conduct may be judged to be chosen by some other person).

At this point it seems feasible and reasonable to characterize a minimal concept of a person by modifying the concept of a reflective subject through (i) allowing the class of interrepresentable subject-phases to contain also non-reflective and unconscious ones and (ii) requiring that the particular which is determined and unified by the interrepresentability class has access to other such particulars through their actions and be accessible to them through its actions. The nature of the unconscious phases – Freudian unconscious experience, Leibnizian *petites perceptions*, etc. – is deliberately left unspecified. The minimal characterization of persons as unified reflective- and other subject-phases and as having access to other persons through interpreting their bodily conduct allows for the possibility of different persons understanding and misunderstanding each other, agreeing and disagreeing with each other, cooperating with and frustrating each other. The claim to have provided a minimal characterization of 'being a person' might, for the sake of argument, be replaced by the weaker claim that what has been provided is merely a conjunction of necessary conditions for the applicability of the concept. Such a replacement – though philosophically important – would not, however, affect the subsequent discussion.

4 *Minds and bodies*

There are obviously three main possible relationships between a person's mind and his body: (i) being a person is *ultimately* being a body, i.e., whereas a person's material attributes are irreducibly material, his mental attributes are reducible to material attributes; (ii) being a person is *ultimately* being a mind, i.e., whereas a person's mental attributes are irreducibly mental, his material attributes are reducible to mental ones; (iii) being a person is *ultimately* being a compound of mind and body, i.e., some of a person's material attributes are irreducibly material and some of his mental attributes irreducibly mental. In order to make this trichotomy more precise, it is necessary to explain on the one hand what is meant by "mental" and "material" attributes, to explain on the other what is meant by "reducibility". The following brief characterization of mental and, hence, of material attributes is indebted to the spirit, if not the letter, of Brentano's analyses, especially those belonging to his late, reistic phase.[3]

It depends on a preliminary distinction between the direct occurrence (occurrence *in modo recto*) and the oblique occurrence (occurrence *in modo obliquo*) of names (or definite descriptions), predicates and sentences. A name occurs directly or referentially if, and only if, it occurs as naming, or referring to, a particular. It occurs obliquely if, and only if, it occurs as an internal component of a predicate to the meaning of which it contributes. Depending on a person's beliefs, some names may occur directly and obliquely, whereas others occur only obliquely. Thus, in the speech of contemporary Englishmen 'Shakespeare' may occur directly and obliquely, while 'Jove' occurs only obliquely (e.g., in 'praying-to-Jove'). Similarly, a predicate occurs directly or applicatively if, and only if, it occurs as applying to one or more particulars. It occurs obliquely if, and only if, it occurs as an internal component of a predicate. Thus, 'being a European' may occur directly or obliquely while 'being a Liliputean' occurs only obliquely (e.g., in 'having a preference-for-being-a-Liliputean-over-being-a-European'). Last, a sentence occurs directly or propositionally if, and only if, it occurs as expressing a proposition and indirectly or obliquely if, and only if, it occurs as an internal component of a predicate (e.g., 'x believes-that-Columbus-discovered-India'). It will sometimes be convenient to say that obliquely occurring names or definite descriptions stand for (merely) "internal particulars", that obliquely occurring predicates stand for "internal attributes" and that obliquely occurring sentences stand for "internal propositions".

Since a person's awareness is always an awareness of something it is characterized by an attribute (expressed by a predicate) of the general form 'x is aware of something' or, schematically,

$$x \, A^\frown y,$$

which becomes a true or false statement if x is replaced by the name or definite description of a person and $^\frown y$ by a locution expressing that of which x is aware. The manner in which x is aware of y is independent of the existence of non-existence of y and is correctly characterized only in so far as the characterization is acceptable to x. The various instances of mental

[3] For details see "On the logic of relations", in *Proceedings of the Aristotelian Society*, 77 (1976), 149–63.

awareness and the mental attributes of which they are instances are usually classified as being cognitive, evaluative and emotive. In order to avoid the ambiguity and vagueness which in ordinary language attaches to the term "emotion", one may distinguish between directed awareness, which is either cognitive or evaluative, and undirected or diffuse awareness. For our purpose it will not be necessary to elaborate this classification or to reject any other – provided that it acknowledges the distinction between expressions occurring *in modo recto* and expressions occurring *in modo obliquo*, i.e., as internal components of a predicate.

Using $\frown a$, $\frown F$, $\frown f$ as "internal" variables standing respectively for internal particulars, attributes, propositions expressed by *obliquely* occurring names (definite descriptions), predicates and sentences, one can characterize a cognitive attribute as being (expressed by a predicate) of form

$$x\ A \frown a \qquad\qquad (1a)$$

$$x\ A \frown F \qquad\qquad (1b)$$

$$x\ A \frown f \qquad\qquad (1c).$$

In order to indicate that an attribute is cognitive, without distinguishing between the three possibilities, one may write

$$x\ CA \frown y \qquad\qquad (1).$$

Each of the three species of cognitive awareness – of internal particulars, attributes or propositions – can be subdivided into subspecies. Thus the awareness of internal particulars may be perceptual awareness, awareness in memory, etc.; and the awareness of internal propositions may be believing, doubting, etc.

Evaluative awareness is directed towards an internal particular, attribute or proposition which is the internal object of cognitive awareness. Thus if we express the general form of an evaluative attribute by $x\ Ev\ A \frown y$ and if we express an evaluative attitude (of preference, indifference, being in favour of, etc.) by *, we can define

$$x\ Ev\ A \frown y\ \overset{=}{_{Df}}\ x\ CE \frown y\ \text{and}\ x\ * \frown y \qquad\qquad (2).$$

Thus a person's favourable attitude towards doubling his size is a compound awareness consisting of his awareness of what is expressed by 'He is doubling his size' and a favourable attitude towards what is so expressed. Again, each species of evaluative awareness – of internal particulars, attributes or propositions – admits of subdivisions into subspecies (depending on the subspecies to which their cognitive components belong).

Undirected or diffuse awareness is neither cognitive nor (*a fortiori*) is it evaluative. An attribute of such awareness, schematically, $x\ DA\frown y$, can thus be defined schematically by

$$x\ DA\frown y \underset{Df}{=} x\ A\frown y \text{ and } not\text{-}(x\ CA\frown y) \text{ and } not\text{-}(x\ Ev\ A\frown y)\quad (3).$$

The clearest cases of such diffuse awareness are cases in which it is unaccountable, e.g., when a person feels happy or depressed without feeling happy or depressed about anything in particular. However, even when a person's diffuse awareness is accountable, e.g., when the cause of his happiness or depression is known, his diffuse awareness though related to a direct awareness does not become direct, i.e., cognitive or evaluative. Thus, if a person is happy about having won a prize because he has won a prize one must distinguish between on the one hand his belief that he has won the prize and his having a pro-attitude towards this belief, i.e., his directed awareness, and on the other hand his merely feeling happy, i.e., his diffuse awareness, whatever may have caused it. The relationship between direct and diffuse awareness may be more intimate, e.g., when a person's feelings are "grounded" in beliefs and evaluations in the sense that if the beliefs and attitudes were different the feelings would also be different. (For a brief discussion of grounded feelings, see chapter 3, section 3).

The preceding remarks on the nature of mental attributes and on their classification would have to be elaborated in order to provide the conceptual apparatus for describing the great variety of types of mental awareness and of their interrelation. Yet they are sufficient to emphasize the general character of mental attributes as expressible by predicates of form $x\ A\frown y$ where x is a place-holder for a directly and $\frown y$ a place-holder for an obliquely occurring expression (the adequacy of which depends wholly on the specific content of x's awareness). They also enable us to define material attributes as nonmental attributes and thus constitute a useful preliminary to discussing the question whether persons are minds (i.e., have ultimately only mental attributes), bodies (i.e., have ultimately only material attributes) or compounds of body and mind.

5 *Persons, minds and bodies*

A person is, or has, both a mind and a body. It is nevertheless possible to reduce mental to material or material to mental attributes. More precisely, it is possible to show that *under certain assumptions* any statement ascribing a material (mental) attribute to a particular is logically equivalent to a statement ascribing only a more or less complex mental (material) attribute to it. For our purpose it will be sufficient to give a very general account of the reducibility assumptions under which material attributes can be reduced to relations between minds, i.e., particulars having only mental attributes, and of the reducibility assumptions under which mental attributes can be reduced to relations between bodies, i.e., particulars having only material attributes.

The mentalist, who is free to assume that there are minds, must explain the difference between mental attributes expressing a mind's awareness of something which is merely internal to it (e.g., its awareness of Mephistopheles or of his having made a contract with Dr Faustus) and mental attributes expressing a mind's awareness of something which is both internal and external to it (e.g., its awareness of a "real" dog). This distinction and the possibility of conferring externality on something which is internal to a mind, is based on what might be called "the assumption of ascertainable intersubjective harmony between minds". According to this assumption a mind's awareness of something which is internal *and* external to it is in harmony with the awareness of any other mind who is, or who under more or less precisely specifiable conditions would be, aware of something sufficiently similar. Conditions of such a harmony have been elaborated by Leibniz and other idealists – subjective, absolute or transcendental.

Whatever elaboration of the assumption of intersubjective harmony is accepted, it must – if the harmony is to be ascertainable – be associated with an effective criterion, which can be applied in practice and which allows for corrigible error. Otherwise the application of the criterion would conflict with the familiar experience of, e.g., mistaking an illusion for an external object or vice versa. In the case of probabilistic criteria the requirement is obviously satisfied. But even if, with Descartes or Brentano, one regards clear and distinct or self-evident judgments as apodictically true, one must allow for the possibility of regarding as self-evident what is not – whether the error, as is held by Descartes, arises from overhastiness, i.e., the will overtaking the understanding (see the fourth Meditation) or in some other way.

The materialist, who is free to assume that there are bodies, must explain the difference between material attributes which, like 'x is a falling stone', have no internal aspect and material attributes which, like 'x is a bodily pain', have such an aspect. This distinction and the possibility of conferring mentality or internality on something which is a material object is based on what might be called "the assumption of intrasubjective recording or recordability". (The term "recording" is used in preference to "observing" since it covers both a mind's and a machine's recording of something.) What – it is assumed – distinguishes a falling stone from a bodily pain is that the latter but not the former can be recorded ("observed") by the body having the pain as well as by another body. One might, of course, assume that a falling stone is attached to a recording apparatus. But, the materialist would say that only certain kinds of material objects are capable of that species of self-recording which amounts to self-observation. He might even make his point by trying to turn a remark made by Leibniz in defence of mentalism against it (see *Monadology*, section 17). Leibniz, he might argue, was right in asserting that if one walked through a human body "as if through a mill" one would notice only material things and processes – just as if one walked, say, through a motorcar factory. Yet the human body – unlike the motorcar factory – is capable of intrasubjective recording.

A dualist who regards mental and material attributes as irreducible to each other might nevertheless accept a version of the mentalist's principle of intersubjective harmony. But he would consider this harmony not as the ground of the difference between that which is merely internal to a mind and that which is also external to it, but as a consequence of the irreducible difference between the mental and the material. A dualist might similarly accept a version of the materialist's principle of intrasubjective record-ability. But he would distinguish between an intrasubjective recording which is nonmental and one that is mental and regard the difference as a difference in kind which follows from the mutual irreducibility of the mental and the material.

6 Thinking about persons as a possible source of immanent metaphysics

Materialism, mentalism and dualism are all compatible with the minimal conception of a person as determined by an equivalence class of inter-representable reflective and other subject-phases and by the requirement of being accessible to other persons and having access to them. This conception thus constitutes a core of which the various versions of materialism, mentalism and dualism are divergent extensions and possible sources of immanent metaphysical principles, i.e., of supreme cognitive principles of a person dominating his other beliefs about the intersubjective perceptual world. Thus any form of materialism imposes considerable constraints on a person's conception of material objects and phenomena since it must be consistent with the assumption that mental attributes are a species of material attributes possessed by a body, capable of recording their possession by itself in a sense in which such intrasubjective observation differs from observation by an external observer.

The assumption that persons are bodies adds to the difficulties of a "natural" classification of material objects, e.g., one which is to serve an extended evolutionary theory concerned not only with the development of lower into higher organisms, but also with the development of species of material objects which are not organisms into species of organisms. Such a theory *might* be served by a classification of material objects into those which are and those which are not mechanisms; of mechanisms into those which are and those which are not self-regulating systems; of self-regulating systems into those which are and those which are not organisms; and of organisms into those which are and those which are not capable of intrasubjective recording. This or a similar classification might, together with the assumption that it represents a temporal and hierarchical ordering of evolutionary stages, not only dominate the biological thinking of some persons, but also function as a supreme principle, i.e., as an immanent metaphysical principle, in their thinking.

Unlike the materialist, the mentalist and the dualist cannot transpose their problems concerning the nature of minds into problems concerning the nature of bodies and of special kinds of material attributes. Yet the problems about irreducible minds are analogous to those about irreducible bodies. Among them are questions about the conditions under which a changing mind continues to be the same; about the conditions under which it continues to belong to the same class of minds; and, last, the conditions under which it ceases to exist. A mentalist will in particular be faced with the need to make decisions about borderline cases as well as with the need – familiar in the case of material objects – for *ad hoc* resolutions of conflicts between competing resemblance-, continuity- and pragmatic requirements.

Just as difficulties in applying the concept 'x is a material object which, though changing, yet persists through time' may lead to the formulation of ideal concepts, such as 'x is a permanent material particle', so difficulties in applying 'x is a mind which, though changing, persists in time' may also lead to the formulation of ideal concepts, e.g., 'x is a permanent soul' ('mental atom', 'monad', etc.). As in the case of material objects and their idealizations, the limited identifiability of human beings who die with eternal mental entities which exist forever does not imply that one rather than the other is fundamental. It is in particular no less possible to be a mental atomist, who holds that ultimately only mental atoms exist, than to be a material or physical atomist, who holds that ultimately only material atoms exist.

There is, however, at present an important difference between physical and mental atomism: physical atomism is through the natural sciences, in particular physics, closely linked to the intersubjectively given world of perception – the link consisting in the empirically testable identifiability of perceptual concepts (e.g., material-object concepts) and ideal concepts (e.g., compounds consisting of physical atoms). Mental atomism on the other hand is not, or only very tenuously, linked to beliefs about the intersubjectively given world of perception. It is, for example, possible for an up-to-date scientist to believe that he has, or is, an immortal monadic soul in such a manner that this belief is consistent with all his beliefs about the world of intersubjective perception. Being neither dominated by, nor yet dominating his beliefs about the intersubjectively given world, the beliefs would not belong to his immanent but might belong to his transcendent metaphysics. In this connection it seems worthwhile to emphasize two points. First, mental atomism, like other transcendent metaphysical beliefs, may be and often is of great practical relevance. Second, just as physical atomism has changed its status from transcendent to immanent metaphysics, so mental atomism may yet undergo a similar development. However, as matters stand at present mental atomism is best considered as belonging to transcendent metaphysics.

CHAPTER 9

ON THINKING ABOUT
SOCIAL PHENOMENA AND HISTORY AS A
POSSIBLE SOURCE OF IMMANENT
METAPHYSICS

Being aware of oneself and of others involves often, if not always, an awareness of social groups and social institutions the existence, nature and individuality of which depends on shared beliefs, attitudes and modes of conduct. That human beings think about themselves and others as social beings is no less obvious than their acceptance of logical principles, of an empirical arithmetic and some more or less radical idealizations of it, or of assumptions about the bearers of material or mental attributes. In examining some assumptions about social phenomena as a possible source of immanent metaphysics, it seems advisable once again to distinguish between a minimal core of beliefs which are common to almost everybody and various mutually inconsistent shells accepted by some people only. Yet, as one moves from logic to social life, the ever-present danger increases of accepting what is characteristic of one's own tradition as characteristic of all mankind. To admit this is at the same time to recall and to stress that in making a statement to the effect that another statement (of logic, mathematics, natural science, etc.) is (for somebody or everybody) a statement of immanent metaphysics, one is making an empirical statement – and not a philosophical statement of some peculiarly nonempirical kind.

The present chapter begins with a minimal characterization of social groups in terms of shared or social beliefs, attitudes and modes of conduct (1). There follows a brief discussion of the ways in which the (shared or unshared) beliefs, attitudes and actions of others are recognized and understood (2). A comparison of social actions and social documents with purely physical phenomena (3) leads to a comparison between the human and the physical sciences (4). In conclusion thinking about social phenomena and history is considered as a possible source of immanent metaphysics (5).

1 A minimal characterization of social groups

A social group is a set of persons with the following characteristics: (i) it is an open aggregate the members (or parts) of which change on the whole only gradually (whether by birth or death or by other ways of gaining or losing their status as members); (ii) the members of the group share some of their more stable beliefs (e.g., a belief in the doctrinal infallibility of the pope, or a belief that increased scientific activity leads to increased economic productivity), some of their more stable attitudes (e.g., a pure pro-attitude towards certain works of art or a moral anti-attitude towards abortion) and some of their acknowledged rules of conduct (e.g., those of a certain legal system); (iii) the beliefs, attitudes and acknowledged rules of conduct which are being shared determine to some extent what the members of the group expect from each other.

There is a difference between sharing a belief or attitude with the other members of a social group and sharing an acknowledged rule of conduct with them. Sharing a belief or attitude with them involves having it oneself, as well as correctly believing that (almost) all members of the social group also have it. Sharing an acknowledged rule of conduct with them involves believing that its violation will result in various sanctions as well as correctly believing that this is also believed by (almost) all members of the social group. It does not mean that one has a pro-attitude towards the conduct enjoined by the rule or that one believes (almost) all members of the group to have such an attitude. Thus acknowledgment of a legal rule implies neither approval nor disapproval of it.

Some changes in the membership of a social group and some changes in the shared beliefs, attitudes or acknowledged rules of conduct are compatible with its continued existence. Others imply that the group has lost its individuality, that it has ceased to be a group of a certain kind or both. The difficulties and flexibilities which have been indicated in discussing the individuation and classification of material objects and persons apply also to the individuation and classification of social groups. A social group which persists in time consists of distinctive group-phases which are inter-representable and form an equivalence class – interrepresentability having to fulfil certain requirements of resemblance, certain requirements of continuity and certain pragmatic requirements (see chapters 7 and 8). As in the case of individuating material objects and persons, the requirements may admit exceptions and conflicts calling for *ad hoc* resolutions. And just as the need may arise for idealizing impermanent material objects into compounds of permanent physical atoms or for idealizing impermanent persons into permanent mental monads, so the need may arise for idealizing actual social groups into permanent, ideal entities.

The shared beliefs, attitudes and acknowledged rules of conduct which characterize a particular social group are obviously not independent of each other. For example, some rules of conduct would not be intelligible without certain beliefs being held by those to whom the rules are addressed and some rules of conduct would not be realizable unless their addressees had certain practical attitudes. Thus, a rule demanding human sacrifice in order to pacify the gods would be unintelligible among people who, not knowing the meaning of 'gods', did not believe in their existence, and unrealizable among people who preferred incurring the anger of the gods to the killing of human beings and whose way of life was completely dedicated to its preservation. Yet it is not necessary to share all beliefs, attitudes and acknowledged rules in order to share some of them or to have similar ones with which in certain contexts they are identifiable.

Thus different social groups may have the same or similar subsystems of beliefs (e.g., religious or scientific beliefs), the same or similar subsystems of attitudes (e.g., sexual morality), the same or similar subsystems of acknowledged rules of conduct. A subsystem of the last kind is also called an institution (e.g., the institution of citizenship, of marriage, or of a certain judicial system). Although belief-systems, attitude-systems and institutions are defined in abstraction from the groups of which they are characteristic, they – like the groups themselves – admit of a great many different ways of individuation, classification and idealization. For the purposes of this essay there is no need to discuss them in detail. But it may be worth noting that the unification of temporarily distinct phases of a social group (belief-system, attitude-system or institution) into a particular social group which, though changing, endures in time presupposes a prior unification of person-phases into particular persons which, though changing, may endure for a lifetime.

Social belief-systems, attitude-systems and social institutions have a certain stability on which predictions about the social group, characterized by them, can be based, bearing some analogy to predictions in the natural sciences. This is particularly so in the case of social institutions. Although the conformity of natural events to the if-then of conjectured laws of nature is on the whole greater than the conformity of the conduct of citizens to the if-then of the law of the land, this need not always be so. To say this is not to prejudge the "ultimate" analysis of social systems, e.g., their reducibility or irreducibility to natural ones.

2 On understanding the beliefs, attitudes and actions of others

Sharing a belief or an attitude with another person implies understanding it. A more or less successful attempt at reaching such understanding involves (i) ascribing a mental attribute to the person; (ii) doing so by interpreting the person's bodily conduct or a result of it; (iii) relating the mental attribute ascribed to the other person to other mental attributes which he is presumed to possess; (iv) empathetically comparing the mental attribute ascribed to the other person with one or more mental attributes possessed by oneself.

Consider, for example, my attempt at understanding another person's belief that Caesar killed Brutus, briefly, that f_0. It (i) involves me in forming the mental attribute 'x believes $\frown f_0$, or, somewhat more colloquially, 'x is an f_0-believer'. This attribute, as has been explained earlier (chapter 8, section 4), is a monadic attribute, in which f_0 occurs *in modo obliquo*, i.e., as contributing to the meaning of the attribute in such a manner that the applicability of the attribute to a person implies neither the truth nor the falsehood of f_0. Moreover, if I assert of some person that he is an f_0-believer, I do not thereby implicitly assert f_0 – except in the case in which the person is myself.

In order to understand that a certain person is an f_0-believer I must (ii) have some evidence for judging him to be an f_0-believer. This evidence may consist on the one hand in the person's linguistic or nonlinguistic bodily conduct, interpreted as the action of a person who is an f_0-believer. It may on the other hand consist in the result of such conduct, interpreted as the result of the action of a person who is an f_0-believer. In some cases the evidence may justify one in ascribing a mental attribute to many persons, e.g., when that which is interpreted is the result of a joint action.

The bare ascription to another person of 'x believes $\frown f_0$' leaves room for a great many misunderstandings. For (iii) our understanding of a particular f_0-believer depends not only on the content but also on the context of his belief that Caesar killed Brutus. For example, it makes a difference to our understanding if he believes what is generally believed history up to the moment in which Brutus tried to kill Caesar, but also believes that Caesar killed Brutus in self-defence; or if he believes that Caesar killed Brutus because the warning about the Ides of March specifically referred to Brutus's murderous intention, etc. Even if the context of a particular f_0-believer's belief that f_0 is irrelevant to our understanding of what it is to be an f_0-believer, it may make a great difference to our understanding of one particular f_0-believer rather than another. There are many circumstances in which we need such understanding, e.g., when we wish to pass a moral judgment on the action described by f_0 in the light of our own or a particular f_0-believer's moral convictions.

The attempt at understanding a particular f_0-believer involves lastly (iv) an empathetic comparison of his belief with one's own. Such a comparison is easy if one is oneself an f_0-believer and thus prepared to assert f_0. If one is not an f_0-believer one may make various attempts at putting oneself "in the f_0-believer's position" by finding one or more beliefs of one's own which in certain contexts can be identified with his belief or by imagining circumstances under which one would oneself be prepared to assert f_0. Understanding another's belief, as here understood, is thus not merely linguistic. It is the kind of understanding which a biographer is trying to achieve of the person whose biography he is writing, which is aimed at in the writing of history and quite generally in the humanities.

What applies to mental attributes ascribing a belief to a person, e.g., 'x believes $\overline{}f_0$', applies similarly to mental attributes ascribing to a person a pure or practical attitude towards what he believes to be logically possible or practicable. An example is the mental attribute 'x has a pro-attitude towards Caesar's killing of Brutus', more briefly, '$x + f_0$', or *somewhat* more colloquially, 'x is an f_0-approver'. Attempts at understanding a particular f_0-approver will involve ascribing '$x + f_0$' to him by interpreting his bodily conduct or a result of it, by relating '$x + f_0$' to other mental attributes he is presumed to possess and by empathetically comparing '$x + f_0$' to one or more of one's own mental attributes. To understand another's attitudes towards oneself or the group to which one belongs may be particularly difficult if they are inimical to oneself or the group to which one belongs. But it is possible to understand another's hatred for oneself – for example, if one comes to see that he regards oneself *as if* one were a murderer.

Just as one understands the beliefs and attitudes of others by interpeting their bodily conduct or its results as actions or the results of actions, so in turn one understands actions by ascribing beliefs and attitudes to agents. For to perform an action is to choose bodily conduct in the light of certain beliefs and evaluations the absence of which would change the nature of the action realized by the chosen bodily conduct. No circularity need be involved in inferring the nature of a person's deliberate action from his beliefs and attitudes and his beliefs and attitudes from his actions, for the beliefs and attitudes from which the nature of a certain action is inferred and the beliefs and attitudes which are inferred from his action need not be the same.

3 On social actions and social documents

To be a member of a social group, as opposed to observing it merely from the outside, is not only to be aware of social actions and social documents, but also to perform social actions and to produce social documents. Social actions are, of course, a species of actions which in turn are a species of happenings or events. Every action involves bodily conduct which is chosen in the light of certain beliefs about its retrospect and its prospect and of certain attitudes towards its prospect. What distinguishes a social action from a solitary one (if indeed there are such actions) is that its constitutive beliefs and attitudes include on the one hand beliefs and attitudes shared by the agent with other members of the social group and on the other hand beliefs about, and attitudes towards, the way in which members of the social group will be affected by the action.

Social documents, which are more or less persistent results of social actions, are a species of documents which in turn are a species of material things. A social document is a material object which has been produced or modified by a social action. Just as social actions may express the beliefs and attitudes of their agents either intentionally, as in the case of many linguistic utterances, or incidentally, so social documents may be intentionally or incidentally expressive of their makers' beliefs and attitudes. Examples of the former type of document are written records of contracts or public meetings; examples of the latter type are motorcars or street litter. Whereas a member of a social group is necessarily an interpreter of actions or documents produced by its members, those who do not belong to it may undertake this task from choice in a professional or amateur manner.

The interconnection between the social actions of the members of a social group is, at least prima facie, extremely complex. This is so because social actions may be deliberately or incidentally cooperative or conflicting; because social actions which appear cooperative may in fact be conflicting and vice versa; because the interpretation or misinterpretation of some people's actions enters the beliefs and attitudes which are constitutive of the actions of others; because social actions which are cooperative in one respect may be conflicting in another, etc. The need to manage this complexity in the service of private or public aims – theoretical, practical or both – calls either for insights which reveal the apparent complexity as merely apparent or for simplifying idealizations which have a limited use in special contexts.

Another way of looking at the complexity of social interactions is to compare (i) sequences of happenings which contain no action; (ii) sequences of happenings which contain only nonsocial actions – if there are such; and (iii) sequences of happenings which contain one or more social actions. The first kind of sequence raises no question about chosen bodily conduct, as compared with unchosen bodily movements or nonmovements, or the movements or nonmovements of material objects in general. If such a sequence is examined scientifically, it becomes the topic of physics or some other natural science.

An example of a sequence of the second kind would be a trivial physical experiment, performed by a solitary physicist in such a way that it does not affect the beliefs and attitudes of other people, say, a retesting of the law of free fall in preparation for an elementary physics lecture. Since the experiment is an action, it has both a physical and a mental aspect, namely, that of being a choice made by an agent who has certain beliefs about, and certain attitudes towards, the retrospect and the prospect of his chosen bodily conduct. Among his beliefs is in particular the belief that his choice is effective in realizing one of at least two different sequences of happenings which he could have chosen and realized. If one wishes to understand the experimenter's action, one must acknowledge this belief of his as well as the other beliefs and attitudes which are constitutive of his action. To ignore a person's belief, e.g., because one believes it to be false, or to ignore a person's attitude, e.g., because one believes it to be unrealizable, is to ignore his possession of a mental attribute and thus an empirical fact about him. And to ignore an empirical fact is in no sense to account for it.

In the case of a social action the person performing it not only believes that he has an opportunity of effectively choosing between different sequences of happenings, but that by choosing to realize one of them he creates or closes similar subsequent opportunities for himself or others or, at least, makes a contribution to the creation or closure of future opportunities of choice for himself or others. Since he usually has no clear idea of all the opportunities for choice which he creates or closes or of the choices which will be made by those for whom the opportunities arise, his conjecture of what will follow his social action will usually be more complex and dubious than the solitary physicist's conjecture of what will follow his trivial experiment. This contrast is fairly obvious and a familiar subject of both pride and self-commiseration, expressed by historians and social scientists. As it stands, it is open to the objection that though in ordinary life a person may believe himself to have, to create and to close opportunities for effective choice, he may yet as a historian, social scientist or philosopher reject this belief. This point is well taken. To do it justice, one might qualify a person's belief in having, creating or closing choices as "ordinary", "practical" or in some other suitable manner.

4 *On the distinction between the human and the physical sciences*

The distinction between the human sciences, the moral sciences or the humanities on the one hand and the natural sciences on the other is based on an uncontroversial difference in their subject matter as well as on various, mutually inconsistent methodological doctrines. The difference in subject matter has its source in the different ways in which a person is aware of human, especially social, actions and their results on the one hand and in which he is aware of physical events and their results on the other – where "physical event" is used in the sense of excluding human actions. In other words, whereas a person's awareness of an action or its result involves the ascription of beliefs and attitudes to the agent, a person's awareness of a physical event or its result involves no such ascription. The distinction does not, of course, imply that the awareness of an action (chosen *bodily* conduct) is limited to the ascription of beliefs and attitudes to the agent. Nor does it imply that a person's awareness of a physical event precludes him from assuming that he shares beliefs about, and attitudes towards, this event with others and, hence, from ascribing these beliefs and attitudes to them. Last, the distinction does not prejudge an analysis according to which the humanities are "ultimately" reducible to the natural sciences or vice versa.

The controversy about the difference in the methods which are, or should be, employed in the natural and in the human sciences centres around the problem whether both kinds of science aim, at least to some extent, at predicting the course of events; and if so, how far this common end is or should be served by common means. In considering these questions, it seems useful to begin by contrasting two apparent extremes, namely, on the one hand physics, which clearly aims at prediction by means of empirical laws and theoretical idealizations, and on the other history, which either does not aim at prediction at all or, if it does, seems to spurn both empirical laws and theoretical idealizations. For our present purpose it is sufficient to remember that in asserting an empirical law (e.g., 'All swans are white' or 'All men die eventually') one is asserting of every bearer of a certain (simple or complex) empirical attribute that it is or will be (with certainty or a given probability) the bearer of a certain other empirical attribute, and that in employing an idealizing *scientific* statement (e.g., $F = dmv/dt$) one is treating certain theoretical attributes, which are idealizations of certain empirical attributes, and these empirical attributes themselves *as if* they were the same.

History, at least according to the traditional and prevalent account of it, aims exclusively at giving a correct and complete account of the human past in its unique concreteness. This definition does not imply that history may not make use of the predictive apparatus of the natural sciences, but merely that, even where this apparatus is available and employed, it cannot by itself achieve history's characteristic aim. Nor does the definition imply that historical knowledge of the human past cannot be used for conjecturing the human future, but merely that such a conjecture is not mediated by the predictive apparatus of the natural sciences. Thus a historian may well use physical methods for the dating of documents and, thereby, of documented historical events. And he may well conjecture that actions of a given kind which had certain consequences in the past will continue to have similar consequences in the future. Yet in so far as history aims at describing the concrete and unrepeatable past, it cannot be content with empirical generalizations which express abstract and repeatable features or with idealizations of actual features which, though different from the actual features of which they are idealizations, are yet – in certain contexts and for certain purposes – identifiable with them.

The inexhaustibility by scientific generalizations and idealizations of the unique and concrete human past is not due to its being human or past but to its uniqueness and concreteness. Human and social phenomena can no less become the subject of scientific generalizations and idealizations than can natural phenomena. Yet, just as it would be a mistake to argue from the difference between social and physical phenomena to the impossibility of a social science, so it would be a mistake to argue from the possibility of a social science to the thesis that social and physical phenomena do not differ from each other. In order to avoid each of these mistaken arguments it seems useful to distinguish clearly between two classifications of systematic empirical enquiries: a classification according to the subject matter and a classification according to the method employed. The former classification corresponds to – and is as unproblematic as – the distinction between purely physical and partly or wholly mental phenomena, especially if it is conceived as compatible with both a materialist reduction of mental to physical or an idealist reduction of physical to mental phenomena. The latter classification corresponds to the distinction between the concrete description of phenomena and their abstract theoretical characterization by means of empirical generalizations and idealizations. The two classifications are independent so that it is possible for an inquiry into mental and social phenomena to be abstractly theoretical and for an inquiry into physical phenomena to be concretely descriptive.

5 *Thinking about social phenomena as a possible source of immanent metaphysics*

Social – no less than physical – phenomena give rise to the tasks of describing, predicting, explaining and influencing their course. The attempts at fulfilling these tasks presuppose in either case a distinction between that which changes and that which endures and, more particularly, a characterization and classification of the changeable and changing entities, as well as of those entities, if any, which – though involved in change – are themselves permanent. If a person's thinking about a social entity, such as a social class, a nation, a collective unconscious, is to involve a principle of his immanent metaphysics, his beliefs about the entity must satisfy two conditions. The first is that his beliefs about the social entity be irreducible, that is to say, do not logically follow from his beliefs about entities which are not social. The second condition is that his beliefs about the social entity be linked to the world of intersubjective experience in the sense that the social entity instantiates intersubjectivity-concepts or idealizing concepts with which they are identified in his social thinking (see chapter 1, sections 3 and 4). It is worth noting that the conditions of irreducibility and empirical linkage apply to all entities which are the subject matter of a person's immanent metaphysical principles, e.g., to material objects or minds. For if, say, beliefs about material objects are reducible to beliefs about minds, they do not contain metaphysical principles (as opposed to consequences derived from premises including them). And in so far as, say, beliefs about minds, e.g., the beliefs that they are immortal, are not empirically linked, they do not belong to an immanent (as opposed to a transcendent) metaphysics.

In the case of beliefs about social entities – even when formulated by philosophers, historians and social scientists – it is frequently unclear whether and to what extent the two conditions are satisfied. Thus it may not be clear whether, say, the working class or the American nation is regarded as a changing set of which certain human beings standing in certain relations are the elements; a changing compound of which these human beings are parts; or a whole which in some way controls the function of its parts (e.g., by having, and being able to realize, a will of its own). Unclarity about the condition of irreducibility is often combined with unclarity about the question of empirical linkage. An example is the idea of human progress which according to Bury "involves a synthesis of the past and a prophecy of the future" and "is based on an interpretation of history which regards men as slowly advancing . . . in a definite and desirable direction and infers that this progress will continue indefinitely".[1] Not only does the subject or subjects to which "men" refers lack any clear determination, but it is also not clear whether the "idea of human progress" is a thesis about a mind-independent Reality which is consistent with any statement about the empirical world or whether it is a historical hypothesis which can be inconsistent with such a statement, so that either the statement or the historical hypothesis must be rejected.

One way of conceiving the idea of human progress as empirically linked would be to characterize the kind and duration of a regression which would be discoverable by a historian and be inconsistent with the idea of progress. Another would be to distinguish between different, discoverable kinds of progress – scientific, political, etc. – so that progress in one respect would not necessarily imply progress in all respects. From the point of view of this essay two concepts of progress are of special interest; the concept of progress of intellectual disciplines, e.g., science or the sciences, within the constraints of an accepted categorial framework; and the concept of the progress of metaphysics itself. (For a discussion of these concepts see chapter 16. In fairness to Bury it should be noted that he is not attempting an analysis of the idea of human progress but to describe its history.)

[1] See J. B. Bury, *The Idea of Progress* (London, 1920), p. 5.

CHAPTER 10

ON DELIMITING A PERSON'S
IMMANENT METAPHYSICS

The principles which together constitute a person's immanent metaphysics and define his categorial framework dominate all his thinking about the world of intersubjective experience (see chapter 1). Yet, although their supremacy is interdisciplinary and not merely intradisciplinary, principles which originally dominate only a certain discipline may eventually become supreme in all fields of a person's thinking. This is particularly obvious in the case of logical principles, but may also hold for other regions of thinking, e.g., instrumental and predictive thinking. Because of this possibility various regions of thought can be treated – and have been treated in the preceding chapters – as possible sources of immanent metaphysics. The aim of the present chapter is to inquire into the conditions in which this possibility is realized and, more generally, into the delimitation of a person's immanent metaphysics within the whole system of his beliefs.

This will be done by examining what is involved in "accepting a proposition" and in "accepting a proposition as true" (1); by comparing various ways in which supreme principles are accepted (2); by considering the relation between central and peripheral supreme principles (3) and the relations of facts to idealized facts and of facts to practicabilities (4). The chapter concludes with some remarks on the borders of immanent metaphysics (5).

1 On accepting propositions

A person's awareness of a proposition (statement, judgment, etc.), say, p, involves a distinction between accepting and rejecting it, in particular between beliefs and actions which would be appropriate to an acceptor of p and beliefs and actions which would be appropriate to a rejector of p. A person accepts p if, and only if, he regards the beliefs and actions appropriate to an acceptor of p appropriate to himself. Thus, a distinction between what is appropriate for an acceptor and what is appropriate for a rejector of p does not imply, but is implied by, its acceptance or rejection.

The statement that a person accepts *p* as true may mean the same as the statement that he accepts *p*. But it also may mean that *p* in addition conforms to a general and effective criterion of truth, i.e., a means by which one can ascertain for any statement (at least "in principle") whether or not it is true. Possession of such a criterion is claimed, for example, by those rationalists who (a) assert that a statement is true if, and only if, it is self-evident or follows from self-evident premises and who (b) ascribe to themselves the capacity of recognizing both features. As has often been pointed out – for example, by Kant in the *Critique of Pure Reason* (B 82 f) and by Leonard Nelson in *Das sogenannte Erkenntnisproblem*[1] – the acceptance of an allegedly general and effective criterion of truth raises the question whether the statement expressing the generality and effectiveness of the proposed criterion is itself true and thus leads to a vicious, infinite regress.

The objection of such a regress need not arise for a definition of truth which, though general, is not associated with an effective criterion. An example is Aristotle's or any other definition of truth as correspondence with fact: two persons of whom one accepts a statement as true while the other accepts its negation as true may well agree that truth is correspondence with fact, without expecting that this agreement will help them in deciding which of the two propositions is true. Again, the objection need not arise for a definition of truth which is not general and is associated with an effective criterion of truth for only a species of true statements. An example is Tarski's semantic definition of truth as a relation between an object-language – such as a language incorporating the expressive means for forming statements of physics – and a metalanguage which enables one to make statements about the object-language. It would be a misunderstanding of Tarski's aims and achievements to assume that this definition was meant to imply a general and effective criterion of truth, including, e.g., an effective criterion of truth *in* physics.

Acceptance of a specific, effective criterion of truth (e.g., the criterion of being a truth-functional tautology for the logical truth of propositions not containing free or bound variables) involves acceptance of the proposition expressing the criterion in the normal way. It is, as was explained, to distinguish between the beliefs and actions appropriate to an acceptor of the proposition (e.g., a logicist) and the beliefs and actions appropriate to its rejector (e.g., an intuitionist) as well as to acknowledge the former beliefs and actions as appropriate to oneself. It is in addition to define, more or less precisely, a class of propositions such that if any proposition is recognized as belonging to the class (as conforming to the criterion, which is its defining

[1] *Ges. Schriften* (Hamburg, 1973), vol. 2, pp. 59–393.

characteristic), it must be accepted. It follows trivially that – since internal consistency is a necessary condition of truth – any proposition which is recognized as being incompatible with any member of the class must be rejected. In other words, the class defined by a person's effective criterion of truth is a subclass of the class which comprises his supreme beliefs (see chapter 2, section 2).

The search for, and the discovery of, a person's specific and effective criteria of truth may be useful in demarcating those of his supreme principles which constitute his immanent metaphysics or, more specifically, demarcate his categorial framework. However, many of the beliefs which conform to his effective criteria will not be supreme *principles*, but less general beliefs which are logical consequences of supreme principles. It is even more important to note that to accept a proposition as supreme is not necessarily to accept it as conforming to an effective criterion of truth. For it is quite possible to accept, say, the principle of causality as supreme and, thereby, to commit oneself to the rejection of any proposition which is inconsistent with it, without claiming to possess or indeed without possessing an effective criterion of truth to which the principle conforms.

Supreme principles, such as the principle of excluded middle or the principle that nature contains (or does not contain) discontinuous change, are sometimes called "negative conditions or criteria of truth". But this manner of speaking may raise problems which are not raised by considering the acceptance of a principle, or any other proposition, as supreme. Among them is the difference between various concepts of truth, in particular those which imply the (impossible) availability of a general and effective criterion of truth; those which imply the availability of an effective criterion of truth for a certain kind of proposition; and concepts which imply that there is a general, noneffective criterion of truth. Concepts of the last kind often express a relation between the world of intersubjective experience within the constraints of some categorial framework and a reality which exists independently of them. Such concepts belong to transcendent metaphysics.

2 On various ways of accepting supreme principles

According to the usage adopted in this essay there is no difference in meaning between 'accepting a supreme principle' and 'accepting a principle as supreme'. The latter locution stresses the difference between the content of the principle and its place in a system of beliefs and, thereby, draws attention to the possibility that two systems of beliefs may contain the same beliefs but differ in their epistemic stratification. To accept a supreme principle or to accept a principle as supreme is on the one hand to accept the principle as one accepts any proposition (as explained in the preceding section); on the other hand, to accept the requirement that any belief which is inconsistent with the principle be rejected. The acceptance of a supreme principle may – like, for example, that of a grammatical rule – be implicit or explicit and admit of various degrees of explicitness. It does in particular not imply its acceptor's capacity to formulate the principle. Yet a philosophical anthropologist may, with the help of a suitable method of questioning, succeed in making a merely implicit acceptance of a supreme principle fully explicit.

The acceptance of a principle as supreme may take a variety of forms which go beyond the mere acknowledgment of their supremacy. The principle may, for example, be judged as absolutely certain. This has been the view of most metaphysicians from Aristotle to Whitehead and beyond. While these absolutist metaphysicians argue that there is *one, and only one*, system of principles the rejection of which is for any thinker unthinkable, others hold that every thinker must take some principles for granted, even if they need not be the same for everybody. Collingwood, who recognized the fundamental importance of such principles to metaphysics, regards them as "absolute presuppositions", which are "not propositions" because for them "the distinction between truth and falsehood does not apply".[2]

That the acceptor of an absolute presupposition in Collingwood's sense cannot conceive its falsehood implies that the principle is one of his supreme principles, i.e., a member of that class of his beliefs which (i) cannot be decomposed into two subclasses, one of which dominates the other, and which (ii) dominates all the beliefs not belonging to it (see chapter 1, section 2). The converse implications, however, are not valid. A principle may well be supreme for a thinker who regards its negation as conceivable, e.g., for the simple reason that he himself had in the past accepted it. And it may well be supreme for a thinker who regards it as true and whose logical principles are inconsistent with the assumption that meaningful propositions can be neither true nor false.

There are situations in which a person would express his confidence in a supreme principle by declaring it to be more or less likely that he will not reject it as a supreme principle or merely as a principle. In some of these situations the degree of a person's confidence in a supreme principle might even be measured (after the fashion of the Ramsey–de Finetti–Savage theories of subjective probability) by his preparedness to lay certain odds on his remaining faithful to the principle. He may or may not have a general

[2] See R. G. Collingwood, *An Essay on Metaphysics* (Oxford, 1940), p. 32.

idea of the circumstances in which he might abandon a supreme principle. Thus, a person who accepts the principle of causality as supreme might admit that he would reject it if he suddenly came to believe in miracles, e.g., as the result of a religious conversion. Indeed if the acceptance of supreme principles at one time was not compatible with the possibility of their rejection at another, there would be no point in trying to argue for their acceptance or rejection. Yet the history of ideas records many such arguments (see chapter 15). A person's high degree of confidence in a supreme principle is, of course, no sure indication of the probability of his remaining faithful to it. One can find examples of thinkers abandoning principles which they considered certain, as well as examples of thinkers who remained faithful to principles to which their attachment was fairly weak.

From weak attachment to a supreme principle one must distinguish wavering between two incompatible principles. Yet the need to make this distinction does not imply that there are no borderline cases between weak attachment and wavering. While faithfulness to a supreme principle may share some features with faithfulness to a person it also takes a variety of other forms. Among them is the possibility of what might be called intellectual or cognitive "akrasia", namely, a state in which a person who has accepted a supreme principle nevertheless, from habit, laziness, thoughtlessness or some other reason, acts on a belief which is incompatible with the principle.

3 On central and peripheral supreme principles

If a person accepts a class of principles as supreme, then he obviously accepts any of its subclasses as supreme. Yet it may be that certain members of a class of supreme principles are, in a sense which can be made clearer, "fundamental to" other members of the class. Thus, if a person accepts the supreme principle that natural phenomena are subject to laws of conservation and the supreme principle of the conservation of energy as defined in classical dynamics, then the former principle is "fundamental to" the latter. The following definition of 'being fundamental to' seems to be both clear enough and general enough for our purpose. Let us assume that somebody has accepted two nonlogical principles, say, f and g. (It does not matter whether he has or has not accepted them as supreme.) Then f is fundamental to g if, and only if, (i) the acceptance of f is consistent with both the acceptance of g and the rejection of g, whereas (ii) the acceptance of g is consistent with the acceptance of f but not consistent with its rejection. The notion of consistency which occurs in this definition is itself defined by the logical principles accepted by the acceptor of f and g. With regard to these logical principles, some of them may be fundamental to others. This can be seen, e.g., in classical logic by starting with the weak principle of non-contradiction as the only condition of consistency and by gradually strengthening this condition through the acceptance of further logical principles until the full classical logic and, hence, the classical definition of consistency is reached (see chapter 5).

There are various ways in which f may be fundamental to g. A trivial kind of this relation arises if g is a conjunction of which f is a member, e.g., when $g = f \wedge h$. Another kind of the relation arises if g is interpretative of f, i.e., if to assert f and g is to apply respectively a concept F and a concept G to the same perceptual phenomenon and if F is interpretative of G (see chapter 1, section 3). Yet another kind of the relation arises if g (noninterpretatively) supplements the characterization of entities characterized by f, e.g., if g is the parallel postulate of Euclidean geometry and f the conjunction of the other postulates of Euclidean geometry.

In terms of the relation of 'x is fundamental to y' one can define two notions which are useful for our purposes, namely, the notions of the core and the periphery of a set of accepted principles, in particular of a set of supreme principles. Let α be a set of (supreme) principles accepted by a person, κ a proper subset of α and π the complement of κ in α (i.e., the class of principles belonging to α but not to κ). Then κ is the core of α and π its periphery if, and only if, (i) every member of κ is fundamental to at least one member π and (ii) for every member of π there is at least one member of κ which is fundamental to it. The definition does not imply that every class α can be divided into a core and a periphery. For it may well happen that a class of principles has neither a core nor a periphery. And it may also happen that while one of its subclasses has a core and a periphery the whole class also comprises members which belong to neither, but are "extraperipheral". It is also clear that if a class α with the core κ and the periphery π is extended into a wider class α_1, the core of α_1 need not be the same as the core of α. Last, one and the same core of principles may be surrounded by different and mutually inconsistent peripheries. Examples are the common core of principles govening the "ordinary" use of 'material object' which may be surrounded by principles interpreting the concept in, say, a Platonic or Humean way; or the common core of Euclidean and non-Euclidean geometries and their mutually incompatible peripheries.

In trying to delimit one's own, another's or "everybody's" supreme principles or immanent metaphysics, the distinction between cores and peripheries is useful and has tacitly been used by systematic philosophers. One method of applying the distinction can be described as follows: it starts by considering (as far as possible) the class of all supreme principles and divides this class, say, α, *if possible* into two mutually exclusive and jointly exhaustive classes of which one is the core of α, say, $\kappa(\alpha)$, and the other the periphery of α, say, $\pi(\alpha)$. (The division is not possible if α contains extraperipheral members – in the extreme case, if all its members are extraperipheral.) One then divides the core $\kappa(\alpha)$, *if possible*, into a core, say, $\kappa\kappa(\alpha)$, and a periphery, say, $\pi\kappa(\alpha)$, and proceeds until one has arrived at a core which cannot be further divided into core and periphery. As regards the periphery $\pi(\alpha)$, one inquires whether, even though it cannot be divided into core and periphery, some of its subclasses, say, $\beta_1, \ldots, \beta_n$, can be so divided. The process must come to an end, but may – depending on one's purpose – be finished earlier.

Kant's *Critique of Pure Reason* involves a tacit application of this method: if α is the class of his supreme principles, then $\kappa(\alpha)$ is his logic and $\pi(\alpha)$ the class of all synthetic *a priori* propositions. The latter class is divided into the classes of mathematical and nonmathematical synthetic *a priori* propositions. Each of these classes is then divided into core and periphery and examined under the headings of the "Transcendental Aesthetics" and the "Transcendental Logic". Leibniz's *Monadology* with his distinction of truths of reason and truths of fact also involves distinctions between cores and peripheries. In the preceding chapters the method was also used. But there its purpose was to emphasize the variety of possible systems of supreme principles or immanent metaphysics. Thus it was shown – or at least argued – that one must distinguish even within logic between core and periphery and that different logical systems, though sharing the same core, differ in their peripheries. Similar distinctions between shared cores and unshared peripheries were made for nonlogical supreme principles.

To draw the distinction between cores and peripheries is to draw attention to the anthropological fact that of the supreme principles and categories, accepted by human beings, some stand in the core–periphery relation to each other. It is not to assert any kind of non-empirical necessity to the effect that a certain core of principles must be accepted, if thinking or, more generally, experience is to be possible. This view of the distinction differs, for example, from the view expressed by Strawson. He holds that "there is a massive central core of human thinking which has no history", that "there are categories and concepts which, in their most fundamental character do not change at all" and that the reason for this lies "in statable conditions of the possibility of experience in general".[3] To state these conditions is according to him *not* to make empirical statements. For the purpose of comparing his view with the view expressed in this essay it is not necessary to raise the more difficult question of the precise status of these nonempirical statements – e.g., whether they have to be regarded as synthetic *a priori* in Kant's or some modified Kantian sense or as somewhat disguised analytic statements. (For a brief discussion of Kant's position see chapter 15, section 2.)

4 On the relations between facts and idealized facts and between facts and practicabilities

If a proposition *f* is fundamental to a proposition *g*, then the acceptance of *g* is inconsistent with the rejection of *f*. Hence the rejection of the core of a class of propositions is inconsistent with the continued acceptance of its periphery. One cannot, as has been pointed out, consistently accept the interpretation of subjectively given perceptual objects as intersubjective, material or mental objects while rejecting the proposition that there are subjectively given perceptual objects; or accept the parallel axiom (or its negation) while rejecting the other Euclidean axioms. Thus the periphery not only depends on its core, but cannot be made independent of it. Not all dependence relations, which are relevant to the delimitation of a person's immanent metaphysics, are thus indissoluble. Among those which can be dissolved, two are of particular interest – not least because their dissolution may turn out to be a source of transcendent metaphysics. These dissolvable relations are the relations between facts and idealized facts and between facts and practicabilities.

Idealization is a species of representation, i.e., the identification under certain conditions of a represented object or attribute, the *representandum*, with a representing object or attribute, the *representans* (see chapter 3, section 2). What distinguishes an idealizing representation or idealization from other kinds of representation is that in it the *representans* has been produced, or is conceived, as an improved version of the *representandum*, where the improvement is judged by the way in which a certain (logical, scientific, legal or other) purpose is served. A kind of idealization, which plays a central rôle in Plato's theory of Forms and which, therefore, might be called "platonic", connects a *representandum*, involving perceptual objects and attributes, with a *representans*, involving nonperceptual objects

---

[3] See P. F. Strawson *Individuals* (London, 1959) p. 14 and *The Bounds of Sense* (London, 1966) p. 120.

and attributes. Examples are the representation of empirical arithmetic and geometry by pure arithmetic and geometry and the representation of the physical world by Newtonian physics or some other idealizing physical theory.

If f is a proposition in which a perceptual attribute is applied to a perceptual object (e.g., a perceptual triangle) and g is a proposition in which a nonperceptual attribute is applied to an idealized representation of the perceptual object (e.g., a Euclidean triangle), then the genesis of g is obviously dependent on the prior acceptance of f. But f is not "fundamental" to g, since one can without inconsistency accept g and reject f. Thus the genetic dependence of pure arithmetic and pure geometry on empirical propositions has not prevented their subsequent independence as intellectual disciplines and as a potential source of immanent and transcendent metaphysics. Their relevance to a person's immanent metaphysics consists (see chapter 6) in their contribution to his categorial framework and to the formulation of the supreme principles defining it. Thus Kant regards the principles of arithmetic and geometry as supreme principles which directly characterize the structure of all perception, whereas Plato regards them as describing not the structure of perception, but nonperceptual structures which are imperfectly approximated by perceptual ones.

The potential relevance of pure arithmetic and pure geometry to transcendent metaphysics is also clearly seen in Plato's theory of Forms, where they are conceived not only as approximative descriptions of intersubjective experience, but also as exact descriptions of mind-independent Reality (see chapter 11, section 4). Conferring independence on platonic idealizations by regarding them as descriptions of transcendent reality is, as will be argued, not the only source of transcendent metaphysics. Nor, as will also be argued, is there only a one-way traffic between transcendent and immanent metaphysics. For just as principles of immanent metaphysics can be separated from their empirical bases, so can transcendent principles (e.g., Democritean atomism) be linked to empirical phenomena (e.g., in the atomic theories of Dalton and his successors).

The relations of cores to peripheries and of perceptual facts to idealizing and ideal facts lie wholly within the domain of thinking about that which is or could be the case. For the purpose of delimiting immanent metaphysics – against both transcendent metaphysics and practical thinking – it is necessary briefly to consider the interdependence of facts on the one hand and actions and practicabilities on the other. The general nature of this interdependence is fairly obvious: a person's chosen actions (including his chosen omissions) depend on some of his factual beliefs, just as a person's factual beliefs depend on some of his chosen actions. He will, for example, not choose to open a door while rejecting the proposition that it is moveable. And he will not believe that it will have been opened by him while choosing not to open it.

An agent's choice may be "illusory" in the sense that the agent is under the impression that his choice was not predetermined by a constellation of facts, whereas both his choice and his impression were so predetermined. For example, an agent may be under the impression that his opening a door and his choosing to do so were not predetermined by a constellation of physical facts, whereas they were so predetermined by his swallowing a drug with his food. And, similarly, a believer's factual belief may be "illusory" in the same sense that what seems to him to be a fact which is independent of his chosen actions is produced by them although he is not aware of it. For example, he may have chosen to take a drug and thereby successfully caused himself to imagine a door and his choosing to open it, as well as to forget the choice made before taking the drug.

The distinction between "illusory" and "nonillusory" choices may give rise to the *empirical* hypothesis that all choices of a certain kind are illusory, i.e., that for every apparently nonillusory choice of this kind there exists an empirically discoverable constellation of physical facts which implies its being illusory. Similarly the distinction between "illusory" and "nonillusory" factual beliefs may give rise to the *empirical* hypothesis that all facts of a certain kind are illusory, i.e., that for every apparently nonillusory fact of this kind there exists a hidden, chosen action by which it was produced. Such an empirical hypothesis must not be confused with the *nonempirical* thesis that *in Reality*, as opposed to mere empirical appearance, all choices made by a person are predetermined facts, or that in Reality, as opposed to mere empirical appearance, all facts observed by a person are the result of actions, *somehow* chosen by him (e.g., his hidden true self). The transformation of these and other empirical hypotheses into nonempirical theses (like the transformation of idealizing descriptions of empirical phenomena into exact descriptions of transcendent reality) is an important source of transcendent metaphysics and must be taken into account when a person's immanent metaphysics is delimited from his transcendent metaphysics (see chapter 18, section 4).

5 On the borders of immanent metaphysics

Within a person's thinking about what is the case we can distinguish his immanent metaphysics, his subordinate objective thinking and his transcendent metaphysics. His immanent metaphysics comprises the supreme principles governing his thinking about the intersubjective world, which is the subject matter of common sense and science. His subordinate objective thinking comprises all his other propositions about that world. His transcendent metaphysics covers his speculations about reality, conceived as existing independently of his immanent metaphysics and his subordinate objective thinking. The borders between a person's immanent metaphysics, his subordinate objective thinking and his speculative metaphysics cannot always be sharply demarcated. This limitation applies not only to Socratic interlocutors, historians of ideas or philosophical anthropologists. For it may well happen that a most skilful Socratic dialogue conducted by a thinker with himself only shows that – at least for the time being – he himself is unable to draw exact borders.

Within the sphere of objective thinking principles may, without being rejected, be demoted from supreme principles to principles of subordinate thinking. Similarly, principles of subordinate objective thinking may become part of immanent metaphysics. The demotions and promotions may happen in all parts of a person's immanent metaphysics – in its innermost core as well as on the extreme periphery. For example, a person may (perhaps under the influence of discussions about the logical structure of quantum mechanics) decide that though classical logic as a whole is valid, the principle of excluded middle can no longer be accepted as a supreme principle since its rejection under certain circumstances has become conceivable. The same person may later come to reinstate the principle as supreme. And again there are borderline cases.

The separation of immanent metaphysics from subordinate objective thinking depends on the place of their principles in the epistemic hierarchy. For their reference to the intersubjective empirical world is not in question. This is not so in the region of thinking where idealizing propositions which are linked to perception border on ideal propositions which are meant to characterize transcendent reality. In the case of some idealizing propositions any decision about their belonging to the region of immanent metaphysics or subordinate objective thinking on the one hand or to transcendent metaphysics on the other may be withheld, postponed or considered useless. Yet whether or not such suspension of judgment is genuine is often difficult to decide. Thus many a pure mathematician would be incapable of deciding how far, if at all, his mathematics is an attempt at describing nonempirical reality, an attempt at idealizing empirically given structures or an attempt at creating structures of independent, e.g., purely aesthetic, interest. The problem of distinguishing between empirical hypotheses and nonempirical theses leads to the undisputed or disputed border of transcendent metaphysics. Having been reached on various routes the border will now be crossed.

TRANSCENDENT METAPHYSICS AND THE APPLICATION OF CONCEPTS

This chapter and the next are devoted to transcendent metaphysics. The present chapter begins by determining its scope and by distinguishing between two ways of pursuing it – one based on the assumption that transcendent reality or some of its aspects are characterizable by concepts, the other based on the assumption that transcendent reality or some of its aspects are not so characterizable (1). The rest of the chapter deals with attempts at using the first approach. They are based on various conjectures, for example, that certain features of empirical reality are approximations to features of transcendent reality (2); that whereas empirical reality comprises particulars and attributes which are in some sense "primary" as well as some that are not, transcendent reality comprises only primary ones (3); that the empirical apprehension of what are facts and what are constructs does not correspond to transcendent reality (4); that transcendent reality is "perfect" in a sense in which empirical reality is not (5). The second approach to transcendent reality forms the topic of the next chapter.

1 On the scope of transcendent metaphysics

Once a person recognizes that his experience of an intersubjective world – i.e., a world of particulars and of attributes which he interprets as not only perceivable by himself, but as intersubjectively given – is constrained by his immanent metaphysics or, more specifically, by the principles constituting his categorial framework, the question arises whether there exists a reality which transcends these constraints (see chapter 4). To propose an affirmative or a negative answer is to engage in transcendent metaphysics, even if the answer remains the only thesis in this field of intellectual endeavour. Entering it cannot be avoided, unless – after the fashion of the sceptics – one suspends judgment. For even the negative answer, namely, that there is no reality except the empirical reality of the intersubjective world, as apprehended within the constraints of one's own or some other categorial framework, transcends this reality.

If there is a transcendent reality, is it, though independent of experience, accessible to it? And if accessible, to what extent, if any, can it be characterized by the application of concepts; and to what extent, if any, can it be grasped in some other manner? The assumption that transcendent reality is accessible in some way or other is shared by transcendent metaphysicians of the most diverse kinds, from naive realists who hold that empirical and transcendent reality do not differ to philosophers who hold that only the concept of not being conceptually characterizable is applicable to transcendent reality, which, therefore, can only be apprehended nonconceptually or not at all.

A thesis to the effect that transcendent reality or some aspects of it cannot be conceptually characterized marks the border between transcendent metaphysics and the nonconceptual apprehension, if any, of transcendent reality. So do the reasons which are given for this inapplicability of concepts. Having noted the border and some borderline cases between immanent and transcendent metaphysics (chapter 10, section 5), one may with some justification locate the domain of transcendent metaphysics between immanent metaphysics on the one hand and attempts at a nonconceptual apprehension of transcendent reality on the other. When it comes to the nature of the nonconceptual apprehension of a transcendent reality, metaphysicians *qua* metaphysicians have to be content with theses as to what it is not and thus, at best, with the removal of obstacles barring access to a reality which exists independently of any differentiation of experience into particulars and attributes, of any categorization of particulars into maximal kinds and of the other constraints which constitute various categorial frameworks – even if the nonconceptual apprehension should in the end legitimate one categorial framework as the only adequate or the most adequate among them.

Anybody who is engaged in some special intellectual discipline or in the most "ordinary" and unspecialized commonsense thinking cannot avoid having an immanent and a transcendent metaphysics. He may (e.g., in so far as he engages in certain kinds of religious worship) in addition consider himself capable of a nonconceptual apprehension of a transcendent reality. The grounds of his confidence in being acquainted with each of these three domains will differ from each other. Thus his confidence in his immanent metaphysics rests most obviously on the internal consistency of its principles, as well as on their connection with the empirical beliefs – scientific or commonsense – which are dominated by these principles. In addition a person's immanent metaphysics may appeal to him on moral grounds, in particular as fitting with his moral convictions and as strengthening them, as well as on aesthetic grounds.

In the case of a person's transcendent metaphysics, the close connection with his empirical beliefs is missing since empirical reality, which is the subject matter of his empirical beliefs and, hence, of his immanent metaphysics, may be wholly different from transcendent reality. In the case of a person's nonconceptual apprehension of transcendent reality even the test of consistency is unavailable. However, a person's confidence in his conceptual or nonconceptual apprehension of transcendent reality may draw strength from his moral convictions, especially if they seem indubitable to him or, at least, less dubitable than his factual judgments. Thus, if he is convinced that he knows what it is to lead a virtuous life, that it is always rewarded, but that in empirical reality it is sometimes not rewarded, then he is committed to a conception or "vision" of transcendent reality which has much in common with the Christian and other religions and which, like these religions, implies that man has an immortal soul.

That this and other attempts at grasping transcendent reality may endow them with features which conform to the thinker's wishes does not, thereby, turn them into wishful thinking. Being aware of this possibility may make the search for access to a transcendent reality more careful, more complex or both. Yet even the strongest conviction that any such search is incurably infected by wishful thinking cannot prevent our engaging in it, except if we decide to suspend judgment about anything which transcends our awareness of what *seems* to be the case and abide by this sceptical decision. The following remarks on various speculations about transcendent reality are intended as an exemplification and not as an exclusive and exhaustive classification.

2 On empirical reality as an approximation to transcendent reality

The "naive realist", as he is sometimes called, does not distinguish between the world as apprehended by him under the constraints of his categorial framework and the world as it exists independently of these constraints and of his own existence. Such naive realism is likely to become implausible when its upholder recognizes that his categorial framework is not the only one. In the face of a plurality of different categorial frameworks he may, for example, turn into an "empiristic realist" who holds that transcendent reality coincides with the world as apprehended under the constraints of *some* categorial framework, even if its formation has as yet not taken place.

Realists of this kind will often express a hope that mankind, the scientific community or some other group of men is consciously or unconsciously working towards the formation of this adequate framework. In other words, the empiristic realist asserts the logically possible and in fact achievable identity of empirical reality, or a clearly discernible aspect of it, with transcendent reality and not merely an approximation of the former to the latter. "The real", says C. S. Peirce, "is that which, sooner or later, information and reasoning would finally result in and which is therefore independent of the vagaries of me and you."[1]

The thesis that there is such an approximation is characteristic of many nonrealist systems of transcendent metaphysics. Some of them remain fairly close to realism by implying that empirical reality clearly manifests the respects or dimensions in which it approximates transcendent reality. They imply that we in some dimensions of our experience distinguish correctly between features which are more or less adequate, in such a manner that their comparative adequacy points to an absolute adequacy which is characteristic of transcendent reality. Thus Plato and Descartes put great weight on the ranking of empirically real features according to their capacity of being more or less precisely apprehended and infer from their intellectual preference for what is more precisely apprehended that transcendent reality is capable of being apprehended with absolute precision, in particular mathematical precision. For them, as has been pointed out earlier, at least some of the approximative idealizations of empirical phenomena are also precise descriptions of transcendent reality. Again the intellectual preference of Plato and other metaphysicians for the comparatively more permanent leads them to conjecture that transcendent reality is absolutely changeless.

At this point it might be objected that some scientific theories, e.g., Newtonian dynamics, are themselves mathematically precise descriptions of an unchanging reality, which, however, is not transcendent, but empirical, and that, consequently, the difference between science and transcendent metaphysics has been misrepresented. The objection is, however, ill founded and based on a failure to discern the rôle of idealization in science (see chapter 7, section 4). Newtonian dynamics no more *describes* empirical reality than does, say, Plato's theory of Forms. The assertion that Newtonian dynamics *describes* an aspect of transcendent reality is as much a thesis of transcendent metaphysics as is the physicalistic thesis that it describes transcendent reality *completely* so that every statement that is true

[1] "Some consequences of four incapacities", in *Journal of Speculative Philosophy*, 2 (1868), 140–57.

of transcendent reality is logically equivalent to a statement of Newtonian dynamics.

The relation between 'comparatively more P' (e.g., 'comparatively more precise', 'comparatively more permanent') and its absolute counterpart is often conceived as analogous to a mathematical relation between 'greater' in some mathematically expressible sense (e.g., 'being ordinally greater', 'being cardinally greater', 'being greater in volume') and a corresponding mathematical notion 'infinitely great'. In that case one would either have to face the problems of infinity, as they arise in mathematics and its immanent metaphysics, or else show that and how this relation and the relevant notion of nonmathematical infinity differ from the mathematical ones. The question of the analogies and disanalogies between mathematical notions of infinity, such as the infinite cardinal number of the set of all integers, and nonmathematical notions of infinity, such as the infinite power of God, is frequently neglected by transcendent metaphysicians. Among the notable exceptions is Leibniz, who distinguishes between mathematical infinity, which he regards as a well-founded fiction, and metaphysical infinity, the nonfictitious nature of which must be understood if God's nature is to be understood.[2] Before discussing conceptions of transcendent reality, characterized by metaphysically infinite attributes, it seems advisable to consider conceptions of this reality which more closely resemble features of empirical reality, as conceived by empirical science and versions of common sense akin to it.

3 On primary attributes as attributes of transcendent reality

Infinitistic metaphysicians regard the attributes of transcendent reality as being at best approximated by empirical attributes. Naive realists believe that the attributes of empirical and transcendent reality coincide. Between these two extremes lies the position of the "semiempiristic realists", as they might be called, who hold that certain attributes are characteristic of both empirical and transcendent reality, whereas others are characteristic only of empirical reality. Such realists may in addition hold that attributes of the latter kind, or "secondary attributes", can in some sense be reduced to attributes of the former kind, or "primary attributes". This reducibility may, for example, be understood as the thesis that to every statement containing secondary attributes there can be found a logically equivalent statement containing only primary ones.

[2] See *Nouveaux Essays*, chapter 18.

A clear distinction between primary attributes, i.e., attributes shared by transcendent and empirical reality, and secondary attributes belonging only to empirical, mind-dependent reality is due to Locke.[3] For our purpose it is sufficient to note that Locke takes it for granted that empirical and transcendent reality comprise bodies having attributes and that within the latter he discerns primary and secondary qualities. The primary qualities of the bodies are "the bulk, figure, number, situation and motion or rest of their solid parts" and "are in them whether we perceive them or not".[4] The secondary qualities "are nothing in the objects themselves but powers to produce various sensations in us by their primary qualities", i.e., sensations, such as "colours, sounds, tastes etc."[5]

Locke's realism, that is to say, Locke's version of arriving at transcendent reality by distinguishing between primary and secondary features of empirical reality and by eliminating the latter, is clearly based on the science of his day. For his assumption that mind-independent reality consists of bodies having the primary qualities which he acknowledges is derived "from the master-builders whose mighty designs in advancing the sciences will leave lasting monuments to the admiration of posterity", i.e., Boyle, Newton and other scientists of his day, whom he hoped to serve as "an under-labourer, in clearing the ground a little, and removing some of the rubbish that lies in the way to knowledge".[6] A semiempiristic realist of the first quarter of the twentieth century who saw himself as an underlabourer of its scientific master-builders might have proposed a rather different distinction between primary and secondary qualities. Thus an underlabourer of Einstein might well have eliminated bodies and their attributes in favour of gravitational and electromagnetic fields and some of their attributes. And an underlabourer of Bohr might have made still other assertions about transcendent, as opposed to empirical, reality.

Reliance upon the science of their day is not the only source from which semiempiristic realists derive their version of the general thesis that in subtracting mere appearance from empirical reality, one is not left empty-handed, but with a description of transcendent reality. An example of such a subtraction, which can be, and has been, proposed independently of science, is based on the distinction between time as divided into past, present and future and time as a tenseless linear continuum of temporal points, of temporal intervals or of temporal points and intervals. Thus some philosophers regard the tensed time series as not being an aspect of transcendent reality, which they conceive as having only a tenseless

---

[3] See, for example, *An Essay Concerning Human Understanding*, book III, chapter 8.
[4] Ibid., section 23.   [5] Ibid., section 10.   [6] Ibid., Epistle to the Reader.

temporal aspect. Defenders of this metaphysical view might, of course, try to draw additional support from physics or other scientific disciplines. But they could equally try to draw additional support from theology, e.g., by arguing with Leibniz that it makes no sense to assert that God created the world at a certain time, while it makes sense to assert that God in creating the world *ipso facto* created its temporal order.[7] Again, one might well argue that a tenseless temporal continuum, by implying universal predetermination, is at best a useful fiction, while the assumption of a tensed temporal order would do justice to one's conviction of open futures – if indeed one has such a conviction.

4 On the transcendent metaphysics of apprehending empirical reality

In considering the delimitation of immanent metaphysics against transcendent metaphysics, attention was drawn to possible difficulties in distinguishing between empirical hypotheses and transcendent theses, e.g., between the empirical hypothesis that all apparently free choices of a certain kind are predetermined in accordance with physical laws, and the thesis of transcendent metaphysics that – in spite of any apparently incompatible physical laws – such choices are free (see chapter 10, section 4). If one allows oneself to regard the apparent difference between what is and what is not chosen as invariably spurious, one may be led to one of two extreme metaphysical views of what it is to apprehend the empirical world and one of two correspondingly extreme views of its relation to a transcendent world comprising selves (spirits, minds, subjects, etc.) by whom the empirical world is apprehended. In one of these views the apprehension of the empirical world is a kind of finding and the self a finder; in the other the apprehension of the empirical world is a kind of making and the self a maker.

Between these extremes there lies a variety of less radical views. For the purpose of comparing them, however briefly and crudely, it will be useful to distinguish between constructs, i.e., constructed or constructible states, and facts, i.e., unconstructed and unconstructible states. This terminology, which is not too far removed from everyday language, ignores the etymology of the world "fact", i.e., its derivation from the Latin *factum*, the meaning of which is fairly close to that of *constructum*. (Thus Vico's famous *factum et verum convertuntur* would in the terminology adopted here be better rendered as *constructum et verum convertuntur*.) A similar distinction

---

[7] See *Correspondence with Clarke*, 3rd letter, section 7.

opposes constructions, i.e., constructed or constructible events, to non-constructive events, which are neither. A fact may wrongly appear to be a construct or vice versa. And it may be controversial whether a state is a fact or a construct.

In everyday life it is on the whole not difficult to draw the line between the finding of facts and the construction of constructs, even if there are borderline cases and even if in the light of experience the line may have to be redrawn. Against this metaphysicians have argued that here as elsewhere transcendent reality is obscured by mind-dependent experience. Let us call those philosophers who hold that at least some apparent findings and at least some apparent facts are in (transcendent) reality makings and constructs "constructivist metaphysicians" or "constructivists". And let us, for want of a better word, call "factualist metaphysicians" or "factualists" those philosophers who hold that at least some apparent makings and at least some apparent constructs are in (transcendent) reality findings and facts.

Kant's metaphysics is a good – possibly the best – example of a thorough constructivism, the influence of which is still widely felt in philosophy and in other fields of inquiry. Kant sees it as a Copernican turning away from the equally thorough factualism of his predecessors, especially Leibniz. One of the main reasons Kant gives for his constructivism is that the necessity and universality of mathematical and other synthetic *a priori* judgments could not be explained unless these judgments characterized not facts found by the thinker, but constructs made by him. The need to explain the very possibility of these necessary and yet nonanalytic judgments was according to Kant not recognized by either his rationalist or his empiricist predecessors because all of them believed that only analytic judgments can be necessary and because this false belief and other equally false beliefs, e.g., that the axioms of arithmetic or the principle of causality were analytic, supported each other. A thorough and still influential factualism is the philosophy of Leibniz. It covers everything except the creator who created *the* world which "in its perfection surpasses all the other possible worlds".[8] This actual world must like all the possible ones conform to *the* laws of logic and, since according to Leibniz mathematics is reducible to logic, to the laws of mathematics.

While there is here no need or room for a detailed description and comparison of Kant's constructivism and Leibniz's factualism, it may be useful to note their influence on two recent philosophers whose views are still widely accepted, namely, Frege and Wittgenstein. Frege was even in his

---

[8] *Theodicée*, section 416.

logicist phase a follower of both Leibniz and Kant, accepting Leibniz's view that arithmetic is reducible to logic and Kant's view that the axioms and theorems of geometry are synthetic and *a priori*. In the last years of his life he abandoned this half-constructivist and half-factualist view of mathematics for a full-blown Kantian constructivism.[9] With regard to the philosophy of Wittgenstein, it can be argued that not only the rather primitive logicism of the *Tractatus Logico-Philosophicus*, according to which all truths of logic are tautologies and all truths of mathematics equations,[10] but the metaphysics of the whole *Tractatus* is a version of Leibniz's factualism. It could similarly be argued that Wittgenstein's later philosophy manifests many characteristic features of Kant's constructivism, which may have entered his thought not only directly, but also indirectly through, e.g., the works of Frege and Schopenhauer, whose influence on himself he gratefully acknowledges.[11]

A comparison between the early and the late philosophies of Frege on the one hand and of Wittgenstein on the other exemplifies the possibility of more or less restricted versions of constructivism or factualism. Thus Frege's philosophical works show mainly changes in his conception of mathematics, whereas Wittgenstein's conversion from factualism to constructivism affects every aspect of the relation between thinking and the world as consisting of facts or constructs. Factualism and constructivism may be restricted not only to mathematics, but also to other fields. When the distinction between "finding" and "making" is applied to a part or aspect, rather than to the whole of reality (as opposed to a possibly illusory experience), then the metaphysical use of these terms may be fairly close to their everyday use. The mathematical intuitionist, for example, need not assume that the constructivist mathematician's self differs from his ordinary self, e.g., in the way in which Kant's transcendental self which constructs experience differs from the empirical self.

Factualism, whether restricted or universal, is prima facie monistic and has on the whole been so regarded by its adherents. They tend to agree with Leibniz that there is only one actual world and that to confuse a *merely possible* world with it is to be mistaken. Constructivism may more easily become pluralistic. Thus, although Kant regarded Newtonian physics and Euclidean geometry as constructs which do not admit of alternatives, the post-Kantian realization of such alternatives led to pluralistic versions of constructivism.

[9] See *Nachgelassene Schriften und Wissenschaftlicher Briefwechsel*, ed. H. Hermes, F. Kambartel and F. Kaulbach (Hamburg, 1976).
[10] See *Tractatus*, 6.22 *et passim*.
[11] See *Vermischte Bemerkungen*, ed. G. H. von Wright and H. Nyman (Oxford, 1977), p. 43.

5 From empirical imperfections to transcendent perfections

The concepts of transcendent metaphysics so far considered are concepts which it shares with commonsense and scientific thinking about empirical reality and its mathematical idealizations. What was distinctive about transcendent metaphysics was the application of these concepts and their complements to transcendent reality. Thus infinistic, idealizing concepts of mathematics are conceived as characterizing not only mathematical structures which in certain contexts and for certain purposes are identifiable with empirical ones, but also that which exists mind-independently. Again, both the primary and the secondary qualities used by philosophical realists are taken from everyday thinking and applied to transcendent reality – the former by being declared applicable, the latter by being declared inapplicable to it. Similar remarks apply to the concepts of fact and finding on the one hand and construct and construction on the other. These concepts too have an everyday meaning, but a different application in transcendent metaphysics, where apparent facts may be judged transcendent constructs and vice versa.

The attributes which are sometimes called "perfect attributes" or, briefly, "perfections" of transcendent reality have no application to empirical reality and are not regarded as applicable to it. In Western philosophy they are usually ascribed to God as the whole or part of transcendent reality. Although often spoken of as infinitistic versions of finite concepts they must – as Leibniz knew and as was pointed out earlier – not be confused with mathematically infinite concepts. Thus God's infinite goodness is not an (ordinal or cardinal) numerical notion or a quantitative notion. To see this one needs only to try to develop an ordinal or cardinal scale for human goodness and, perhaps, to recall the very limited success of attempts at developing such a scale for the very much simpler notion of economic utility.

Similar remarks apply to perfection conceived as activity or richness of cognitive content. The former conception is exemplified by Spinoza's thesis to the effect that "in proportion as each thing possesses more of perfection, so it is more active and less passive; and *vice versa*, in proportion as it is more active, so it is more perfect".[12] The latter conception is exemplified by Leibniz's thesis that "one created thing is more perfect than another when we find in the first that which gives an *a priori* reason for what occurs in the second".[13] Yet even if an ordinal scale for comparing goodness, activity or cognitive content were available, the perfection of God is conceived as lying

[12] See *Ethics*, part V, prop. 40.   [13] See *Monadology*, section 50.

not only in one of these dimensions, but in all of them and by some, such as Spinoza, also in other dimensions, of which human beings are not aware.

The radical difference between the concepts of a perfection or of a perfect being and other concepts manifests itself, according to some metaphysicians, also in logic. Thus it is held by Anselm of Canterbury that whereas any concept other than the concept of a perfect being does not logically imply that an instance of it exists, the concept of a perfect being logically implies its existence. And it is held by Leibniz that "God alone (or the Necessary Being) has this prerogative that if he be possible he must necessarily exist." [14] For the present purpose, namely, the exemplification of concepts which are regarded as characterizing transcendent reality but are not applicable or, through *as-if* identifications, linked to empirical reality, it is not necessary to decide whether Anselm's, Leibniz's or other proofs of their nonemptiness are valid as they stand or, if not, whether they can in one way or another be validly reconstructed (see chapter 18, section 5).

If one admits that a concept of a perfection, of a specific perfection (such as perfect goodness, perfect knowledge, perfect power), of a perfect being or any other concept which, though not applicable to empirical reality, is alleged to be applicable to transcendent reality is not logically impossible, then the following questions arise: can one justifiably assume the purely existential thesis that the concept is transcendently not empty or applicable, even if that to which it is applicable is not and, possibly, cannot be given? If the concept is transcendently not empty, can one justifiably assume that an instance of it or perhaps its only instance is accessible? If so, how is an instance or the only instance accessible? Various answers have been given: empiristic realists, even if they admitted that the assumption of an empirically but not transcendently empty concept is not logically impossible, would have to deny the existential thesis. Others, e.g., Spinoza, not only assert the existential theorem but ascribe to all or some human beings a capacity of apprehending the bearer of such an attribute in a manner which – like Spinoza's *scientia intuitiva* or Cusanus's *intellectus* – differs from ordinary perception and ordinary thinking. All these answers imply the possibility of applying concepts to transcendent reality.

In concluding this chapter it seems proper to emphasize once again that its distinction between various kinds of transcendent metaphysics – based respectively on regarding empirical reality as an exact or approximative representation of transcendent reality, on opposing primary to secondary qualities, on radically redrawing the line separating facts from constructs and on contrasting imperfect empirical with perfect transcendent reality –

[14] Ibid., section 45.

must not be taken as exclusive or exhaustive. Nor must it be taken as implying that other approaches to transcendent metaphysics, e.g., one that, roughly speaking, regards all metaphysics as prescientific, wishful thinking, may not shed light on the structure of various metaphysical systems.[15]

[15] See, for example, *Erkenntnis und Illusion*, by Ernst Topitsch (Hamburg, 1979).

CHAPTER 12

TRANSCENDENT METAPHYSICS AND THE LIMITS OF CONCEPTUAL THINKING

The versions of transcendent metaphysics which have been exemplified, as indeed all transcendent metaphysics in the strict sense of the term, are based on the assumption that transcendent reality can be characterized by concepts. The claim that a conceptual grasp of transcendent reality has been, or can in principle be, achieved has been denied by philosophers of different kinds. Among them are sceptics, antimetaphysical mystics and what, for want of a better term, may be called "metaphysical mystics" or "aesthetic metaphysicians". The sceptics hold that no proposition which transcends its propounder's purely subjective experience is rationally justifiable. The antimetaphysical mystics hold that any attempt at a characterization of transcendent reality by the application of concepts to particulars is wholly inadequate. The metaphysical mystics or aesthetic metaphysicians hold that transcendent reality can, at best, be aesthetically represented, more precisely that it can be represented by conceptual structures borrowed from immanent metaphysics, but used in a nonpropositional manner bearing some similarity to poetry.

The present chapter examines, within the limits set by this essay, philosophical scepticism (1); reports on mystical experience (2); some relations between mysticism and transcendent metaphysics (3); attempted representations of the apprehension of transcendent reality which are aesthetic as well as metaphysical (4) and attempted representations of this reality itself (5).

1 Scepticism, immanent and transcendent metaphysics

The most radical form of scepticism is Pyrrhonism, as described by Sextus.[1] It is according to him "an ability, or mental attitude which opposes appearance to judgments in any way whatsoever ($\delta\acute{u}\nu\alpha\mu\iota\varsigma$ $\dot{\alpha}\nu\tau\iota\vartheta\epsilon\tau\iota\kappa\grave{\eta}$ $\phi\alpha\iota\nu\omega\mu\acute{e}\nu\omega\nu$ $\kappa\alpha\iota$ $\nu oo\upsilon\mu\acute{e}\nu\omega\nu$, $\kappa\alpha\vartheta'$ $o\acute{\iota}o\nu\delta\acute{\eta}\pi o\tau\epsilon$ $\tau\rho\acute{o}\pi o\nu$) with the result that owing to the equipollence ($\iota\sigma o\sigma\vartheta\acute{e}\nu\epsilon\iota\alpha$) of the objects and reasons thus opposed, we are

[1] See, for example, *Sextus Empiricus* with an English translation by R. G. Bury (London and Harvard, 1956).

brought first to a state of suspension of judgment (ἐποχή, which Bury translates by 'mental suspense') and next to a state of unperturbedness or quietude (ἀταραξία)".[2] The sceptical attitude is compatible with seeing "that we can not remain wholly inactive" and, thus, with "adhering to appearances" and "living in accordance with the normal values of life, in an undogmatic manner (ἀδοξάστως)".[3]

This brief characterization raises exegetic as well as philosophical questions which are relevant to the tasks of immanent and transcendent metaphysics, in particular questions about the nature, scope, and legitimacy of suspending judgment and about the possibility of engaging in practical life in spite of suspending judgment. Sextus contrasts what appears to himself and what he announces in an undogmatic way with making assertions about "the underlying external entities" (περὶ τῶν ἔξωθεν ὑποκειμένων) – assertions which, together with the corresponding negations, he refrains from making. In suspending judgment on "the underlying entities" on the ground that mutually incompatible judgments about them are equipollent, Sextus assumes an account of interpretative stratification, especially objectivization, which resembles the account given earlier in this essay (chapter 1, section 3). Thus 'x is a wholly subjective chair-appearance' and 'x is an (externally underlying) chair' are characteristic examples of two concepts, the second of which is interpretative of the first. Moreover, 'x is a wholly subjective chair-appearance' is compatible with 'x is a chair' and also with 'x is not a chair.' It is equally compatible with the concepts 'x is a chair as conceived by Plato' and 'x is a chair as conceived by Aristotle' even though these two concepts of "dogmatic metaphysics" are mutually incompatible. The question whether what appears to the sceptic and is announced by him in an undogmatic way as being a merely subjective appearance can be so announced without any interpretation is (it seems to me) not clearly answered in Sextus's text. But that, according to him, all transsubjective, intersubjective or objective statements are interpretative is clear enough. And that what is suspended is not the undogmatically announced appearance, but the judgment interpreting it, is no less clear.

If the sceptical suspension of judgment acknowledges the rôle of interpretation – in particular the conferment of objectivity on subjective appearances – it ipso facto acknowledges the differentiation of experience into particulars and attributes. For without some such differentiation attributes implying transsubjective, intersubjective or objective validity could not be assigned or refused to any appearance. Nor could their assignment or refusal be suspended. To assume that it could, is to confuse the mere absence of

---

[2] Ibid., vol. 1, chapter 4.   [3] Ibid., vol. 1 (*Outlines of Pyrrhonism*), chapter 11.

assignment or refusal with withholding or suspending them. To acknowledge the differentiation of experience is in turn to acknowledge the weak principle of noncontradiction and, thus, a minimum of deductive organization, since the differentiation would be pointless if every attribute were correctly assignable and correctly refusable to every particular (see chapter 1, section 2). Although the sceptic's "equipollence of the opposed objects and reasons" which leads to his suspension of judgment restricts his acknowledgment of epistemic domination of one class of judgments by another, it does not exclude it altogether: his appeal to argument implies the epistemic supremacy of the logical principles employed. And some passages of Sextus's work seem (to me, sometimes) to indicate that the class of undogmatic announcements of pure subjective awareness is also supreme for him.

The sceptical suspension of judgment about the "external entities" which allegedly underlie what appears to him supports to some extent the general purpose of this essay and some of its results. For in order to suspend judgment about immanent and transcendent metaphysics, a sceptical inquiry must, no less than the present philosophico-anthropological one, exhibit their structure, as determined by the manner in which a person's beliefs are organized through the differentiation of experience into particulars and attributes, its deductive organization and the rest. To say this is, of course, not to say that Sextus has anticipated the results of the present inquiry, but rather that his attempt at suspension of judgment is compatible with them.

It must further be noted that the sceptical suspension of judgment about external entities and, hence, about immanent metaphysics is not unqualified since it is not meant to lead to inactivity or to justify it. It is purely theoretical in that it allows the sceptic to "live in accordance with the normal rules of life", i.e., in accordance "with the fourfold regulation" of which "one part lies in the guidance of Nature, another in the constraint of the passions, another in the tradition of law and customs, another in the instruction of the arts".[4] Such a life requires, at least, a provisional or undogmatic acceptance of a more or less closely organized body of beliefs and, hence, of an immanent metaphysics or categorial framework (see chapter 10, section 1).

Does the Pyrrhonian sceptic also have a transcendent metaphysics? He clearly is not a philosophical realist of a Lockean or any other persuasion. Nor is he a naive realist whose naive identification of the mind-dependent world of objects with mind-independent reality is as dogmatic as any philosophical realism. But the sceptic does – and *qua* sceptic should – conduct himself *as if* he were a naive realist. Whether such a purely pragmatic realism is to be

[4] Ibid., vol. 1, chapter 11.

classified as being a transcendent metaphysics is of little consequence. For it is either not transcendent metaphysics at all, as was suggested earlier, or a vanishingly feeble version of it.

2 Mystical experience and transcendent reality

To the sceptic the claims of transcendent metaphysics must appear illegitimate because he considers it correct to suspend judgment on all matters beyond his subjective experience. To the mystic the claim of transcendent metaphysics to reveal reality must appear illegitimate because he believes any characterization of reality by means of concepts to be inadequate. Yet in spite of their very different estimates of the aims and achievements of immanent and transcendent metaphysics both the sceptic and the mystic may throw light on their structure and function. The sceptic may do so by comparing the application of descriptive concepts to subjective appearances with the application of interpretative concepts ascribing intersubjectivity or objectivity to these appearances. The mystic may do so by comparing the conceptual characterization of conceptually characterizable entities with a mystical experience which is not so characterizable.

Mystics belonging to different cultural backgrounds, holding different religious beliefs and possibly differing in some features of their experience agree nevertheless to a remarkable extent in their hints at what it is and in their statements as to what it is not. Although the hints, like the sentences in some poems, take the form of statements, they are nonpropositional and must not be confused with statements. Otherwise the hints may be taken to assert what the statements clearly deny. Thus when Plato, Plotinus and mystics using their language say that transcendent reality is "on the other side of being" (ἐπέκεινα τῆς οὐσίας)[5] they do not wish to assert that 'transcendent reality' denotes one of the particulars and 'on the other side of being' one of the attributes which result from the differentiation into particulars and attributes of ordinary perception and thinking within the constraints of a categorial framework or of conceptual thinking of some other kind. Indeed they frequently deny this explicitly or implicitly by opposing mystical experience to sense-perception and to discursive thinking. When a mystic uses the language of transcendent metaphysics to hint at his experience, the danger of confusing his nonpropositional hints with statements is greater than when he uses, say, the poetic or emotional languauge of love for another human being. For the positions of the mystic

[5] *Republic*, 509B.

and the transcendent metaphysician are closer to each other than the positions of a mystic and the lover of another human being.

The need to distinguish nonpropositional hints at mystical experience from statements about it is clearly seen, expressed and justified by William James. He draws attention to the frequent occurrence in mystical literature of "such self-contradictory phrases as 'dazzling obscurity', 'whispering silence', 'teeming desert'" and remarks that "not conceptual speech, but music rather, is the element through which we are best spoken to by mystical truth", adding that "many mystical scriptures are indeed little more than musical compositions".[6] A rough guide for distinguishing between a mystic's nonpropositional hints and statements might point out that sentences which apparently express self-contradictory or affirmative statements are more likely to be nonpropositional hints than sentences which apparently express negative statements.

William James's own characterization of a common core of mystical experience is in line with what others who have inquired into the historical evidence have said about it – provided that one makes allowances for his tendency towards a pantheistic, rather than a monotheistic interpretation or terminology. Among the features of mystical experience mentioned by him, the following are relevant in the context of this essay: first, in our mystical states we *somehow* "become one with the Absolute" and "become aware of our oneness". In saying that we *somehow* become one with the Absolute and *somehow* aware of one oneness, we imply our own and other people's inability precisely to describe the manner and the content of the awareness. Neither the "That art Thou" of the Upanishads nor Spinoza's "intellectual love of God" which "depends on the mind, as its formal cause, in so far as the mind itself is eternal" replaces the nonpropositional hint of "somehow" by definite statements. The same holds for the reports given by Christian mystics, for example, by Saint Teresa – whom James regards as the expert of experts in describing mystical experience – when she says of the soul that so "long as she is united with God" she "neither sees, hears, not understands".[7]

Second, mystical states defy expression and are in this respect "more like states of feeling than like states of knowledge". To try to impart to another in what "the quality or worth" of a mystical experience consists is like trying to impart the quality or worth of being in love to somebody who has never been in love. "One must have been in love oneself to understand a lover's state of mind".[8] At the same time mystical states "seem to those who experience them to be also states of knowledge . . . and states of insight into depths of

---

[6] See the chapter on mysticism in *Varieties of Religious Experience* (New York, 1902).
[7] Ibid., p. 40u.   [8] Ibid., p. 371.

truth unplumbed by the discursive intellect".[9] A third feature of mystic states is their passivity, i.e., the mystic's feeling " as if his own will were in abeyance, and indeed sometimes as if he were grasped and held by a superior power".[10] James also notes a fourth feature of mystical states which is for our present purpose of less importance, namely, that mystical states cannot be sustained for long – "an hour or two" appearing to "be the limit beyond which they fade in the light of common day". The access, if any, through mystical experience and the access, if any, through metaphysics to transcendent reality are thus radically different.

3 Mysticism and transcendent metaphysics

Although the mystic and the transcendent philosopher aim at apprehending transcendent reality, the latter's conceptual and the former's nonconceptual approach are so different that it is not at all obvious how far, if at all, the two approaches aid or hinder each other. Mystical experiences may be quite independent of any prior transcendent philosophizing and may be regarded as such by mystics, by transcendent metaphysicians and even by those who combine the mystical and the metaphysical approach in their persons. Among the many examples of reports on alleged mystical experiences whose subject is untouched by purification or pollution through metaphysical thinking is the following passage from *The Epistle of Privy Counsel* by the unknown author of the *Cloud of Unknowing*:

Look that nothing remain in thy working mind but a naked intent stretching unto God, not clothed in any special thought. Well is this work likened to a sleep. For as in sleep the use of the bodily wits is ceased, that the body may take his full rest in feeding and strengthening of the bodily nature; right so in this ghostly sleep the wanton questions of the wild ghostly wits and all imaginative reasons be fast bound and utterly voided, so that the silly soul may softly sleep and rest in the lovely beholding of God as he is, in full feeding and strengthening of the ghostly nature.[11]

There are other roads which allegedly may lead to mystic experience. One of them is drunkenness – from alcohol, not from transcendent metaphysics. One can hardly do better than repeat the sympathetic words of William James at some length:

Sobriety diminishes, discriminates, and says no; drunkenness expands, unites, and says yes. It is in fact the great exciter of the *Yes* function in man. It brings its votary from the chill periphery of things to the radiant core. It makes him for the moment one

---

[9] Ibid., p. 371.   [10] Ibid., p. 371.
[11] Quoted from *Varieties of Mystic Experiences – An Anthology and Interpretation*, by Elmer O'Brien, SJ (New York and San Francisco, 1964), p. 212.

with truth. Not through mere perversity do men run after it. To the poor and the unlettered it stands in the place of symphony concerts and of literature . . . The drunken consciousness is one bit of the mystic consciousness.

It should be emphasized that James speaks only of "the fleeting earlier phases" of drunkenness, which "in its totality" he regards as a "degrading . . . poisoning".[12]

The author of the *Cloud of Unknowing* and James's fortunate drunk in the initial states of drunkenness approach awareness of transcendent reality without formulating propositions of immanent or transcendent metaphysics. For others the road to mystic experience leads through metaphysics. The long list of philosophers who took it includes Plato, Plotinus, Nicolaus of Cusa and, in our own time, Wittgenstein. Their journey can be divided into three stages: the first is the stage of immanent metaphysics. It consists of the philosopher's explicit recognition of his categorial framework and possibly of the general principles which govern the organization of a person's beliefs into a categorial framework. These general principles are, of course, of special interest in the context of this essay, since it is one of its tasks to exhibit them.

The second stage consists of the denial that the principles of conceptual and propositional thinking, employed in the constitution of the philosopher's immanent metaphysics or categorial framework (of any immanent metaphysics or categorial framework), are – except possibly as symbolic hints – helpful in the apprehension of transcendent reality. This denial, together with the specification of the principles in question, belongs to transcendent metaphysics. As part of the road towards the non-conceptual apprehension of transcendent reality, it might in conformity with medieval usage be called the *via negativa*. The third and last stage consists of the apprehension of transcendent reality and, possibly, of conveying this apprehension.

Unlike the sceptic, the mystical philosopher does not merely suspend judgment about the claim that thinking within the constraints of an immanent metaphysics or categorial framework can gain access to mind-independent, transcendent reality, but declares the claim to be invalid. This declaration is often based on a negative characterization of transcendent reality which at the same time exhibits what is common to any immanent metaphysics. Thus Nicolaus of Cusa says of the "divine unity" that it "precedes all plurality" and hence "all diversity, difference, opposition, inequality, division and anything that accompanies plurality", that it "belongs to no kind, has no name, no shape even though it is all within all".[13] He acknowledges that commonsense, mathematical and scientific

---

[12] Ibid., p. 378.   [13] *De Conjecturis*, part I, chapter 5, section 17.

thinking imply the acceptance of the principle of contradiction but holds that there is a higher form of awareness for which the principle is not valid since in it contradictions coincide.[14] He distinguishes between, on the one hand, *ratio*, which proceeds by differentiating experience into particulars and attributes, by organizing them in accordance with a deductive logic and by conforming to the other principles of organization which result in categorial frameworks, and, on the other hand, *intellectus*, which is an altogether different awareness, namely, the awareness of the divine unity, or, more generally, of transcendent reality. (My reason for using the Latin words is that using English ones might add to the confusion which is caused by *ratio* and *intellectus* being sometimes translated as "reason" (*Vernunft*) and sometimes as "understanding" (*Verstand*).)

What Cusanus says about the *intellectus* applies also to other versions of nonconceptual and, one may add, nonperceptual awareness of transcendent reality. Not being subject to even the weak principle of non-contradiction and, hence, incapable of being characterized by the application of concepts and the assertion of propositions, the content of the awareness cannot be expressed by true sentences. To that extent Wittgenstein is right when at the end of the *Tractatus* he declares what only shows itself is unsayable and that "whereof one cannot speak, thereof one must be silent". Yet whereof one cannot speak in sentences expressing true propositions, of that one might be able to speak in sentences used as poetic or other nonpropositional representations.

4 On attempts at representing the apprehension of transcendent reality in a manner which is both aesthetic and metaphysical

It is occasionally claimed by poets and composers and, much more often, by others on their behalf that they have more or less successfully attempted to represent the apprehension of a transcendent reality or this reality itself. The claim, whatever its precise meaning, is widely regarded as making sense or, at least, as not being wholly absurd. In the context of a discussion of transcendent metaphysics and the limits of conceptual thinking it raises two issues. First, can the nature of the aesthetic representation in question be made clearer; and, if so, how? Second, can such a representation be both aesthetic and metaphysical in a sense which implies a clear distinction between it and aesthetic representations belonging to poetry – including so-called metaphysical poetry – painting, music and the arts in general?

An aesthetic representation of apprehending a transcendent reality

[14] See ibid., part II, chapter 2, section 81, for example.

involves, like any aesthetic representation, a *representans*, or aesthetic object, i.e., a person's conduct or product in so far as it evokes a certain feeling, and a *representandum*, or aesthetic meaning, i.e., the feeling which the aesthetic object is intended or meant to evoke. And the aesthetic object, more or less adequately, represents the aesthetic meaning for a person who treats the feeling evoked *as if* it were the feeling intended. (This characterization of aesthetic representation is taken from chapter 4, section 3, where the relevant meaning of "feeling" is further explained.) In the case of aesthetically representing the apprehension of a transcendent reality the *representandum* is the feeling which for the person representing it is, or is characteristically involved in, what he takes to be his apprehension of transcendent reality. The *representans* is the feeling evoked, in himself or another person, by a certain piece of music, a painting, a poem, a dance, etc. It may in particular also be a piece of "nonpropositional, metaphysical prose", i.e., a piece of prose comprising expressions transferred from a context in which they are used propositionally into a context in which they are not so used. It is not difficult to distinguish between the ways in which a metaphysical poet, a metaphysical mystic and a mystic who is neither a poet nor a metaphysician represent what they take to be their apprehension of transcendent reality. From the point of view of the present investigation it is important to consider somewhat more closely the aesthetic use of metaphysical language by metaphysicians.

This use is closely connected with their approach to transcendent reality. Whereas, as has been pointed out earlier, St Teresa approaches it independently of all philosophizing, Spinoza, Nicolaus of Cusa and others approach it *via* metaphysical thinking. Because of this, St Teresa in representing her apprehension of transcendent reality uses words like "seeing", "hearing", "understanding", which in their propositional use express commonsense concepts; whereas Spinoza uses words like "God" (in the sense of *deus sive natura*) or "scientia intuitiva", which in their propositional use express technical terms of metaphysics. For St Teresa metaphysics is irrelevant to the apprehension of transcendent reality; and the aesthetic use of metaphysical language irrelevant to representing this apprehension. For Spinoza metaphysics is an indispensable or, at the very least, a helpful stage in approaching the apprehension of transcendent reality; and the aesthetic use of metaphysical language an indispensable or, at the very least, a helpful aid in representing this apprehension.

St Teresa is an example of a nonmetaphysical mystic in a sense which implies not only the irrelevance of metaphysics to the apprehension of transcendent reality, but also of the aesthetic use of metaphysical language to its representation. Some nonmetaphysical mystics are more radical in that they reject metaphysics and even the aesthetic use of metaphysical language as a more or less serious obstacle to the apprehension of transcendent reality. Spinoza may be called not only a "metaphysical mystic", but also an "aesthetic metaphysician", depending on whether one wishes to emphasize his approach through metaphysics to the apprehension of transcendent reality or his aesthetic use of metaphysical language in representing the apprehension. To these examples other equally clear ones may be added. Thus, if a mystic tells us without qualification that what he experienced was at the same time brilliantly light and utterly dark and the bearer of other mutually exclusive attributes, his mysticism is clearly nonmetaphysical. The same sentences, preceded by a metaphysical argument which tries to establish that the apprehension of transcendent reality is not conceptual (propositional, discursive, etc.), may constitute an essential part of a metaphysical mystic's message to those whom he wishes to inform and possibly also to convert.

And there are, of course, borderline cases. For example, a mystic and the person to whom he relates his claim to have had a vision of God may not be clear whether the term "vision" is being used as expressing a kind of apprehension which resembles ordinary seeing; whether it is used as a technical philosophical term expressing what Kant and others call an "intellectual intuition", i.e., an apprehension which is neither perceptual nor conceptual (discursive, etc.); and whether, if it is used in the latter way, the concept of an intellectual intuition is at all applicable to any experience. That there are borderline cases between nonmetaphysical mysticism and metaphysical mysticism or aesthetic metaphysics is not surprising. Taking note of them serves the demarcation of transcendent metaphysics from metaphysical mysticism, which tries to represent what cannot be stated.

5 On attempted aesthetic-cum-metaphysical representations of transcendent reality

Because the conceptual characterization of mystical experience is restricted to negative statements, its positive aspects can only be expressed and conveyed through aesthetic representation. Because mystical experience somehow involves a union of subject and object, any aesthetic representation which separates the apprehension of the transcendent reality by the mystic from this reality does in this respect misrepresent his experience. This need not detract from its value since some misrepresentation is common to all aesthetic representations (e.g., in poetry or painting), all of which require for their success that features of the *representans* which are not to be included in its identification with the *representandum* are acknowledged as such. Yet mystical experience is not the only nonconceptual and, hence, the only aesthetically representable apprehension of transcendent reality. There are others – and more common ones – in which the person who believes himself to apprehend transcendent reality fully preserves his individual distinctness. In representing such a reality the distinctness of subject and object must not be obscured but, on the contrary, clearly exhibited.

Whereas the preceding remarks were mainly devoted to attempts at a metaphysical-cum-aesthetic representation of the manner in which a transcendent reality is apprehended, the following remarks will be mainly concerned with such representations of the apprehended reality itself. As before the *representans* comprises words which in their propositional use express technical terms of metaphysics and which could not be used in the aesthetic representation of transcendent reality unless their technical, propositional use is well understood. A characteristic set of examples uses "logic" in this way: the person for whom the representation is intended is assumed to have a more or less clear conception of logic (Aristotelian or other) and is reminded of it. He is then asked to *imagine* something which as a finite being or for other cogent reasons he is incapable of conceiving, namely, a superlogic which in some respects resembles and in others surpasses ordinary logic. He is lastly told that what ordinary logic is to reality as constrained by his immanent metaphysics, the superlogic is to transcendent reality, i.e., that the former relation represents the latter.

A specific version of using logic in an aesthetic representation of an aspect of transcendent reality is based on imagining that the relation of deducibility which is characteristic of (any) logic has been replaced by a notion of "coherence" characteristic of the superlogic. We are told that whereas according to ordinary logic not every true proposition logically implies every other, according to the superlogic every proposition which is true of transcendent reality "superlogically" implies, or "coheres" with, every other such proposition. Those who have a more or less clear conception of logic and who can imagine, but not conceive, the required superlogic, are supposed to understand the aesthetic-cum-metaphysical representation of an aspect of transcendent reality, whether it satisfies them or not. There are, not surprisingly, also philosophers who hold that the superlogical implication in question is an applicable concept and that their "coherence theory" is conceptual and not aesthetic metaphysics.[15]

---

[15] Among the more recent defences of his view is Brand Blanshard's *The Nature of Thought* (London, 1939), vol. 2.

Another version of using logic in an aesthetic representation of an aspect of transcendent reality is based on imagining that the relation of deducibility which is characteristic of logic is replaced by an "ampliative deducibility" characteristic of the superlogic. We are told that whereas according to ordinary logic the premises of a deductive inference are richer in content than its conclusion, the converse is true in the superlogic. While some can imagine, but not conceive, the required superlogic, others hold that its ampliative deducibility is an applicable concept and that their superlogic constitutes a conceptual metaphysics. An early defender of this view is Descartes, who in this respect can be regarded as a forerunner of Hegel and the neo-Hegelians. There are other kinds of "superlogic" the status of which as conceptual metaphysics, aesthetic metaphysics or even nonsense is controversial.

What has been said about attempts at the aesthetic representation of transcendent reality by an imaginable, but not conceivable superlogic holds also for its representation by a supermathematics, a superphysics, a superhistory and other imaginable, but inconceivable, superdisciplines. A detailed discussion and classification of them would have to consider various combinations, e.g., of a superlogic with a superphysics or super-history or with both of them. It would also have to take note of claims that these superdisciplines are not aesthetic representations, but conceptual characterizations of transcendent reality, of claims that in order to understand their nature it is necessary to distinguish between concepts and superconcepts or "Ideas", which are not subject to the principle of noncontradiction and other logical principles; and of a variety of other claims about ways of expressing the nature of transcendent reality, which are neither conceptual characterizations nor aesthetic representations.

Transcendent, no less than immanent, metaphysics consists of statements, i.e., the application of concepts to its subject matter. In considering the possibility of a nonconceptual and nonconceptually representable access to transcendent reality, one crosses the border of transcendent metaphysics. And trying to cross the border which separates transcendent metaphysics from nonconceptual modes of grasping reality may serve the understanding of transcendent metaphysics.

CHAPTER 13

ON ANTIMETAPHYSICAL
ERRORS AND ILLUSIONS

Any person who in one way or another distinguishes between particulars
and attributes, employs at least the weak principle of noncontradiction,
interprets part of what is given subjectively by applying intersubjectivity-
concepts to it, and acknowledges that some beliefs are dominated while
others are supreme has *ipso facto* accepted an immanent metaphysics or a
(more or less clearly demarcated) categorial framework. And any person
who explicitly or implicitly assumes some relation between his beliefs as
constrained by his immanent metaphysics and a reality which is independent of his beliefs has *ipso facto* accepted a transcendent metaphysics.
If such a person rejects *all* metaphysics as erroneous or illusory and believes
his thinking to be free from metaphysical assumptions, he is guilty of what
may be called the "antimetaphysical error" or suffers from what may be
called the "antimetaphysical illusion".

The present chapter examines some versions of this error or illusion. It
begins by considering rejections of metaphysics based on identifying
metaphysics with specific kinds or systems of metaphysics (1); with a
primitive form of thinking which can, and should, be replaced by thinking
that is more advanced (2); or with ideological propaganda, masquerading
as true insight into the nature of reality (3). There follows a critique of the
antimetaphysical arguments propounded by Hume and his empiricist
successors (4); as well as by Wittgenstein and his followers (5).

1 On antimetaphysics and the mistaken identification of metaphysics with
one of its kinds or systems

The simplest and most simple-minded antimetaphysics is based on the
assumption that metaphysics consists of supreme principles which are
inconsistent with one's own. If one makes this assumption one can easily
come to believe that metaphysics is a kind of superstition. A more interesting
cause of the antimetaphysical error is the identification of metaphysics with
transcendent metaphysics. Those who make this identification normally

assign the various principles of immanent metaphysics to the disciplines in which they are most obviously employed and which provided the ground for their acceptance and the reason for their formulation. Thus an "antimetaphysician" who, with, e.g., Leibniz or Kant, accepts the principle that nature makes no jumps and that consequently all laws of nature must be expressible as continuous functions will assign this principle to physics. If, with, for example, Cantor and Gödel, he accepts the principle that there are actually infinite sets, he will assign it to mathematics. And if, with, for example, Aristotle and Frege, he accepts the principle of excluded middle, he will assign it to logic. Having thus disposed of immanent metaphysics he may, for example, with Kant, regard the questions of God, freedom and immortality as the subject-matter of transcendent metaphysics and then, unlike Kant, declare these questions, for one reason or another, as being spurious, unanswerable or, at least, as being of no concern to him.

Although the preceding chapters of this essay imply that our anti-metaphysician has accepted both an immanent and a transcendent metaphysics, it may be useful very briefly to indicate the outline of a Socratic dialogue designed to make this clear to him. Such a dialogue would start by showing that, and how, his own logical, mathematical, scientific and other beliefs are organized through a distinction between particulars and attributes, the acceptance of the weak principle of noncontradiction and the other ways by which structure is imposed on what would otherwise be a mere aggregate of beliefs. It would next emphasize the rôle of epistemic stratification, the difference between supreme principles and subordinate principles, and show how his own supreme principles define his (more or less precisely demarcated) categorial framework. Having explained this notion it would draw attention to categorial frameworks in which one or more of his supreme principles – e.g., the principles of continuity in nature, of the existence of actual infinities or of the principle of excluded middle – are replaced by others. It would show the need to distinguish between his categorial framework and the general notion of a categorial framework and suggest that the notion of a categorial framework is a clarification or analysis of what Kant and others have called "immanent metaphysics". If well conducted, the first part of the dialogue should end with establishing that there is no point in regarding one's own categorial framework as part of nonmetaphysical, e.g., scientific, thinking and in regarding other categorial frameworks as "metaphysical" in a more or less derogatory sense of the term.

Once the beneficiary of the Socratic dialogue has seen that not only other or inferior thinkers, but also he himself has an immanent metaphysics or thinks within the constraints of a categorial framework, the question of the adequacy of his or any other categorial framework to a reality which is independent of his awareness can be raised. If in answer to this question he asserts that his own categorial framework does not distort that reality or distorts it less than any other, it should be easy to convince him that in holding such a view he is making an assumption of transcendent metaphysics. He might find this acceptable, especially if he acknowledges that there is no point in regarding what one believes to be the relation of one's own categorial framework to reality as not being metaphysical, but, e.g., as part of scientific thinking, and in regarding what others believe about the relation of their categorial framework to reality as "metaphysical" in a more or less derogatory sense. But he might also find that he has always tended to be a sceptic or agnostic with respect to transcendent metaphysics and approve of this tendency. Such a position is, as we have seen (chapter 12, section 1), perfectly tenable. For one can think within a certain categorial framework and live *as if* the beliefs which guide one's conduct were true, while following Sextus in suspending judgment about their truth or falsehood.

The categorial frameworks which are most widely accepted in contemporary culture have their source in the natural sciences, especially in physical theories, embedded in infinitistic mathematics and classical logic. And the most widely accepted theses of transcendent metaphysics belong to some version of realism, implying that the principles which constitute a categorial framework are also adequate characterizations of reality. This is why the imagined beneficiary of the Socratic dialogue was somebody who believed not only in the value of natural science, but also in its incompatibility with metaphysics. A more cunning and more effective strategy might be first to enlist our scientific antimetaphysician's help in exhibiting the metaphysics of some opponent of scientific thinking and then to show that the organization of both, the beliefs of the opponent and the beliefs of the defender of science, implies the acceptance of an immanent metaphysics and – unless they are sceptics – of a transcendent metaphysics.

2 On antimetaphysics and the mistaken identification of metaphysics with prescientific thinking

Another reason for the antimetaphysical error or illusion is the mistaken identification of metaphysical thinking with prescientific thinking. An early, clear and influential version of this view is due to Auguste Comte.[1] He believed himself to have discovered "a great, fundamental law", namely, that "each of our fundamental conceptions, each branch of our knowledge passes through three different states: the theological or fictitious state, the Metaphysical or abstract state, and the Scientific or positive state".[2] Comte emphasizes the interdependence of observation and theory in scientific thinking. He notes that in the primitive stages of thinking mankind is faced with two difficulties: having "to observe in order to form *real* theories" and having "to form *theories of some sort* before it could apply itself to a connected series of observations".[3] Theological conceptions offered one – Comte holds the only – way out of this conundrum in that they "presented a rallying point for the efforts of the mind and furnished materials for its activity".[4] The theological philosophy presents phenomena "as being produced by the direct and continuous action of more or less numerous agents, whose arbitrary intervention explains all the apparent anomalies of the universe".[5] Theological philosophy, which includes the "attractive chimeras of Astrology or the powerful deceptions of Alchemy", provided a "stimulus for our intellectual development", the need of which was, according to Comte, "felt long ago by Kepler in the case of astronomy".[6]

The great achievements of Kepler and Newton, of Comte's contemporary Fourier, and of their scientific successors belong to the Positive Philosophy, the task of which is to "consider all phenomena as subject to invariable natural *Laws*" and to aim at "the exact discovery of these Laws" and their reduction "to the least possible number of them".[7] An example of such a law is the Newtonian law of gravitation according to which the force with which two particles attract each other is directly proportional to their masses, as ascertainable by their weight, and indirectly proportional to the square of their distance. Comte rightly emphasizes that the questions of "determining what attraction and weight are in themselves or what their causes are" lie outside the domain of science and, hence, of Positive Philosophy. Positive philosophers, therefore, "rightly abandon them to the imagination of the theologians or the subtlety of metaphysicians".[8]

Comte characterizes metaphysics as the transitional stage between theology and science or Positive Philosophy. It consists in "substituting in the study of phenomena, a corresponding inseparable entity for a direct supernatural agency" even though "at first, the former was only held to be

---

[1] See his *Cours de Philosophie Positive* 6 vols. (1830–43). The following quotations in this chapter are taken from an English translation of the first two chapters of his work by Paul Descours and H. Gordon Jones (London, 1905).
[2] Ibid, section 4.   [3] Ibid., section 15, italics mine.   [4] Ibid., section 15.   [5] Ibid., section 15.
[6] Ibid., sections 18, 19.   [7] Ibid., section 23.   [8] Ibid., section 24.

an off-shoot of the latter".[9] As mankind became gradually more scientific and less theological "the ideas of these metaphysical agents gradually became so dim that all right-minded persons only considered them to be abstract names of the phenomena in question". The metaphysical stage is, according to Comte, a necessary stage in passing from "the Theological to the Positive *regime*". He regards the "combined influence of the precepts of Bacon, the conceptions of Descartes, and the discoveries of Galileo" as one of the main reasons why the "Positive Philosophy began to assert itself in the world, in evident opposition to the Theological and Metaphysical spirit" and why "Positive conceptions disengaged themselves clearly from the superstitions and scholastic alloy, which had more or less disguised the true character of all the previous scientific work".[10] Comte held that in the field of natural phenomena Positive Philosophy had, through the natural sciences, replaced "theological and metaphysical methods . . . either as a means of investigation or even as a mode of reasoning", but that "these discarded methods are . . . still exclusively used for both purposes in everything which concerns social phenomena".[11] To replace theological and metaphysical speculation about social phenomena "by the foundation of Social Physics" seemed to him "the greatest and most pressing of our mental needs".[12] And in trying to fill this need he became the founder of sociology.

Comte, like Berkeley before him, distinguishes between two apparent intellectual tasks: the task of science, which is to describe phenomena and their regular connection; and the task of theology and other kinds of nonscientific thinking, which is to explain *why* phenomena occur in the way they do – in a sense of "why" which requires the indication of causes, essences, or other notions which are not needed for the description of phenomenal regularities. It is a thesis of Berkeley's transcendent metaphysics that human beings are not only capable of fulfilling the first task, but that they are also capable of more or less adequately fulfilling the second. It is a thesis of Comte's transcendent metaphysics that the second task cannot be fulfilled by human beings because it surpasses their capacity. In order to avoid confusion Comte's Positive Philosophy with, for example, logical positivism, it is important to emphasize that Comte does not reject theology as being devoid of linguistic meaning, that is, as consisting of utterances which merely look like statements, and that he does not reject them as logically impossible. That he rejects them as false and asserts their negations follows from his account of theology as the predecessor of science and as a guide to action for those who believe in theological propositions.

[9] Ibid., section 2.   [10] Ibid., section 28.   [11] Ibid., section 31.   [12] Ibid., section 32.

Comte accepts supreme principles – immanent to logic, mathematics, and natural science – which together constitute a categorial framework. This follows from what he says about the law of gravitation, about physics, and about the natural sciences in general. An inquiry into his work would, it seems, reveal that his categorial framework shows similarities to Berkeley's philosophy – provided one subtracts Berkeley's theology from it; and to Kant's *Critique of Pure Reason* – provided one abandons the distinction between phenomena and noumena. Comte or a modern Comtean might well argue that since he reserves the name "metaphysics" for various nonscientific or antiscientific philosophies, his own immanent and transcendent metaphysics should not be called "metaphysics" simpliciter, but, for example, "positivist metaphysics". If this expression is not considered a contradiction in terms, it seems unobjectionable.

3 Antimetaphysics and the identification of metaphysical systems with ideologies

Just as in Comte's view metaphysics is inadequate to reality because it is prescientific and, hence, unscientific, so in the view of Marx, Engels, and other Marxist philosophers it is inadequate to reality because it is ideological and, hence again, unscientific. And just as Comte fails to recognize the implicit metaphysical assumptions in scientific thinking, so the critics of ideology fail to see that their critique also implies such assumptions.

A person's system of beliefs, including in particular his metaphysics, and of practical attitudes, including in particular his morality, is considered an ideology if it satisfies the following conditions: the person shares the system of beliefs and practical attitudes with the other members of a social group to which he belongs (see chapter 9, section 1). Having the beliefs and practical attitudes serves the interests of this group and causes its members consciously or unconsciously to impose the beliefs and attitudes on all members of their society and not only on the members of their social group. The beliefs and attitudes which belong to the system need not, and normally are not, correct in a sense of the term which may differ from one school of social philosophers to another. According to Marx and Engels every ideology accepted by the members of a ruling social class corresponds to "a definite stage of development of the material mode of production", determining "the relations of production" and thus "the economic structure of society – the real foundation, on which rises a legal and political superstructure", and with it, "definite forms of social consciousness".[13]

---

[13] *Zur Kritik der politischen Ökonomie* (Berlin, 1959), in Karl Marx and Friedrich Engels, *Werke* (Berlin, 1962), vol. 13, p. 8.

Marx and Engels claim to know that, and how, an ideology which corresponds to a definite stage of production distorts reality in ways of which those who accept the ideology are not aware.

They claim, moreover, that what provides this knowledge is a scientific theory explaining the nature of social being, of consciousness, and of the relation between them – as summarized by the famous dictum that "it is not the consciousness of men that determines their being, but on the contrary, their social being that determines their consciousness".[14] Thus the "fog-formations (*Nebelbildungen*) in men's brain", namely, "morality, religion, metaphysics and all other ideology", are also "sublimates of their life process, which is material, empirically ascertainable and connected with material presuppositions".[15] Yet men's social being determines not only their ideology which is the outcome of speculation, but also their true beliefs which are the outcome of science. "Where speculation ceases, i.e., with real life, begins real, positive science, the representation of practical activity, of practical process of human development."[16]

This real science implies that "the class which has the means of material production at its disposal thereby also disposes of the means of mental production, so that the thoughts of those who lack the means of mental production are thereby on the average subject to this class".[17] A "class engaged in revolution acts from the beginning, because it opposes a *class*, not as a class but as representative of the whole of humanity".[18] This is particularly so in the case of the proletariat, which acts as the representative of the whole of humanity, since the result of its successful revolution is the classless society, the social being of which will no longer determine an ideology but the truth – a truth which scientific Marxism can anticipate.

In discussing Comte's Positive Philosophy it was pointed out that his conception of science is too narrow since it excludes all immanent metaphysics from it or, in other words, since it ignores the way in which scientific thinking is constrained by the thinker's categorial framework. The Marxist conception of science, on the other hand, is too wide since it includes in it not only an immanent, but also a transcendent metaphysics. A full exposition and critique of Marx's "real science" or dialectical materialism falls outside the scope of this essay, especially as very different versions of this philosophy are claimed to embody its central insights.

Marxism in all its versions is both an immanent and a transcendent metaphysics. With regard to the former – at least as understood by Engels, Marx's close collaborator, and by Lenin, his politically most influential

---

[14] Ibid., p. 8.
[15] Karl Marx and Friedrich Engels, *Deutsche Ideologie*, in *Werke*, vol. 3, p. 26.
[16] Ibid., p. 27.   [17] Ibid., p. 46.   [18] Ibid., p. 47.

disciple – its maximal kinds are material entities, to which all mental ones are reducible.[19] With regard to transcendent metaphysics, Marxist materialism implies, at least, a realist assumption to the effect that what is given to experience, if correctly interpreted by the "real science", is a part or aspect of mind-independent reality. Marxist dialectics, whatever its precise meaning, involves even stronger assumptions, belonging to transcendent metaphysics. To see this it is enough to consider quite generally the Marxist, and the similar Hegelian, opposition of ampliative, dialectical to deductive formal logic and the corresponding opposition of dialectical to formal reasoning.

The critics of metaphysics, so far considered, reject it on the ground that it contains utter falsehood or, at least, serious distortions of the truth. They do not imply that even the "powerful attractions of alchemy" mentioned by Comte or the "fog-formations" mentioned by Marx and Engels are meaningless.

4 On the alleged meaninglessness of metaphysics

The thesis that metaphysics is meaningless was central to the philosophy of logical positivism, which flourished in the first half of this century. It was influenced by Comte, for whom metaphysics was prescientific, by Hume, for whom it was "sophistry and confusion", and by modern logic, the rigour of which it tried to emulate. A. J. Ayer, who has since abandoned logical positivism in favour of what might be considered a logical pragmatism, made the case as follows: he rightly states that metaphysical sentences (in a sense of the term which excludes logical principles, e.g., the principle of excluded middle), express neither tautologies (in the sense of logically valid propositions) nor empirical hypotheses. He further propounds what is either a false assertion or a perverse stipulative definition to the effect that a sentence is meaningful if, and only if, it either expresses a logically valid proposition or an empirical hypothesis. And he concludes that "since tautologies and empirical hypotheses form the entire class of significant propositions, we are justified in concluding that all metaphysical assertions are nonsense".[20] It has often been pointed out that the logical positivists' thesis is by its own criterion nonsensical or meaningless since it is neither logically necessary nor an empirical hypothesis. If somebody should insist that every example of a metaphysical proposition given in the preceding

---

[19] For the possibility of such reduction, though not its details, see chapter 8, section 5.

[20] *Language, Truth and Logic*, 2nd edn (London, 1946), p. 41. For a more detailed criticism of Ayer's view on metaphysics from his early views to the present see my *Ayer on Metaphysics*, in *Perception and Identity*, ed. G. F. Macdonald (London, 1979), pp. 262–76.

pages is meaningless, then his sense of "meaninglessness" is, to say the least, highly idiosyncratic. Retelling, however briefly, the all too familiar story of the rise and fall of logical positivism can be justified if it suggests questions which it leaves unanswered. Among them the following are relevant to the present inquiry: first, how, if at all, can one distinguish between the linguistic and some other philosophically useful sense or senses of "meaninglessness"? Second, what is the relation between a theory of linguistic meaning and metaphysics? Because the logical positivists ignored the first question or wrongly identified the linguistic with some other sense of "meaninglessness", their answer to the second question was simply that their theory of meaning showed that metaphysics was meaningless, that it therefore was no intellectual discipline and thus could not *qua* existing intellectual discipline be related to a theory of linguistic meaning or any other discipline.

Within the limits of the present inquiry it is sufficient to distinguish logical, metaphysical and linguistic meaninglessness (and, hence, meaningfulness). In doing so it will be possible to look back on what has been said earlier about logic and metaphysics – but not on any discussion of linguistics. However, for the limited purposes of this inquiry the place of such a discussion will be taken by proposing a fairly obvious requirement which any satisfactory theory of linguistic meaning would have to fulfil.

By accepting a logic one also accepts a notion of logical impossibility with respect to this logic, e.g., classical or intuitionist logic. If this notion of logical impossibility is clear and if "meaninglessness" is defined in the narrow sense of being synonymous with "logically impossible", then no more needs to be said except possibly that for a sentence to be logically meaningless it must be *linguistically* meaningful.[21] Philosophers frequently assert or imply that a linguistically and logically meaningful sentence may yet be meaningless, or – more precisely – metaphysically meaningless. Thus Kant asserts that a linguistically and logically meaningful proposition which is incompatible with the principles exhibited in the Transcendental Analytic would yet be meaningless. For, Kant argues, no cognition (*Erkenntnis*) can contradict these principles "without losing all its content, that is to say all reference to any object and, thereby, any truth".[22] The meaninglessness to which Kant refers and which consists in the incompatibility with *his* immanent metaphysics is easily extended with respect to any categorial framework: a linguistically and logically meaningful proposition is metaphysically meaningless or irrational with respect to the principles defining a categorial framework if, and only if, the proposition is by virtue of

---

[21] For a discussion of logical validity, see chapter 5.   [22] *Kritik der reinen Vernunft*, B 87.

the logic underlying the framework incompatible with it. Briefly, if F are the framework principles and L the principles of its logic then a proposition f is metaphysically meaningless or irrational with respect to F if, and only if, f is L-inconsistent with F (see chapter 4, section 1).

It is a principal task of linguistics to propose explicit criteria of linguistic meaning and thus, among other things, to prevent confusing it with, e.g., logical or metaphysical meaningfulness – even though every linguistic theory, like any other theory, will be constrained by a more or less explicit categorial framework and its underlying logic. An obvious requirement which prevents such a confusion is the following: if a sentence, say, f, is accepted as logically or metaphysically meaningful and its negation, say, $\neg f$, is rejected as logically or metaphysically meaningless, then both f and $\neg f$ are linguistically meaningful. Put more loosely, *linguistic* meaning must be neutral between competing metaphysical or logical theories – as it must be between other nonlinguistic, e.g., physical, theories. To insist on this requirement is, among other things, to insist on the distinction between speaking a language and holding a theory. Thus two speakers of German of whom one is an adherent of Leibniz's while the other is an adherent of Kant's philosophy (of whom one adheres to Einstein's while the other adheres to Born's interpretation of quantum mechanics) do speak the same language and would not cease to do so if either underwent conversion to the other's theory.

5 On the antimetaphysical views in Wittgenstein's later philosophy

In comparing the transcendent metaphysics of factualism, according to which the world of experience is found and not made by the person who experiences it, and of constructivism, according to which the world of experience is, at least partly, made, Wittgenstein's later philosophy served as an example of constructivism (see chapter 10, section 4). Wittgenstein would have rejected this characterization since he regarded his account of thought as embodied in language and of language as exemplified by a variety of language games as purely descriptive, more particularly as belonging to descriptive anthropology or, as he puts it, "natural history".[23] As was the case with the discussion of the Positive Philosophy and of logical positivism, the critique of Wittgenstein's antimetaphysics must be based on a very brief summary and the hope of its proving adequate to his own remarks.

Language games, which are their principal subject, are rule-governed

---

[23] See *Philosophische Untersuchungen* (Oxford, 1953), section 25.

social practices in which the use of words is interwoven with other activities and which are part of a way of life. If one agrees with the account of predictive and instrumental thinking, and of thinking about persons and mental phenomena, given earlier in this essay (chapters 7 and 8), one is bound to agree with many of Wittgenstein's philosophical remarks about "ordinary language" games. In describing them he pays particular attention to some features which are almost systematically neglected by Hume, by applied mathematicians and by formal logicians in the tradition of Frege and Russell. Among them are the distinction between what may be called "subsumptive rules", the range of whose applicability is determined before their application, and "creative rules", the range of whose applicability is to some extent determined in the course of their application; the emphasis on the need for, and the function of, vague concepts and family resemblances; the distinction between "depth grammar" and "surface grammar"; the insistence that there can be no private language and that every language game implies some standards of certainty; and, last, an interesting opposition between criteria and symptoms.

Wittgenstein holds that by ignoring these features of ordinary language, philosophers have developed the tendency "to ask and answer questions in the way science does" – an approach which, as he characteristically puts it, is "the real source of metaphysics and leads the philosopher into complete darkness".[24] It is worth noting that the very features which scientists and philosophers playing their kind of language games ignored were quite familiar to – and well described by – the Roman jurists and their successors. That this is so should not be surprising since, e.g., the judicial process is to a large extent governed by rules which differ from rules governing ordinary language games only by being incorporated into the law of the land.[25]

In attacking metaphysics as complete darkness or as lying on the road to it, Wittgenstein does not distinguish between immanent and transcendent metaphysics and, consequently, does not consider the borderline between them or the possibility of its being redrawn in the course of a thinker's lifetime. Yet Wittgenstein's description of language games and of a person's language as one language game implies the acknowledgement of principles which constitute a more or less clearly demarcated categorial framework. For he implicitly acknowledges that the thinking embodied in ordinary language involves a differentiation between attributes and particulars and a deductive organization by logical principles, even though these principles

---

[24] See *The Blue Book* in *The Blue and Brown Books* (Oxford, 1958), p. 18.
[25] See my "Über Sprachspiele und rechtliche Institutionen", in *Proceedings of the 5th International Wittgenstein Symposium* (Vienna, 1981), pp. 480–91.

admit inexact predicates and neutral propositions (see chapter 5). And he implicitly acknowledges a classification of intersubjective particulars into maximal kinds, even though the constitutive and individuating principles associated with them lack the precision of the corresponding principles employed in mathematics and the sciences (see chapters 5 and 6).

That Wittgenstein also acknowledges epistemic stratification and, hence, the supremacy of some rules in a language game, follows from his remarks on certainty. He holds that although a language game may involve the incomplete testing of doubtful conjectures and the acknowledgement of unachievable certainties, its being played is *ipso facto* the acknowledgement of something as certain. For "when we test anything we are already presupposing something that is not tested".[26] Wittgenstein's examples of certain and, hence, of supreme assumptions do not, for the most part, refer to principles but to more specific beliefs, e.g., the historian's certainty about "history (and all that is connected with it) and even whether the earth has at all existed a hundred years ago".[27] Yet the certainty in question covers *at least* the logical principles of the language game. It should be noted that, according to Wittgenstein, "the certainty" of supreme principles is based not on their being accepted as beyond Cartesian doubt, but as "beyond all reasonable doubt"[28] and as being rooted in "our praxis (*Handeln*), which lies at the bottom of the language game".[29]

It may thus be assumed that Wittgenstein's antimetaphysical position is mainly directed against transcendent metaphysics. Although he sees his task – and the proper task of all philosophy – as consisting in the description of language games, his description of metaphysics as being, or leading to, utter darkness implies that he diagnoses it as an illness and that he wishes to cure its victims. It consists in the separation of language from other activities with which, in its healthy state, it is interwoven. Wittgenstein describes the illness as "language resting" (*wenn die Sprache feiert*) or as "language running idle", as opposed to "language working".[30]

The main cause of the illness, though possibly not the only one, lies, Wittgenstein holds, in the ignorance or hubris of philosophers who, instead of describing language, try to interfere with it. Yet it may be doubted that "language running idle" is always an illness. For it may happen that what started as "mere" metaphysical speculation (e.g., the Democritean theory of atoms) may later be "put to work", for example, by being woven into the conceptual net of some scientific theory (e.g., a scientific atomic theory).

---

[26] See *Über Gewissheit*, ed. E. Anscombe and G. H. von Wright (Oxford, 1974).
[27] Ibid., section 311.   [28] Ibid., section 416.   [29] Ibid., section 204.
[30] See *Philosophische Untersuchungen*, sections 38 and 132.

And in so far as transcendent metaphysics is language running idle, which can be put into gear and to work, its creation is not causing an intellectual illness, but may eventually improve the intellectual health of its creator or his descendants. To make this point is not to imply that the only justification of transcendent metaphysics is the possibility of its being incorporated into the conceptual net of some scientific theory.

PART III

STABILITY AND CHANGE
IN METAPHYSICS

CHAPTER 14

ON INTERNAL STRAINS

The first two parts of this essay were in the main devoted to exhibiting the structure and function of metaphysical systems. The third and last part will be chiefly devoted to changes in them. Chapter 14 examines changes resulting from internal strains and attempts to remove them through reflection on possible rearrangements and modifications. Chapter 15 considers changes resulting from external pressures, exerted by competing metaphysical systems, and attempts to remove these pressures through arguments. Chapter 16 discusses the scope and limits of metaphysical pluralism and the problem of progress in metaphysics. The concluding chapter contains a brief outline of some transcendent speculations, which, although not implied by the preceding discussion, are yet to some extent suggested by it.

The present chapter begins with an explanation of the notion of internal metaphysical strains and an indication of their range and intensity (1). It then considers strains arising from conflict between a person's immanent and his transcendent metaphysics (2); strains arising from conflicts between different logics (3); and strains arising from interdisciplinary, especially interscientific, conflict (4). The chapter ends by outlining some general methods for removing internal strains (5).

1 On the notion of internal, metaphysical strains

The acceptance of a set of metaphysical beliefs by a person is an empirical fact. So is its being subject to change. In recent times both these facts were in one way or another emphasized not only by historians of philosophy, but also by philosophers, in particular by Wittgenstein, who, as has been mentioned (in chapter 13, section 4), regarded his way of philosophizing as belonging to natural history, and by Collingwood, who regarded his and any genuine metaphysics as belonging to history. Although Collingwood's account of metaphysics as consisting of absolute presuppositions differs greatly from the account given in this essay (see chapter 10, section 2), his remarks on metaphysical change as resulting from "strains" may serve as a useful starting point for a discussion of metaphysical change due to inner conflict rather than external pressure. Collingwood holds that in metaphysics, as in history generally, "one phase changes into another because the first phase was in unstable equilibrium and had in itself the seeds of change and indeed of that change". He opposes metaphysics with its internal strains to the "strainless structure" of "a body of propositions in mathematics" because "mathematical propositions are not historical propositions". And he likens the subject matter of metaphysics because of its intricacy and restlessness to "the subject matter of legal or constitutional history".[1]

Although Collingwood's notion of internal strains causing unstable equilibrium in metaphysical systems is stimulating and suggestive, it must be modified in a number of ways before it can be adopted for our purpose. One modification consists in distinguishing internal strains, which may sometimes be removed by reflection, from external pressures, which may sometimes be removed by argument. The opposition of internal strains and reflection on the one hand to external pressures and argument on the other does not, of course, exclude the possibility of borderline cases and interactions. Thus an external pressure may draw attention to an internal strain which has so far been neglected, while becoming aware of an internal strain may add weight to an external pressure. Yet even if reflection may metaphorically be described as an argument which a person conducts with himself and argument as a way of receiving other beliefs – at least potentially – into one's own system of beliefs, it must be admitted that some objections from outside may be such that they could not have arisen from solitary reflection and that the converse also holds.

Another, no less important, modification consists in rejecting the erroneous and misleading contrast between the historical character of metaphysics and the nonhistorical character of mathematics. For just as mathematical theorems and systems, though nonhistorical, have a history expressed in historical propositions about them, so metaphysical principles and systems, though equally unhistorical, have a history. Contrasting Dedekind's mathematical theory of real numbers as nonhistorical with Leibniz's acceptance of the doctrine of pre-established harmony as historical is no less justified than contrasting Dedekind's acceptance of his theory of real numbers as historical with the metaphysical theory of pre-established harmony as nonhistorical. In either case the theory is nonempirical and,

[1] See R. J. Collingwood, *Essay on Metaphysics*, pp. 74–7.

hence, nonhistorical, while the acceptance or rejection of the theory or the wavering between its acceptance or rejection is a historical fact.

Last, one must object to Collingwood's characterization of mathematics as essentially strainless and of metaphysics as essentially involving strains. The cause of this impression is very likely that whereas his knowledge of metaphysics was that of an insider, he knew mathematics only as a distant outsider. The strains within mathematics are painfully obvious to many mathematicians, especially those who, not content to work within existing theories, try to create new ones. Thus according to Lebesgue "mathematicians always considered their epoch to be a period of crisis". And Weyl held that classical analysis, far from being a "secure rock", was a "house built essentially on sand", the "fluctuating foundations" of which badly needed "supports of reliable firmness".[2] Indeed, to ascribe strainlessness to mathematics and strains to metaphysics is to ignore that mathematics may contain supreme, i.e., metaphysical, principles and is, in any case, subject to them.

The most extreme cases of internal strains are, of course, acknowledged internal inconsistencies. Less extreme cases range from suspicions that, though inconsistencies have not yet arisen from the acceptance of certain supreme principles, they are likely to arise in the future, to more or less indefinite discomforts. A ranking of internal strains in order of their intensity is hardly possible. But it is advisable to exemplify their variety. Internal strains which have their source in the acknowledgement of *potential* inconsistencies are of particular interest to the understanding of metaphysical change and, hence, to the history of ideas. Such a strain may, for example, arise between a person's religious and his scientific beliefs, if the person's religious, but not his scientific, beliefs are supreme and if – although at present his religious and his scientific beliefs are consistent with each other – he fears that he may in future acquire a scientific belief which may be inconsistent with his religious beliefs and which he will find difficult to reject. A similar strain may arise if, because of this fear, or for some other reason, the person wavers between regarding his religious or his scientific beliefs as supreme. Again, wavering between two sets of principles may undermine the person's confidence in acknowledging either set as supreme. And there are many other ways in which potential inconsistencies between principles which are acknowledged as supreme, or as candidates for supremacy, may result in strains calling for modifications which would remove or, at least, alleviate them.

[2] See H. L. Lebesgue, *Oeuvres* (5 vols., Geneva, 1973) vol. 5, p. 300, and H. Weyl, *Das Kontinuum* (Göttingen, 1918), preface.

Another type of internal strain arises from practical or intellectual difficulties in conforming to one's metaphysical principles. Thus a categorial framework involving a great many maximal kinds or highly complex constitutive and individuating principles, associated with them, may give rise to the uncomfortable suspicion that it violates the precept – if accepted – that entities and kinds of entities be not multiplied beyond need (*entia non sunt multiplicanda praeter necessitatem*) and that in general avoidable complexities be avoided. Such a suspicion may well manifest itself as a strain on a person's categorial framework which, in Collingwood's words, has "in itself the seeds of change".

To the strains mentioned so far one must add such as arise from aesthetic dissatisfaction as well as from dissatisfactions which are not clearly characterizable and appear to be removable by metaphysical changes the nature of which is as yet also unclear. The difficulty, perhaps even the impossibility, of devising an exact and complete classification of internal strains does not justify their being lumped together. Failure to distinguish acknowledged logical inconsistencies in one's metaphysics from other strains may be particularly confusing if it leads to the absorption of a logic which proscribes inconsistency into a "Logic" of conflict or opposition in general.

2 On internal strains resulting from conflicts between immanent and transcendent metaphysics

The strains resulting from the joint acceptance of a transcendent and an immanent metaphysics may range from the acknowledgement of a logical inconsistency, which must be remedied, to mild discomfort about some possible disharmony. In so far as statements about transcendent reality and supreme principles which dominate thinking about the experienced intersubjective world have a different subject matter, no logical inconsistency can arise between them. A real or apparent logical inconsistency may, however, arise if transcendent reality is assumed to manifest itself in some way in the world of experience, more precisely, if transcendent reality is assumed to manifest itself through an attribute which it does not appear to possess or the possession of which appears to be logically incompatible with the attributes it does possess. Examples of such conflicts are familiar from the thought of theologians, philosophers and others who believe in a perfectly powerful and perfectly good God and whose experience includes mental and physical suffering as well as the awareness of the suffering of other living creatures. (A similar – real or apparent – conflict arises from trying to reconcile God's goodness and power with human immorality.)

What makes our example particularly useful is that it does not admit two otherwise tempting manoeuvres for avoiding the difficulty. One is to argue that since mind-independent reality is one thing and mind-dependent appearance another and since suffering clearly belongs only to the latter, the task of overcoming an inconsistency is wholly spurious, since there is no inconsistency to overcome. This argument is of no avail because an all-powerful God is the creator of both mind-independent reality and mind-dependent appearance and is, thus, responsible for any shortcomings they may have in themselves or as parts of his total creation. The other manoeuvre is to argue that pain is an illusion. This argument is also of no avail. For though it may sometimes be in order to distinguish between a real and an imaginary pain, the distinction has nothing to do with the painfulness of either. And it is this painfulness which is one of the evils calling for a theodicy, i.e., for a justification of its existence in a world created by an omnipotent and wholly benevolent God.

The first step in dealing with the apparent conflict between the evil of suffering, as manifested in the mind-dependent world, and God's unlimited power and goodness is to determine whether or not the conflict is a logical inconsistency. If it is so judged, then one or both of the incompatible theses will have to be rejected or modified. If it is judged to be a merely apparent logical inconsistency, then this judgment must be capable of being backed by a suitable interpretation. No sharp line can be drawn between modification and interpretation. Their effectiveness in removing the strain resulting from the conflict between the theses will depend on the extent to which they give the impression of being "natural" or "artificial".

Leibniz, who believes himself to have demonstrated the existence of an omnipotent and perfectly benevolent God (see, for example, *Monadology* sections 37–41), does, as he must, regard the conflict as merely apparent and certainly not as a logical inconsistency and argues – among other things – that the mistaken belief to the contrary arises from confusing the best of all possible worlds, as created by God, with the world as it may appear to a suffering human being, who, understandably, may think it capable of much improvement. This line of argument is for our purposes best put in Leibniz's own words, as translated into English from his *De Rerum Originatione Radicali* of the year 1697:

Yet out of so little experience we rashly make judgments about the immeasurable and the eternal, just as men who had been born and bred in prison or in the subterranean salt-mines of Sarmatia might think that there was no other light in the world than the treacherous flicker of torches, which was hardly sufficient to guide their footsteps. Look at the most lovely picture, and then cover it up, leaving uncovered only a tiny scrap of it. What else will you see here . . . but a kind of confused medley of colours, without selection, without art! . . . What happens to the eyes in painting is equally experienced by the ears in music.[3]

A philosophically minded prisoner of the Sarmatian salt-mines might well accept this part of the Leibnizian theodicy and deplore his own place in the best of all possible worlds. He might also examine Leibniz's argument for the existence of God and reject it as fallacious or, perhaps more plausibly, as correct but based on some premise which he finds unacceptable. He might, in particular, doubt the Leibnizian assumption that existence is better than nonexistence and might be inclined to think that, because of the suffering it contains, the world's not having been created would be preferable to its having been created. There is no need here to elaborate these and a variety of other reactions to the thought expressed in the quoted passage – reactions ranging from a more or less convinced rejection of Leibniz's theological thesis to a more or less convinced acceptance of it.

Transcendent theses expressing a person's religious convictions or closely connected with them are not the only ones which frequently retain their supremacy in conflicts with immanent metaphysics. The same may happen in the case of transcendent theses which serve the justification of certain social or political institutions, since political convictions may be held with a fervour resembling religious fervour in strength as well as in some of its manifestations, such as the desire to make converts or to persecute dissidents. But transcendent theses which have no special connection with a person's religious or political convictions – for example, the principle of moral freedom as held by some Kantians or neo-Kantians – may also manifest great survival value, while transcendent theses grounded in religious or political convictions may, like these convictions themselves, succumb to the strains caused by conflicts between them and principles of immanent metaphysics.

The transcendent thesis of realism, i.e., that mind-dependent reality, as constrained by a categorial framework, and mind-independent reality are no different, seems to be most suitable to protect immanent metaphysics from conflicts with transcendent. The transcendent metaphysics of realism may even survive a complete change of categorial framework, since the transcendent realist's reaction to such a change may merely be that the new categorial framework is better fitted to secure access to mind-independent reality than the old one. Yet science and its immanent metaphysics may come into conflict with specific types of realism, e.g., a realism which

---

[3] See *Philosophical Writings by Leibniz*, selected and translated by Mary Morris (London, 1934), p. 38f.

identifies the mind-independent world with the world of Newtonian physics. Thus it has been argued that quantum mechanics is in conflict with the "doctrine that the world is made up of objects whose existence is independent of human conciousness".[4]

3 On metaphysical strains arising from conflicting logical principles

Thinking involves the differentiation of experience into particulars and attributes and – since the differentiation would otherwise not serve its purpose – the acceptance of the weak principle of noncontradiction (see chapter 1, section 2). What distinguishes the various logical systems from each other are mutually incompatible principles, accepted in addition to the weak principle of noncontradiction. It is the acceptance of these additional principles which define the opposition between exact and inexact, finitist and infinitist, constructive and classical logics, etc. (see chapter 1, section 2 and chapter 5). The inclination to accept both members of one or more of these pairs of opposites or the inability to decide between the opposites are examples of internal strains. So is the inclination to accept one member as a supreme principle and the other as secondary or merely auxiliary, if combined with an inability to decide the question of supremacy. Although in each of these cases the choice which will remove the conflict and the strain is a choice between logical principles, the reflection about the conflict is not limited to comparing the opposing logical principles *qua* logical principles, but will also draw support from extralogical thinking. This can be seen from considering the conflict between exact and inexact logics as a typical example.

To do so briefly we may imagine a scientist of whom we assume that in his everyday life and in cooperating with his laboratory-helpers, who lack his theoretical training, he uses inexact, commonsense concepts, as expressed by the ordinary language which he shares with the scientists and nonscientists of his society; that in his scientific work he uses only exact mathematical and scientific concepts; and that he acknowledges the need to use both kinds of concepts – at least for the time being, which is likely to cover his whole life. If he feels impelled to reflect on the problem of the primacy of exact concepts over inexact ones, of inexact over exact ones or on their equal status, his reflection might draw on a great variety of beliefs, especially philosophical beliefs. It *might* – depending on the place of his

---

[4] For a recent version of such an argument see Bernard d'Espagnat, "The quantum theory and reality" in *Scientific American*, vol. 241, no. 5 (November, 1979). See also d'Espagnat, *The Conceptual Foundations of Quantum Mechanics*, 2nd revised edn (Reading, Mass., 1976).

scientific work in the context of his other beliefs – draw on transcendent beliefs about a reality which though mind-independent is yet accessible to thinking; on epistemology, i.e., on beliefs about the nature of knowledge; or on philosophical linguistics, i.e., beliefs about the nature of language. (There is no need to trespass on the sociology of knowledge to show that even scientists whose formal university training did not include philosophy or intellectual history are likely to have explicit philosophical beliefs, even if they themselves call them "antiphilosophical".)

If the scientist is inclined towards a Platonic ontology, according to which reality is a region of eternal, mathematical or mathematically precise forms, which admit of no borderline cases, and according to which the commonsense world with its fluidity and unsharp borders is not "really real", he is likely to accept only the principles of exact logic as supreme. If he is inclined to a Heraclitean ontology, he is likely to regard it as supporting the principles of inexact logic as supreme. Again, if he has accepted a version of the Cartesian epistemology, according to which clarity and distinctness is considered as a criterion of knowledge, which is absent from perception but attainable by science, he will find his epistemology in harmony with exact rather than inexact logic. If, on the other hand, he holds an empiricist theory of perception, while agreeing with Descartes on its indistinctness, he may regard his epistemology as pointing towards the supremacy of an inexact logic.

If the scientist was a student in the fifties or sixties of the present century, he may hold that the ancient philosophers were mistaken in regarding ontology as the fundamental or even as a feasible philosophical discipline; that the moderns were mistaken in regarding epistemology as the fundamental or even as a feasible philosophical discipline; and that the truly fundamental philosophy is the philosophy of meaning or of language. Yet on the issue of exact or inexact logic, the philosophy of language is no more united than ontology or epistemology. For our present purpose it will be sufficient briefly to compare the views of Frege, a protagonist of exact logic, with those of (the later) Wittgenstein, a protagonist of inexact logic.

For Frege an inexact logic, admitting of borderline cases or of indeterminate cases, is a contradiction in terms (see chapter 5, section 2). This follows from his principle of completeness, which includes the principle of exactness, i.e., the requirement that "the definition of every concept determine for every object whether or not if falls under it".[5] Frege agrees that the concepts expressed in ordinary language frequently fail to satisfy this requirement. But he holds that thought and its linguistic expression, though inseparable for human beings, are logically independent and that it

[5] *Grundgesetze der Arithmetik*, vol. 2, p. 69.

is possible to construct a formal language, such as his *Begriffsschrift*, which, though it too is not capable "of purely representing a thought", can nevertheless reduce the deviations of the linguistic expression of a thought from the thought itself to "what is unavoidable and harmless".[6] It can, unlike ordinary language, represent the exactness of exact concepts or, more precisely, of concepts *simpliciter*, since according to Frege so-called "inexact concepts" are not concepts at all.

Wittgenstein agrees with Frege's characterization of everyday language as admitting inexact concepts or, as Frege would say, "concept-like fomations" (*begriffsähnliche Gebilde*), which do not satisfy the requirement of exactness. But he disagrees with Frege's thesis of the logical separability of thought and language. Since he further holds that only limited parts of ordinary language can for limited purposes be replaced by exact formalizations and that ordinary language as a whole is not so replaceable, it follows for him that Frege's logic or any exact logic misrepresents language and that, because of the inseparability of thought and language, it *ipso facto* misrepresents thought. This does not mean that Wittgenstein would be satisfied with any particular version of inexact logic which goes beyond acceptance of the weak principle of noncontradiction.

By itself, the employment of both exact and inexact concepts by one person does not imply any strain in the system of his beliefs. What does imply such a strain is the acknowledgment of an actual or potential claim that only exact concepts or only inexact concepts are legitimate (as opposed to heuristically useful, fictitious, etc.) concepts, i.e., acceptable from the point of view of logic, ontology, epistemology, theory of meaning or any other discipline which implies, or suggests, a stratification of principles and the consequent acceptance of some principles as supreme. The issue of the acceptance or rejection of Frege's principle of exactness is only one example of alternative principles which can peacefully coexist if their sovereignty is limited to certain regions of a person's system of beliefs, but which lead to conflict and strain when they are claimed to dominate the whole system. Similar remarks apply, e.g., to contrasts between finitist and infinitist or constructivistic and classical logic.

4 On metaphysical strains arising from interdisciplinary, especially interscientific conflicts

In so far as one distinguishes between different intellectual fields or disciplines, one may distinguish between metaphysical strains resulting from intradisciplinary and from interdisciplinary conflicts. The distinction is

---

[6] *Begriffsschrift* (Halle an Salle, 1879), p. xiii.

useful and convenient, provided that one remembers that the demarcation of the various disciplines is neither rigid nor unchangeable. This is particularly so in the sciences. Thus if an inquiry of the kind undertaken here had been conducted in the nineteenth century, it would very likely have considered physics and chemistry as separate sciences and conflicts between them as interscientific. If the reduction or reducibility in principle of chemistry to physics is generally accepted, they are from the point of view of an inquiry into metaphysical strains more conveniently regarded as one science and the conflicts between them as intrascientific. Physics and biology are, it would seem, more conveniently classified as separate sciences and conflicts between them as interscientific, as is shown by the following examples.

A person who accepts Darwin's theory of gradual evolution may also accept or feel inclined to accept the principle of natural continuity or the metaphysical principle that nature makes no jumps (*natura non facit saltus*). This principle or, to be more careful, such a principle was accepted by Leibniz and by Kant. A person who accepts modern quantum mechanics in its dominant interpretation will accept the denial of the principle of natural continuity and might accept, or be inclined to accept, the stronger principle that nature not only makes quantum jumps, but that all natural processes are in their ultimate analysis discontinuous. A person who accepts both scientific theories is likely to suffer a strain caused by the real or apparent incompatibility of the biology-inspired and of the physics-inspired principle. In trying to remove the strain by reflection he is likely first of all to inquire whether the apparent conflict between them is or is not a logical incompatibility.

The answer to this question depends, of course, on what is meant by jumps or discontinuities in natural processes and on the difference, if any, between the biological concept of continuity, which according to Darwin is exemplified by the processes of natural evolution, and the physical concept of continuity, which is characteristic of Newtonian dynamics, but not of quantum physics. Quite apart from considering either biology or physics, it is possible and useful to distinguish between what may be called "phenomenal" and "ideal, mathematical" concepts of continuity. To accept a phenomenal concept of continuity is to require that two classes which are continuous with each other have common borderline cases – a requirement which implies the acceptance of inexact concepts and, hence, an inexact logic. To accept an ideal, mathematical concept of continuity is to define the continuity of two classes within an exact logic – as was done by Dedekind, who admits neither borderline nor indeterminate cases and thus accepts

Frege's principle of exactness and the principle of excluded middle, or by Brouwer and his intuitionist followers, who, though rejecting the principle of excluded middle by admitting indeterminate cases, do not admit borderline (or neutral) cases.[7]

Darwin's concept of continuity is phenomenal. His evolutionary taxonomy is based on a thesis of gradualness which implies not only that there are borderline cases between classes of animals, namely, between pairs of species the first member of which evolves into the second, but also borderline cases between classes of classes of animals, namely, between the class of species and the class of varieties. With regard to the latter type of borderline cases, Darwin implies their occurrence by asserting that the "amount of difference considered necessary to give any two forms the rank of species", rather than that of variety, "cannot be defined".[8] The existence of borderline cases between two species, i.e., of animals which with equal correctness can be assigned membership in either, is generally admitted. These borderline cases are usually "hybrids" which result from the interbreeding of species and may not only be viable but also fertile when back-crossed to either parental species.[9] The phenomenal continuity of the evolution of species is regarded as fundamental by Darwin and many of his modern successors.

The concept of continuity used in Newtonian dynamics is an ideal, mathematical concept whether it is expressed in the classical or the intuitionist theory of real numbers. The former theory involves not only the acceptance of Frege's principle of exactness and thus the rejection of borderline and indeterminate cases, but also the acceptance of non-denumerable actual infinities which are far removed from perception. The intuitionist theory of real numbers involves, apart from the rejection of borderline cases, the acceptance of "infinitely proceeding sequences" which, though less removed from perception than actual infinities, are still clearly mathematical rather than phenomenal. Similar remarks apply to statistical theories which, using more or less sophisticated mathematics, define two populations as continuous with each other if it can be shown that each of them has a subpopulation such that the relevant and statistically significant difference between the populations is statistically insignificant or negligible for the subpopulations.

A person who accepts the Darwinian theory of evolution with its thesis that biological nature is (phenomenally) continuous and the Newtonian

---

[7] For the difference between indeterminacy and neutrality see chapter 5, section 2. For a discussion of empirical continuity see chapter 4 of *Experience and Theory*.

[8] *The Origin of Species*, 6th edn (London, 1884), p. 47.

[9] See T. Dobzhansky, *Evolution, Genetics and Man* (New York, 1953), p. 174.

theory of dynamics with its thesis that physical nature is (mathematically) continuous is unlikely to be disturbed by the difference between the two concepts of continuity, which may even escape his attention. If it does not, it will not be difficult for him to find that the two theses are not only logically compatible with each other, but logically independent. Having recognized the logical independence of the two theses, he may yet for aesthetic or other reasons be well satisfied with the parallel between biological nature making no phenomenal jumps and physical nature making no mathematical jumps. Since the two theses are logically independent, no logical incompatibility will result if one of them is replaced by its negation. Yet a certain strain may arise from such a replacement. Thus a person who, while remaining a Darwinian in biology, has replaced Newtonian dynamics by quantum dynamics with its theses that atomic energy-changes are discontinuous or represent "quantum jumps" may come to suspect that a justified attempt at unifying physics and biology will introduce assumptions which, when conjoined with his biological and physical beliefs, produce an internal inconsistency. Similar remarks apply to strains resulting from conflicts between doctrines of continuity in physical and discontinuity in biological nature. An example would be the beliefs of a person who accepts Schrödinger's view that there are no quantum jumps or other discontinuities in nature, but who has also come to accept the anti-Darwinian view of Gould and Eldridge that evolutionary processes involve phenomenal discontinuities.[10]

For our purpose it is not necessary to elaborate the examples given, to add further examples to them or to show at length that interscientific conflicts resulting in metaphysical conflicts, i.e., in conflicts between supreme principles, become thereby *ipso facto* intrascientific conflicts. It seems equally superfluous to show that interdisciplinary conflicts – and the metaphysical strains resulting from them – need not be interscientific, but can arise between nonscientific disciplines, such as jurisprudence and art criticism (e.g., on the issue of pornography), or between a specific science or science in general and some nonscientific discipline such as history. The last-mentioned conflict, which has been touched upon earlier (chapter 9, section 4), may take the form of an apparent or real incompatibility between the claim that all events, whether or not they involve human actions, are subject to prognostically effective, deterministic or probabilistic, laws and the claim that some human actions are in principle unpredictable. It should

---

[10] See, for example, Schrödinger, "Are there quantum jumps?" parts I, II, *British Journal for the Philosophy of Science*, 3 (1952), 109–23, 233–42, and S. J. Gould and N. Eldridge, "Punctuated equilibria, the tempo and mode of evolution reconsidered", *Paleobiology*, 3 (1977) 115–45.

be noted that the assumption of immanent metaphysics that all actions are (are not) predictable must be distinguished from the assumption of transcendent metaphysics that there are (are not) actions which manifest man's freedom – an assumption to be considered later (chapter 17, section 4).

5 On some general methods for removing internal, metaphysical strains

The aim of reflecting on an internal, metaphysical strain is to identify the actually or potentially offending metaphysical principles or sets of principles and to remove the strain by wholly rejecting them, by partly modifying their content, by changing their place in the system of beliefs or by combining these methods in various ways. The following ways of removing metaphysical strains are frequently employed. To characterize and exemplify them is not to imply that their classification is complete.

The most radical step is, of course, to replace an offending supreme principle by its contradictory or a contrary. Yet this step is not always feasible if one wishes to continue an inquiry which was successfully begun and, however defectively, pursued under the aegis of the offending principle. As Descartes puts it at the beginning of the third part of his *Discourse on Method*, it will not do "to pull down the house in which we live before commencing to rebuild it" since it "is necessary that we be furnished with some other house in which we may live conveniently (*commodément*) during the operations". A less radical step is to change the meaning of the principle so as to restrict its range of application. An example would be the replacement of the general principle that nature makes no (phenomenal or ideal, mathematical) jumps by the principle that nature makes no ideal, mathematical jumps, or the restriction of the principle of excluded middle to finite domains. The measures so far mentioned are especially appropriate if a specific principle or conjunction of principles is identified as the source of an actual, rather than a merely potential, incompatibility.

If a principle or conjunction of principles is identified as a potential source of a metaphysical strain – e.g., because of a suspicion that it may turn out to be incompatible with some beliefs which will be acquired in the future – the strain may be removed or mitigated by depriving it, or a wider class of principles to which it belongs, of its supremacy. Another way of characterizing this modification is to describe it as the demotion of the principle, conjunction of principles or class of principles from the class of supreme principles (as defined in chapter 1, section 2) to a class of dominated principles, i.e., to a lower stratum in the stratified system of beliefs. An example would be the demotion of the principle of mathematical continuity to a principle of physics which is assumed in Newtonian mechanics, which is denied in the Copenhagen interpretation of quantum physics and which may after a reinterpretation or reconstruction of quantum physics, e.g., on the lines of Schrödinger's thought, at some time in the future regain its status as an assumption of physics.

From the demotion of a principle to a lower stratum, one must distinguish its demotion to the status of a provisional fiction, i.e., a provisionally accepted idealization, intended to serve as a stop-gap until such time as it can be replaced either by a principle which is not an idealization or else by an idealization the acceptance of which is not provisional. A provisional fiction must thus be distinguished from a mathematical idealization, e.g., a geometry or theory of sets, since mathematical theories can be, and have been, replaced by others which were judged more suitable for all or some purposes. A provisional fiction must also be distinguished from a simplifying fiction, which can be used to simplify complex reasoning through replacing complex concepts by simpler ones in such a way that the results of the simplifying reasoning are demonstrably the same as the results of the original reasoning, as is, e.g., the case when the limit-concepts of a Cauchy-type analysis are replaced by the concepts of nonstandard analysis.[11] Last, and obviously, provisional fictions must be distinguished from those idealizations which, like Plato's Forms, are regarded as characterizing transcendent reality. An example of the demotion of a supreme principle to the status of a provisional fiction would be provided by a person who has come to reject the concept of quantum jumps as absurd, but who for the time being uses them for making useful predictions.

Reflection about a conflict between supreme principles may in the end result in an acknowledged inability to choose between them. If the conflicting principles are contradictories, then the wavering between them cannot be solved by accepting their disjunction. If on the other hand the conflicting principles are contraries, then the acceptance of their disjunction is not without content since it excludes some possibilities. The same holds for conflicts of other kinds, provided that their resolution results in the acceptance of a disjunction of principles which together are not exclusive and exhaustive of all possibilities. An example of such a disjunctive pluralism of principles would be the acceptance of the disjunction consisting of the principle that nature makes only phenomenal jumps and of the principle that it makes only mathematical jumps – if the disjunction is accepted by a person at the end of his reflection about his

[11] See A. Robinson *Non-Standard Analysis* (Amsterdam, 1970).

inclination to accept either principle to the exclusion of the other and the acknowledgement of his inability to decide in favour of one of these principles. It should be noted that the removal of an internal metaphysical strain resulting from the conflict of principles by the cautious acceptance of their disjunction must be distinguished from metaphysical perspectivism, i.e., the thesis that incompatible principles may embody different aspects of transcendent reality. (For a discussion of metaphysical perspectivism see chapter 17.)

CHAPTER 15

ON EXTERNAL PRESSURES
EXERTED BY METHODOLOGICAL AND
OTHER ARGUMENTS

Whether or not a conflict of one's own metaphysical beliefs with those of another person is taken seriously depends on whether one respects the actual or potential opponent as a thinker, whether one regards his beliefs as harmfully influential, whether one feels inclined towards accepting them, as well as on a variety of other reasons. So does the decision not to be satisfied with removing the external pressure by reflection, but to engage in an argument intended to justify one's own metaphysical beliefs or, at least, to discredit those of the opponent. Like all arguments, metaphysical arguments require some understanding of what one's opponent believes (see chapter 9, section 2) and some agreement with him about what is permitted and what forbidden when engaging in such an argument. Metaphysical arguments differ from deductive arguments in two important respects. First, whereas deductive arguments consist in the derivation of a conclusion from an accepted premise or conjunction of premises, metaphysical arguments are (or include) arguments for the acceptance of a premise, namely, a supreme principle. Second, whereas deductive arguments proceed in accordance with a clearly defined and agreed method, the method for the establishment of supreme principles is either much less clearly defined or not defined at all.

   The purpose of this chapter is to examine some historically important, and still influential, general methods for establishing metaphysical principles, as well as to consider metaphysical arguments which are not based on any general method. The chapter begins by discussing the Cartesian method of doubt (1), the Kantian transcendental method (2) and Husserl's phenomenological method (3). It then briefly considers the dialectic and the so-called "scientific" and "linguistic" methods for establishing metaphysical principles (4). It ends by describing some varieties of what may be characterized as honest, or nonsophistic, metaphysical rhetoric (5).

1 On Descartes's method of establishing metaphysical principles

For our limited purpose it will be sufficient to compare two versions of Descartes's method for achieving certain knowledge of metaphysical principles or for demonstrating their "scientific truth". The first and strong version is expressed by the rule that in order to acquire scientific truth (*scientia*) we "must seek that which we can see clearly and with evidence (*clare et evidenter*) or deduce with certainty (*certo deducere*)".[1] Descartes's notion of deduction, whatever its precise meaning, must be distinguished from logical deduction, since it is intended not only to explicate, but also to amplify the content of its premises. It is based on a necessary connection between two simple things which consists in "one thing's being . . . so implied in the concept of the other in a confused sort of way that we cannot conceive either distinctly, if we judge them to be disjoined from each other (*ab invicem sejunctas*)". It is exemplified by such implications as 'shape implies extension', 'my existence implies God's existence', 'my knowing implies my having a mind which is distinct from my body'.[2] Because Cartesian deduction is, at least sometimes, amplifying, intuition does not suffice for the establishment of metaphysical principles.[3]

A weaker version of the method is given at the beginning of the third Meditation.[4] It is expressed by the general rule that "all that is true which I perceive very clearly and distinctly (*valde clare et distincte*)". The second version is weaker since perceiving something very clearly and distinctly ranks below perceiving it clearly and with evidence. The weaker version admits some slight doubt. It does so because it leaves open the possibility of God's having it brought about that "I am mistaken also in those matters of which I believe myself through my mind's eyes to have the most evident intuition (*ut errem etiam in iis quae me puto oculis quam evidentissime intueri*)." The doubt is slight. In Descartes's words, "since I have no occasion to hold that there is a God who is a deceiver and since so far I do not sufficiently know whether God exists, the reason for my doubt is tenuous (*tenuis*) and so to speak 'metaphysical'".[5] The transition from the weak rule, and the corresponding nonmetaphysical certainty, to the strong rule and the corresponding metaphysical certainty requires more than a proof of a perfect God's existence. It requires in addition the proof that a perfect God would never deceive us – for example, because, even though such a God has

---

[1] See *Rules for the Direction of the Understanding*, rule III.   [2] Ibid., comments to rule XII.
[3] For a discussion of some difficulties in Descartes's view of the relation between intuition and deduction see *Fundamental Questions of Philosophy*. 4th edn (Brighton, 1979), pp. 21f.
[4] See *Meditations on the First Philosophy*.   [5] Ibid.

created a world containing suffering and other real or apparent evils, unjustified reliance on the strong version of Descartes's method is not among them.

Neither method provides a criterion of truth. This follows from the possibility of error resulting from an incorrect application of the method in either version.[6] For if, as can always be done, the possibility of error is admitted and the correct application of the method called in question, then the correctness of the application can only be established by applying the method to its application, and so on *ad infinitum*. This regress, which is characteristic of all *general* criteria of truth (see chapter 10, section 1), can only be halted by postulating that genuine self-evidence is somehow self-authenticating and renders any further question of correctness illegitimate. Neither the weak nor the strong version of the method provides an effective method of argument by which the acceptor of a proposition can convince a rejector of the proposition of his error. For if two people disagree as to whether a certain proposition is or is not self-evident, then the appeal to self-evidence will be useless. And if they agree that a certain proposition is self-evident, then the appeal to self-evidence is superfluous.

Descartes's view of the relation between a person's acceptance of a proposition as certain, because it has passed the test of the method of doubt, and the person's judgment that the proposition is therefore true, contains an important insight into the relation between the manner in which a proposition is accepted as belonging to a system of beliefs and its epistemological status in the system. More precisely, Descartes's meta-physical certainty or the lesser certainty, which is not supported by a proof of the existence of a God who is not a deceiver, unilaterally implies supremacy, as defined in this essay (chapter 1, section 2). Thus a person who accepts Descartes's doctrine of the mind's distinctness from the body as supreme and who is aware of the inconsistency of this doctrine with any version of materialism will reject materialism because it is inconsistent with one of his supreme principles – whether or not he agrees with Descartes that the principle passes the test of the method of doubt and whether or not he accepts Descartes's claim that the method can serve as a test of absolute, necessary truth.

Just as every person's system of beliefs is stratified and thus includes a set of supreme principles (at least his logical principles), so every system of beliefs, which are shared by the members of a community, contains shared supreme beliefs. Thus, any personal or social system of beliefs contains *ipso facto* beliefs, held with certainty in a sense which is definable in terms of

[6] See the fourth Meditation.

consistency, domination and supremacy. That in this sense of the word every social practice, including the employment of a common language, involves certainty has been emphasized by Wittgenstein and would, it seems, have been admitted by Sextus Empiricus (see chapter 13, section 5). Various kinds of social cooperation may gain in effectiveness by extending the agreement on supreme principles of those engaged in cooperating with each other. The extension of such agreement is, however, not achieved by appeals to self-evidence, but by philosophical arguments which can be described as employing the method of honest or nonsophistic rhetoric (see section 5, below).

2 On Kant's transcendental method of establishing metaphysical principles

To Descartes's claims that there are metaphysically certain propositions, that there is one and only one set of them and that their certainty and uniqueness can be demonstrated by the method of doubt correspond Kant's claims that there are synthetic *a priori* propositions, that there is one and only one set of them and that their necessity and uniqueness can be demonstrated by the transcendental method. For our purpose it is sufficient to recall that according to Kant a proposition is synthetic if, and only if, its negation is not self-contradictory and *a priori* if, and only if, it is logically independent of any proposition describing sense-experience (as opposed to objective experience). This definition covers the axioms and theorems of the mathematics accepted by Kant, as well as certain other supreme principles of his system of beliefs, e.g., the principles of causality, continuity and the conservation of substance. As has been mentioned earlier (chapter 13, section 4), the necessity of the synthetic *a priori* principles consists in their being necessary conditions of objective experience, or the experience of objects, for anybody accepting these principles (which according to Kant is everybody). Since the so-defined necessity is not based on formal logic, but on what Kant calls "transcendental logic", it may be called "transcendental necessity". Transcendental necessity, like Cartesian certainty, implies, but is not implied by, epistemic supremacy. The implication is even more obvious since transcendental necessity, unlike Cartesian certainty, is explicitly defined in terms of inconsistency.

Just as the Cartesian certainty of a proposition is tested, not by any failed attempt at doubting, but by a specific philosophical method of doubt, so the transcendental necessity of a proposition is tested, not by any failure to negate while preserving objective reference, but by the transcendental method. In so far as the method covers the (Kantian) nonmathematical synthetic *a priori* principles, it is intended to show that only by conforming to these principles can one become aware of objective phenomena, as distinct from merely subjective impressions. Briefly, Kant argues that certain concepts – the so-called Categories – are applicable to subjective experience; that in so applying them one confers objectivity on subjective experience; and that the synthetic *a priori* principles express the conditions of their applicability, that is to say, demarcate the scope of possible objective experience (*die Möglichkeit der Erfahrung . . . also das was allen unsern Erkenntnissen a priori objektive Realität gibt*).[7]

Kant distinguishes between the fact of his using certain Categories in his thinking about objective phenomena and the justification or legitimation of this fact by what might be called the "objectivity- and the uniqueness-theses", which – as he puts it in the terminology of jurisprudence – are answers not to *quaestiones facti*, but to *quaestiones iuris*. The former thesis asserts that there can be no objectivity without Categories, the latter that there can be no objectivity without the Categories listed by him. The uniqueness thesis is central to his philosophy because it links *the* Categories to *the* logical forms of judgment which are characteristic of logic, not of *a* logic. The statement that there are alternative sets of Categories would be just as unacceptable to him as the statement that there are alternative logics – e.g., various extensions of the logical core, as constituted by the weak law of noncontradiction. That the "deduction" of the Categories or "pure concepts of the understanding", i.e., the justification of their use, is meant to establish not only the objectivity- but also the uniqueness-thesis is made quite clear in the summary of the deduction which refers to *the* "concepts of the pure understanding" and not to one set or other of such concepts.[8]

In claiming that our thinking and belief-systems involve the acceptance of supreme principles, Descartes and Kant agree with the position defended in this essay. In claiming that there is one and only one such set, including one and only one set of logical principles, their views differ radically from that position. Moreover, if their uniqueness claim must be rejected, then neither the method of doubt nor the transcendental method – whatever their precise nature and employment – can be valid methods for the discovery of the unique set of supreme principles, for the simple reason that there is no such set.

Yet when Kant's objectivity-thesis is separated from his uniqueness-thesis, it can be considered as a restricted version of the account given (in chapter 3, section 3) of interpretative stratification and *a priori* concepts, especially concepts of intersubjectivity. Thus according to Kant the dif-

---

[7] *Kritik der reinen Vernunft*, B 195.   [8] See ibid., B 168, 69; also, for example, Prolegomena section 39.

ference between the judgment that something is a subjectively experienced change and the judgment that it is an objective change consists in the concepts which are applied in making the second, but not also the first, of these judgments. The concepts which describe the perceptual features of the experienced change are the same for both judgments, e.g., a change of colour, shape, etc. What distinguishes the second from the first judgment is that in making the former one also applies the concept of causality and, therefore, also the concept of continuity, i.e., the concept of an "alteration which is possible only through a continuous action of causality".[9]

Kant's account can be expressed by saying, in the terminology of this essay, that the concept of an objective change is interpretative of the concept of a subjectively experienced change and that the *a priori* difference between them is the *a priori* concept 'x is caused' – in a sense in which causality implies continuity.[10] Kant's account of this objectivizing interpretation implies the further doctrine that there is one and only one valid way of conferring objectivity on what is subjectively experienced, namely, the application of causality and the other Kantian categories to it. If one accepts Kant's doctrine that not only is objectivity conferred by the application of the Kantian Categories, but that it is not conferred by any other *a priori* concepts of objectivity, then one must regard, e.g., the statement that in "black-body" radiation energy is emitted discontinuously in discrete amounts as being "without content, that is to say without reference to any object and, thereby without any truth" (see chapter 13, section 4). If in accordance with the position of this essay one rejects the uniqueness thesis, then the statement about black-body radiation, which is inconsistent with Kant's supreme principle of causality, must for that reason be judged metaphysically meaningless *with respect to Kant's metaphysics*. It cannot be judged linguistically meaningless, logically meaningless or without qualification metaphysically meaningless (see chapter 13, section 4).

3 On Husserl's phenomenological method of establishing metaphysical principles

The so-called phenomenological method, as developed by Husserl, is in both aim and strategy indebted to Descartes's method of doubt and to Kant's transcendental method. Husserl shares with his teacher Brentano the conviction that evidence and certain truth are gained through pure description, as opposed to interpretation of experiencing and of what is experienced. A late version of Husserl's method has been summarized by

---

[9] *Kritik der reinen Vernunft*, B 253   [10] See Ibid., B 253.

him in the article *Phenomenology*, which he contributed to the 1929 edition of the *Encyclopaedia Britannica*.[11] Phenomenology is according to Husserl "a new descriptive philosophical method which has established . . . (1) an *a priori* psychological discipline . . . and (2) a universal philosophy, which can supply an organum for a methodological revision of all the sciences". The subject matter of phenomenology are mental phenomena, i.e., consciousness, which is always consciousness of something, and the content of this consciousness. Husserl calls the former "Noesis" and the latter "Noema".

The phenomenologist, *qua* phenomenologist, employs successively three so-called "reductions": the phenomenological reduction which "reveals the phenomena of actual internal experience"; the eidetic reduction which reveals "the essential forms constraining psychical existence"; and, lastly, the transcendental reduction which "reduces the already psychologically purified to the transcendental, that most general subjectivity which makes the world and its 'souls' and confirms them". The three reductions are meant to result in judgments which are *a priori*, in a sense in which a judgment is *a priori* if, and only if, it is logically or nonlogically necessary and unique, i.e., not admitting of alternatives.

The phenomenological reduction consists in an ἐποχή, "a suspension of judgment about what Sextus calls "any underlying external entities" (see chapter 12, section 2). As Husserl puts it, in practising the ἐποχή, one "must inhibit any ordinary, objective 'position', and partake in no judgment concerning the objective world". As a result of the ἐποχή, "the experience itself" (as opposed to the objectivity claim based on it) "will remain what it was, an experience of this house, of this body, of this world in general, in its particular mode". The phenomenological reduction is thus the converse of any objectivizing interpretation, such as the application of the Kantian Categories. If the application of the Categories confers objectivity on what is subjectively experienced, then the phenomenological reduction withdraws the so-conferred objectivity-claim. It thereby achieves subjective certainty or, at least, greater subjective certainty, since a person's claim to have experienced something which, in addition to having certain experienced qualities, is also part of an objective, external world is more likely to be mistaken than the person's more modest claim to have experienced something which has the same experienced qualities, but is not judged to be or judged not to be part of an objective external world. In suspending objective experience the phenomenological reduction suspends also the

[11] The article has been reprinted in *Realism and the Background of Phenomenology*, edited with an introduction by R. M. Chisholm (Glencoe, 1960), from which the following quotations have been taken.

Kantian conditions of its possibility, i.e., the Kantian synthetic *a priori* principles.

Where then does Husserl locate the *a priori?* The answer is provided by the eidetic reduction which consists in "the expert recognition, comprehension and description of the manifold 'appearances' of what are no longer 'objects', but unities of sense". Now the unity of sense, as well as its form, or structure of which I am aware without objectivization or any other kind of interpretation, is *necessary for me* in the sense that it cannot be changed by me without losing its identity. Yet the necessity of the *a priori* as understood by Kant, Husserl and many other philosophers is intersubjective and unique. Husserl sees no difficulties in making the transition from subjectivity to unique intersubjectivity. He simply asserts that "as a similar 'bracketing' of objective, and description of what then 'appears' ('noema' in 'noesis'), can be performed upon the 'life' of another self, which we represent to ourselves, the 'reductive' method can be extended from one's own self-experience to one's experience of other selves". The transcendental reduction is taken as a further strengthening of the intersubjective necessity, allegedly established by the eidetic reduction. Since, however, the transcendental is based on the eidetic reduction and since the validity of this reduction will be presently called into question, no more needs here to be said about the transcendental reduction.

The invalidity of the eidetic reduction follows from the possibility of providing counterexamples. Thus Husserl's phenomenological and eidetic reductions reveal to him uniquely necessary principles which, as in Kant's philosophy, include *the* principles of logic. If, as we may assume, the principle of excluded middle is among them, then its necessity cannot be established for an intuitionist logician who rejects this principle. Indeed an intuitionist's intuition – which may well be considered as involving a phenomenological and an eidetic reduction – will to him reveal a unique and intersubjectively necessary logic, which is incompatible with the logic as revealed to Husserl by the phenomenological method.

Since in the determination of unique and intersubjectively necessary principles intuition is for Husserl, as for Descartes, the highest court of appeal, a person's deviant intuition cannot be refuted by an appeal to another person's correct intuition. Yet even if the possibility of divergent intuitions is admitted, one might still argue that the phenomenological method (or some other method relying on intuition) is preferable to its competitors. Husserl regards so-called "psychologism" as the most – possibly the only – serious competitor to the phenomenological method and thus joins Frege, Brentano, Meinong and others in trying to refute it.

Psychologism, as conceived by these thinkers, is the attempt at reducing logical, mathematical and other types of apparently nonempirically necessary statements to empirical statements.

It is here sufficient to consider an example from mathematics and logic. A classical, as opposed to an intuitionist, mathematician would accept the mathematical thesis that since, as has been proved by Cantor, not all real numbers are algebraic (i.e., are roots of polynomial equations of form $a_0x^n + a_1x^{n-1} + \ldots + a_n = 0$, where the coefficients are integers), there exists at least one transcendent (i.e., non-algebraic) number. Because Cantor's – unlike, for example, Liouville's – proof of the existence of transcendent numbers does not enable one to construct such a number, the classical mathematician's acceptance of the thesis would be based only on the proof that not all real numbers are algebraic and on the principles of logic, in particular the principle of excluded middle in the form: $(\forall x)\, P(x)$ or $(\exists x)\, \neg P(x)$. An adherent of psychologism would hold that the logical proposition 'If not all real numbers are algebraic then there exists a transcendent number' is reducible to the empirical proposition 'If anybody believes that not all real numbers are algebraic then he cannot as *a matter of psychological fact* help believing that there exists a transcendent number.' And he would also hold that the principle of excluded middle is reducible to the empirical proposition 'Nobody can help believing that either all things possess a certain property or that there is at least one thing not possessing it.' Against this Husserl and other opponents of psychologism rightly point out that a mathematical thesis or a logical principle must not be confused with an empirical generalization.

Yet rejecting the psychologistic analysis does not commit us to accepting Husserl's doctrine of the unique and intersubjective necessity of classical logic, mathematics and whatever else he finds revealed through the phenomenological and eidetic reductions. It is possible to argue for a view which is neither psychologistic nor phenomenological, namely, the view expressed in this essay (see, for example, chapter 5, section 1). Briefly, to assert a mathematical or logical proposition *is not* to assert either an empirical proposition or else a proposition which is uniquely and inter-subjectively necessary for every human being, or necessary in some even stronger sense of absolute necessity. To assert that a mathematical or logical principle has been accepted by some, or even by all, human beings is indeed to assert an empirical proposition. However, in asserting *an empirical proposition about a nonempirical (e.g., logical or mathematical) proposition* one does not deprive the former of its empirical or the latter of its nonempirical character. Conflating them may well be the source of spurious notions of absolute necessity of which the Cartesian, the transcendental and the phenomenological are examples.

4 On the dialectic, scientific and linguistic methods of establishing metaphysical principles

The methods so far discussed are all claimed to establish principles which are and, in accordance with their user's beliefs, ought to be supreme. Yet even though the purpose for which they are being used is either the legitimation of their user's own supreme principles or the conversion of others to them, the connection between the required methodological procedures and the results established by following them is fairly tenuous. Thus the method of doubt – instead of enabling one to accept the doctrine of a nondeceiving God – might well be used to justify agnosticism; the transcendental method, to justify a principle of discontinuity and other principles incompatible with Newtonian physics; the phenomenological method, to justify principles of intuitionist logic and mathematics. Against this, the methods to be briefly discussed in the present section are more closely connected with the results established by their employment: the dialectic method of inference is implied by the very conception of Reality which it is used to justify. The linguistic method of distinguishing between the meaningful and the meaningless is based on the implicit acceptance of the very principles which it establishes as meaningful. And the scientific method, which conceives of philosophy as a part of science, conforms to the supreme principles by means of which the user of the method demarcates the scope of science and of the scientific theories accepted by him.

That the dialectical method – unlike deductive or inductive reasoning, unlike the Cartesian and the phenomenological methods and to a lesser degree unlike the transcendental method – is not to be regarded as a metaphysically neutral strategy of discovery, but as an aspect of Reality, is made quite clear by Hegel. Thus to give an example of many statements making this point, he says of the method that it is "nothing else but the structure of the whole put up in its pure essence" (*nichts anderes als der Bau des Ganzen in seiner reinen Wesenheit aufgestellt*).[12]

Although Marx's materialist conception of Reality differs from Hegel's absolute idealism, the Marxist dialectical method is related to Marxist Reality as the Hegelian dialectical method to Hegelian Reality. In Marx's words, "the mystification which the dialectic suffers in Hegel's hands, in no way prevents (*verhindert in keiner Weise*) that he represented its general

[12] *Phanomenologie des Geistes Vorrede Jubilaums Ausgabe* (Stuttgart, 1927), vol. 2, p. 45.

forms of motion (*Bewegungsformen*) for the first time in a comprehensive and conscious manner".[13]

In order to characterize the common nature of the Hegelian and Marxist dialectical methods it is useful to compare dialectical with Cartesian inference. Both are assumed to start from indubitable premises, both are ampliative (as distinct from deductive in the sense of formal logic) and both determine for any premise or conjunction of premises one and only one conclusion. But whereas Cartesian inference depends for its validity on a necessary connection between premise and conclusion which consists in the impossibility of either being clearly conceivable without the other, dialectical inference is further characterized by means of a concept of "negation", which is as central to the philosophies of Hegel and Marx as it is controversial and difficult to understand. For the present purpose it is sufficient to note that the Hegelian differs from the Marxist negation and that both differ from the negation of formal logic. According to both Hegel and Marx the premise of a dialectical inference dialectically implies its dialectical negation. Some commentators hold that dialectical reasoning proceeds in triads, i.e., that it begins with a thesis, which dialectically implies its dialectical negation or antithesis; and that thesis and antithesis together dialectically imply their synthesis.[14] Both Hegelian and Marxist dialectical reasoning reach a final stage which, since it in some way preserves the preceding phases, can only be grasped if the whole road leading to it has been taken.

The interdependence of the dialectical method and the – Hegelian or Marxist – conception of Reality invalidates any claim that the correct employment of the method results in establishing *the* supreme principles which are, or ought to be, accepted by everybody. It might, of course, be argued that before being forced into serving the defence of a specific metaphysics, the dialectical method was an autonomous and metaphysically neutral type of ampliative inference which, when correctly used, could achieve the aims which the Cartesian method was not strong enough to realize. Yet the "necessary connection" between a dialectical premise and its dialectical negation must, like the "necessary connection" of the Cartesian method, in the end rely on a shared intuition, the appeal to which is superfluous if the intuition is shared and useless if it is not shared. This does not mean that dialectics, like the method of doubt, cannot be useful, in metaphysics as elsewhere, when its claims are realistically reduced. The precept that one should not accept as indubitable what is open to

[13] *Das Kapital*, vol. 1, *Postcript* to the 2nd edn.
[14] For example, W. T. Stace in *The Philosophy of Hegel* (London, 1924).

reasonable doubt is as useful as the precept that both sides in a dispute should be given a hearing.

Little needs to be added here about the scientific and linguistic methods of establishing metaphysical principles, since the use made of these methods in attempts to replace metaphysics has been examined earlier. What has been said about attempts at replacing metaphysics by science, after the fashion of Comte and his successors, or by descriptive linguistics, after the fashion of the later Wittgenstein and his successors (in chapter 13), can with obvious modification be applied to attempts at using these or similar methods in putting metaphysics or philosophy generally on a secure basis or on the right road. Thus to assert, as did Brentano in one of his "*Habili-tationsthesen*", that "the true method of philosophy is no other than that of the natural sciences" is to accept what one takes to be the supreme principles of the natural sciences, in general or at a certain stage of their development, as supreme principles *simpliciter* and, in so far as they demarcate one's categorial framework, as constituting one's immanent metaphysics. Again to assert, with Ryle and other so-called "ordinary language" philosophers or defenders of so-called "informal logic", that certain statements though not logically absurd are yet "incoherent", "logically odd", etc.,[15] is to accept the general criteria of such oddity as supreme. Whether, and to what extent, the proposal that metaphysics or philosophy is, or should be, based on science or the informal logic of ordinary language implies a uniqueness claim depends on the proponent's conception of science and ordinary language. It could be argued that in Brentano's case it does imply such a claim and that in Ryle's case it probably does.

5 On nonsophistic, metaphysical rhetoric

Metaphysicians who do not claim to be in possession of absolutely cogent metaphysical arguments must, in order to justify their own supreme principles, resort to honest persuasion or nonsophistic rhetoric. Such argumentation consists in justifying supreme principles which its proponent has himself accepted, by reasons which he himself finds acceptable. It may include stretches of deductive argument, e.g., pointing out that the person whom the proponent is trying to persuade has accepted mutually incompatible principles. It may also include weakened versions of the above-mentioned methodological arguments, e.g., pointing out that a statement is not above reasonable doubt; that though a belief is claimed to

[15] See, for example, G. Ryle, "Ordinary language", in *Philosophical Review*, 57 (1953), 167–86.

be objective, the claim is not borne out by any clear reference to any objective entities; that what is claimed to be a mere description depends on a dubious interpretation; that the apparent cogency of a thesis derives from wilful neglect of reasons supporting the antithesis; that what would be rejected on scientific grounds should not lightly be accepted on nonscientific ones; that the content of a statement which sounds odd might with advantage be re-examined.

The following remarks about nonsophistic rhetoric in metaphysics apply both to arguments in favour of their proponent's immanent metaphysics, in particular of supreme principles demarcating his categorial framework, and to arguments in favour of his transcendent metaphysics, i.e., his beliefs about transcendent reality. The types of argument to be mentioned are not exclusive of each other. Nor are they to be regarded as exhausting all possibilities.

One of these types, which is at least as old as the Socratic dialogues, consists in trying to persuade another person that although he is not aware of his having accepted a metaphysical thesis and might even think that he rejects it, he does as a matter of fact accept it. The persuasion may consist in simply making an implicit belief explicit; in clarifying and thus modifying an implicit belief so that the explicitly formulated and accepted belief differs from the original belief, which it, however, still resembles in respects which both the proponent and the opponent regard as important; in changing the implicit belief in important respects. Since the Socratic method covers all these species of persuasion, it differs from "exhibition analysis", which aims at making implicit assumptions explicit without changing them in any way in the process and which *qua* analysis is not meant to persuade.[16]

A second type of nonsophistic rhetoric in favour of the acceptance of certain supreme principles may be called "the argument from so far inconceivable alternatives", which could be regarded as a much weakened, but plausible, version of Kant's transcendental deduction. An example will suffice. Kant argued that, without accepting the principles of causality and continuity, thinking about objects, in particular scientific thinking, would be impossible. He might have defended the weaker thesis that, as far as he could judge from his own experience and the documents available to him, scientific thinking was impossible without accepting these principles. This argument could have been won by Kant through challenging any opponent to produce a scientific theory not involving the principles. It would not have

---

[16] See *Fundamental Questions in Philosophy*, chapter 2. For a brief outline of a Socratic dialogue in favour of distinguishing between a particular metaphysical system and metaphysics in general see chapter 13, section 1.

been invalidated by the correct point that what is inconceivable at one time may be conceivable at another and that therefore inconceivability at, or up to, a certain time does not imply absolute inconceivability. Although quantum mechanics in its standard interpretation invalidates the transcendental deduction, it does not invalidate the argument from so far inconceivable alternatives.

A third kind of nonsophistic, rhetorical argument for the acceptance of a metaphysical principle is "pragmatic or practical argument". The proponent of such an argument appeals to a common moral or, at least, not immoral aim which he shares with his interlocutor, in order to tip the otherwise equal balance between the acceptance or rejection of the principle. He may, for example, argue that a principle which is likely to decrease human suffering or which is likely to further the production of certain commodities should be accepted rather than rejected – provided that there are no other grounds which together support a different decision. A pragmatic moral argument must be distinguished from a purely moral argument, which is not put forward to tip an otherwise equal balance between the acceptance or rejection of a metaphysical principle, but which is put forward as an independent ground for accepting or rejecting it. The proponent of a pragmatic argument must not appeal to a common aim which he considers immoral since in this case his argument would not be honestly, but dishonestly, rhetorical.

In concluding this very brief and incomplete discussion of nonsophistic or honest rhetoric it should be mentioned that no sharp borderline can be drawn between honest and dishonest rhetoric and that there are degrees of dishonesty. The proponent of a rhetorical argument in favour of one of his metaphysical principles crosses the border-region between honest and dishonest rhetoric if he employs a reason which carries no conviction for himself but which, he assumes, will appeal to his opponent. A case in point would be an agnostic's or atheist's defence of predetermination (or free will) on religious grounds which are based on his opponent's religion. Such an argument is, however, not wholly dishonest since it does not try to "make the weaker case appear stronger"[17] but merely to make the stronger case appear stronger to the opponent than it appears to the proponent.

[17] Plato, *Apology*, 2, B.

CHAPTER 16

ON METAPHYSICAL PLURALISM, INTRAMETAPHYSICAL AND METAPHYSICAL PROGRESS

The present chapter is devoted to three related tasks. The first is retrospectively to summarize the scope and limits of metaphysical pluralism and, thereby, to underline the approach of this essay which, in its attempt to propound empirical theses about systems of nonempirical propositions, belongs to philosophical anthropology. The second is to exhibit the frequently neglected rôle played by a person's metaphysics in his judgments about scientific progress – or progress in other disciplines – pursued within the constraints of his metaphysics or, at least, viewed from its standpoint. The third task of this chapter is to consider the problem of metaphysical progress.

The chapter begins with a brief retrospective look at the concepts of metaphysical pluralism (1) and a brief discussion of the general concept of progress (2). It then considers some problems arising from multidimensional concepts of progress (3). There follows an examination of scientific progress within the constraints of a categorial framework (4). The chapter ends with a discussion of metaphysical progress (5).

1 A retrospective look at the plurality of metaphysical systems

To ask whether the approach of this essay is pluralistic or monistic is like asking a natural historian whether, in distinguishing between various species of a genus, he has committed himself to pluralism or monism. While he might reject the question as pointless, he might also give a more conciliatory answer. Thus, he might say that in making the distinction, he is neither a pluralist nor a monist since he distinguishes a plurality of species within one genus; that he is both, namely, a pluralist with regard to the species and a monist with regard to their genus; or that whether he is one or the other is a matter of emphasis, that he finds it necessary or convenient to say at some times that he distinguishes *many* species within one genus, at other times that he distinguishes many species within *one* genus. Similar remarks apply to mathematicians who distinguish between different geometries, each of which is a geometry, and to jurists who distinguish between different legal systems, each of which is a legal system. All these distinctions are compatible with a personal preference for one of the distinguished species – for example, for an animal species, because it conforms to certain evolutionary criteria; for a geometry, because it is most helpful in physics; for a legal system, because it conforms to certain criteria of morality; for an immanent or transcendent metaphysics, because for some reason or other (such as the reasons given in the next chapter) it gives its acceptor greater intellectual or emotional satisfaction than its competitors.

One of the main tasks of this inquiry has been to characterize and to exemplify the notion of an immanent metaphysics or, more precisely, a categorial framework. The general characterization consists in exhibiting the empirical fact that (almost) every human being organizes his beliefs in certain ways, resulting in the acceptance of certain principles which together constitute his categorial framework. That (almost) all human beings – be they philosophers or nonphilosophers, scientists or nonscientists, experts in other fields of inquiry or nonexperts in them – employ the organizing principles mentioned and that the employment of these principles results in categorial frameworks, accepted with varying degrees of explicitness and assurance, is an empirical thesis for which the evidence seems to be abundant. The writings of philosophers and scientists as well as other written documents contain, however, a great deal of support for the assumption that what is common to various categorial frameworks is more than their being categorial frameworks. The preceding chapters (especially part II) contain an attempt at showing this by distinguishing, within the principles accepted by various thinkers, between those belonging to a common core or common cores and those which are peripheral.

In the course of this inquiry it has frequently been pointed out that there is a danger of regarding a set of supreme principles as a permanent feature of all human thinking and, more particularly, of every culture and intellectual tradition, when as a matter of empirical fact it is local rather than global. The danger of making this mistake, as was also pointed out, increases as one moves away from the minimal principle of noncontradiction to more peripheral principles of logic and from there to what was propounded as the core of empirical and idealized mathematical thinking, of predictive and instrumental thinking about nature, of thinking about persons and mental phenomena, of thinking about social phenomena and history. From mistakes about the class of human beings who accept a certain principle or set of principles – such as classical logic, Euclidean geometry, the Kantian analogies of experience – one must distinguish mistakes about the content of the principles and their relation to the other beliefs of their acceptors.

It would have been easy to avoid empirical mistakes about the class of acceptors of a certain categorial framework or of certain principles contributing to its constitution. Thus, instead of asserting or, rather, confidently conjecturing that certain principles and other propositions have been generally accepted and instead of analysing the so-accepted propositions and their interrelations, one might well rest content with merely analysing these propositions without deciding the question of their acceptance. A similar, empirically noncommittal strategy might be adopted when distinguishing between various types of thinking, such as logical, mathematical or instrumental thinking, and when distinguishing within each of these types between principles which belong to a more or less common core and principles which belong to a more or less varied periphery.

Yet such caution is unnecessary when the empirical evidence is easily accessible and when, once certain questions are clearly formulated, the answers are fairly obvious. A more important reason for facing empirical questions as to whether certain principles are accepted by (almost) everybody or by some groups of people only is the need to counteract spurious arguments for the unique necessity of certain principles, when in fact viable alternatives exist. While the emphasis on alternative possibilities seems appropriate at a time in which exaggerated uniqueness-claims are made by transcendental and phenomenological philosophers, other times might require a change of emphasis. Thus, if for some reason or other a thesis of limitless pluralism became dominant, it would be advisable to emphasize more strongly that the range of alternative categorial frameworks is limited by the deductive organization, epistemic stratification and the other methods by which human thinking is organized. In examining human thinking one is, of course, not implying that other ways of apprehending the world – subhuman, superhuman or simply nonhuman – are not possible.

2 On the concept of progress

When thinking about social and historical phenomena was considered as a possible source of metaphysics (chapter 9, section 5), the concept of human progress and the thesis that mankind is progressing, i.e., that, in Bury's words, it "advances in a definite and desirable direction", were used as examples. It was then pointed out that the assumption of a progression of social or historical states which manifests progress may not only function as a supreme assumption within sociology or some other special discipline, but that it may also become a principle of immanent metaphysics. In either case the concepts of social or historical states must be empirically linked. If the principle is to be part of a person's categorial framework, the concept of a social or historical state (event, process, etc.) must, moreover, be acknowledged as defining a maximal kind with which the assumption of progress is associated as a constitutive principle.

For the purpose of discussing the progress of a specific natural science, of natural science in general or of some other field of inquiry within the constraints of an immanent metaphysics, as well as for the purpose of discussing metaphysical progress, if there be such, it is useful to be aware of the formal structure of any kind of progress. It is, first of all, obvious that progress – as well as regress or stagnation – is manifested by a process which is divided into temporally distinct phases. Second, any two phases are comparable with respect to a relation xRy, expressing that x constitutes progress over y or, with regard to progress, does not differ from y. The relation has the same formal properties as $x \geq y$, where x and y are natural numbers. This means that one can define a relation, xPy, which corresponds to $x > y$. It defines 'x constitutes progress over y' by '(xRy) and not (yRx)'. Third, this relation must be the object of a positive attitude which may be practical or pure and which often is a moral attitude. It seems fair to assume that the three mentioned necessary conditions of any kind of progress are contained in Bury's concise formulation. However, in stating them explicitly, one draws attention to features and possible variations which might otherwise be overlooked.

One of them is the distinction between a strong and a weak sense of progress. In the strong sense of "progress" a process is progressive if, and only if, every phase of the process constitutes progress over each preceding phase. In the weak sense of "progress" a progress is progressive if, and only if, every phase has at least one successor which constitutes progress over all its predecessors and if, in the case of a finite sequence of phases, the last phase constitutes progress over all its predecessors. Progress in the weak sense is implied by, but does not imply, progress in the strong sense. Whether or not a process which manifests progress in the weak sense also manifests progress in the strong sense depends on its division into phases. It is always possible to change a weakly progressive into a strongly progressive process by changing its division into phases. However, the question whether a process manifests progress and, if so, whether it manifests weak or strong progress is usually asked after the process has been divided into phases on grounds which are independent of these questions.

To believe that a process manifests – weak or strong – progress is not necessarily to know the ordering relation. Indeed some historically important conceptions of progress imply no more than the belief that there is such an ordering relation without any knowledge of its nature or with only a most fragmentary knowledge of it. Thus a believer in divine providence may, from the fact of social change, from the existence of an infinitely benevolent creator and from the inability of human beings to understand his ways, infer that the process which is human history is progressive, that there consequently exists a relation which renders it so and that this relation is either unknowable or else not yet known. An elaboration of this sketch would show that, from the point of view of logic, the reasoning which leads from the (mainly theological) premises to the theological existence-theorem is no less sound than the reasoning by which mathematical existence-theorems are established.

An example of an assumption of human progress which goes beyond the mere assertion of its existence is found in Darwin's *The Descent of Man* (first edition, 1871). In this work Darwin distinguishes sharply between the process which led to the origin of the human species and the progress of that species. It seems best to quote his own words:

Important as the struggle for existence has been and even still is, yet as far as the highest part of man's nature is concerned there are other agencies more important. For the moral qualities are advanced, either directly or indirectly, through the effects of habit, the reasoning powers, instruction, religion *etc*, rather than through natural selection; though to this latter agency may be safely attributed the social instinct, which afforded the basis for the development of moral sense.[1]

A more definite and less cautious characterization of human progress is found at the end of his earlier work, *The Origin of Species* (first edition, 1859), in which the Struggle for Life and Natural Selection is taken to be the sole cause of all progress, be it nonhuman or human. As has been the case throughout the animal kingdom, so one can

foretell that it will be the common and widely-spread species, belonging to the larger and dominant groups within each class, which will ultimately prevail and procreate new and dominant species . . . And as natural selection works solely by and for the good of each being, all corporeal and mental endowment will tend to progress towards perfection.[2]

---

[1] Charles Darwin, *The Descent of Man*, part III, chapter 21.
[2] *The Origin of Species*, chapter 15, p. 428, quoted from sixth edn, London, 1884.

These two views of Darwin on the nature of biological and specifically human development differ widely from each other. But they both imply that development manifests progress in, at least, the weak sense of the term. Although this relation is acknowledged to result from development in various respects, directions or dimensions – physical strength, mental power, happiness, morality, etc. – it is regarded as unproblematic. Thus the question of the way in which the linear order or one-dimensionality of ever-increasing perfection is imposed on the many directions or dimensions of development is not raised. It is worth noting that T. H. Huxley raises this question and answers it by the thesis that ethical progress is overriding, that is to say that if x is morally preferable to y, x manifests progress over y even if y is superior in respect of physical strength, mental power, etc. Indeed Huxley's way of imposing linear order on many-dimensional progress makes him reject Darwin's theory. He holds that "the cosmic process has no sort of relation to moral ends" and that "the ethical progress of society" – which he takes to be a fact – "depends not on imitating the cosmic process, still less in running away from it, but in combating it".[3]

3 Dimensions of change and progress

A belief in "progress towards perfection" is compatible with – and usually implies – an acknowledgement of different aspects, directions or dimensions of progress or regress and of the possibility that progress in one of them may strengthen or weaken progress in another. It is the highly complex interaction between changes in different dimensions which tends to empty the notion of a linear overall progress of its content and to support the view that the meaning of "progress towards perfection" can be understood only very imperfectly, since it reveals itself only in the course of time. Even the relation between progress in two directions may be controversial. An example is the relation between progress in knowledge, especially scientific knowledge, and progress in happiness or the absence of sorrow. There is first of all the view of Ecclesiastes that "he that increases knowledge increases sorrow" (Ecclesiastes, 1:18). There is, next, the belief of the Enlightenment that, at least since the beginning of organized and institutionalized search for scientific knowledge, he that increases knowledge decreases sorrow. And there is, last, a more recent view that the applicability of science for destructive purposes is rapidly increasing and that consequently, from a certain stage onwards, the increase of *scientific* knowledge leads to an increase of sorrow.

[3] *Evolution and Ethics* (1893), reprinted in T. H. Huxley, *Collected Essays*, (9 vols., London, 1894), vol. 9, p. 83.

Before examining the way in which an overall linear ordering of historical states by means of a relation 'x is as perfect as, or more perfect than, y' results from specific linear orderings by means of a relation 'x is with respect to a certain dimension of change indifferent or preferable to y', it is necessary to distinguish between various dimensions of change. The distinctions must, moreover, be made in the light of our present purpose, which is to exhibit the rôle of metaphysics in determining criteria of specific progress and of overall progress as well as to tackle the question of metaphysical progress, if there be such progress. The distinction between various dimensions of change may be more or less fine. It must, however, take note of the possibility that progress in one dimension may well cause regression in another and must, at least, avoid obscuring this possibility.

For our purpose it seems useful to distinguish between three broad dimensions of change connecting the various states or stages in the development of a society, a civilization or mankind, namely, cognitive, technical and evaluative change. Cognitive change is change in the available information about what is the case, in the available predictions and retrodictions and in the explanations of facts and happenings. Technical change is change in the instruments for the satisfaction of human needs such as food, health, movement, communication. Evaluative change is change in the system of evaluations. To distinguish between progressive and regressive change, as opposed to mere change, evaluative criteria must be introduced, which may be internal criteria that are accepted by the social group or civilization which is being judged, external criteria, i.e., those accepted by an outside observer, or criteria which are both internal and external.

The problem of determining whether one social state represents progress over another would be easily solved if there were available a method or instrument which, after the fashion of a thermometer, measuring degrees of temperature, would measure degrees of progressiveness. The desired instrument would either have to be capable of measuring the degrees of progressiveness of an overall state or of its different dimensions. In the latter case the overall progressiveness or regressiveness of any state would be the result of performing certain simple additions or subtractions. However, not even the most sanguine believer in progress is likely to claim that he possesses such a progressometer. He might, however, claim to be able to compare any two states with respect to their greater or equal progressiveness in certain dimensions by means of a progressometer resembling a crude thermometer which enables him to determine only whether of any two bodies one is hotter than the other, colder than the other or whether they do not differ in temperature.

Such a progressometer is available, if one restricts oneself to the dimension of change in information about matters of fact and makes two assumptions which in some cases – e.g., in the more formal sciences, in which the axiomatic method is, or can be used – are not unrealistic. One is that the information which is available at any stage can be expressed by an internally consistent set of propositions. The other assumption is that the information available at one stage is preserved at the next. If these two assumptions are justified, progress in information coincides with growth of information – every set of informative propositions being contained in its successor. Similar remarks apply to progress in predictions and retrodictions if the set of reliable predictions and retrodictions associated with an earlier stage of development is contained in its successors. Here an increase not only in the set of predictive and retrodictive conjectures but also an increase in their reliability may be taken to represent progress. Technical progress may also be measured by the increase in the number of instruments for the satisfaction of human needs and by an increase in their efficiency (defined in such a way that the two kinds of increase cannot hinder each other).

Agreement about progress in the informative, the predictive and retrodictive, and the technical dimension is on the whole reached with comparative ease. Such agreement is, however, compatible with profound disagreement about progress in the explanatory and the evaluative dimension. A follower of Comte or the Enlightenment and a believer in the wisdom of Ecclesiastes may well agree that the store of factual information, the power of prediction and retrodiction, and technical ability have much grown since the seventeenth century. Yet while this growth for the Comtean is accompanied by a growth in the power of explaining what can be explained and by a moral improvement of humanity, it may for the believer in the wisdom of Ecclesiastes involve a decay in understanding and morals. In examining the concepts of explanatory and evaluative progress, it is of the utmost importance clearly to distinguish explanatory progress *within* a categorial framework and evaluative progress *within* a morality from explanatory or moral progress due to change *of* a categorial framework or a morality. Before the latter questions can be raised it is necessary to discuss the former. Both kinds of question are best considered with reference to a specific example. The question of scientific progress seems particularly suitable – not least because of the central rôle played by science in recent discussions about progress.

4 *On scientific progress within the constraints of a categorial framework*

Scientific thinking consists in the construction, reconstruction and replacement of scientific theories and in their application in the service of information (including prediction and retrodiction), of technical use and of explanation. According to a widely accepted view, the so-called "deductivist" or "hypothetico-deductivist" view of science, a scientific theory is, or approximates, a system of axioms of the form "If so and so is the case at time t_1, then such and such is the case at time t_2' (where t_2 may equal t_1 and the *if-then* expresses either a certainty or a degree of probability). The axioms permit the deduction of theorems of the same form. And the axioms and theorems, together with initial conditions of the form 'So and so is the case at time t_1' permit the deduction of conjectures of the form 'Such and such is the case at time t_2' (with certainty or a given degree of probability). This so-called "deductivist account" is not the only one. Among the alternatives there is in particular the more recent "structuralist" view of Sneed and Stegmüller, according to which a scientific theory is not regarded as a set of statements which are true or false, but as a complex predicate which is correctly or incorrectly applicable.[4] Both deductivism and structuralism suffer from the defect of ignoring the rôle of idealization in scientific thinking. It will be sufficient to show this in the case of the deductivist account, since what will be said about it can be easily extended to the structuralist account of the rôle of scientific theories.

In so far as a scientific theory does not describe empirical phenomena, but idealizes them, one can distinguish the following steps in its use for the purpose of increasing the available information. First, from the store of statements expressing the already available information in common language one or more are replaced by statements of the theory with which they are linked in the sense of being in certain specified contexts identifiable with them. Second, the statements of the theory are used as premises from which, together with axioms or theorems of the theory, a conclusion is derived which is, of course, expressed in the language of the theory. Third, the conclusion is replaced by a statement expressed in the common language, with which it is linked, and thus extends the previously available information. The steps may be briefly called "idealization", "theoretical inference" and "de-idealization".[5]

The extension of information by means of scientific theories is thus not direct, but leads through the region of theory, or rather theories, which may

---

[4] See, for example, W. Stegmüller, *The Structural View of Theories* (Berlin, 1979).
[5] See chapter 8, section 3 and, for a more detailed discussion, *Experience and Theory*, chapter 12.

conflict with each other. To be more precise, we assume that at a certain time the available information about, say, the physical world, expressed in commonsense language, consists of an internally consistent set of propositions P_0 some of which have been acquired by applying the hitherto available physical theories $T_1, \ldots, T_n$. (The internal consistency of P_0 does not imply the internal consistency of the set consisting of $T_1, \ldots, T_n$, since two mutually inconsistent theories may be linked to the same empirical propositions – as when Euclidean and a non-Euclidean geometry are linked to propositions about perceptual phenomena.) Let us now further assume that by adding a new physical theory, T_{n+1}, to $T_1, \ldots, T_n$, the set of informative propositions P_0 is extended to P_1.

Although the addition of T_{n+1} represents informative progress over the stage in which only $T_1, \ldots, T_n$ were accepted, it is worthwhile to distinguish between the following varieties: one of them, which might be called "theoretically unifying, informative progress", and which is often meant by historians of science when they speak of progress, is characterized by T_{n+1} logically implying the conjunction of $T_1, \ldots, T_n$ without being implied by it. Another variety of informative progress, which might be called "theoretically consistent, informative progress", is characterized by the consistency of T_{n+1} with the conjunction of $T_1, \ldots, T_n$. Last, informative progress may be "theoretically conflicting" in the sense that T_{n+1} is inconsistent with the conjunction of $T_1, \ldots, T_n$. (Finer distinctions are possible but not needed here.) Positivists and others for whom the rôle of science is purely informative will regard the differences between these varieties of informative progress as irrelevant or negligible, while others will have to weigh, e.g., "small", unifying against "large", but theoretically conflicting, informative progress.

What has been said about informative progress by means of scientific theories applies with obvious modifications to technical progress, i.e., in the provision of instruments for the satisfaction of human needs, in the wide sense of the term in which the needs of different people may conflict and in which their satisfaction may lead to disaster, such as nuclear war. Informative and technical progress clearly overlap since a great deal of scientific information is technical information. Indeed if, with the pragmatists, one regards every belief or, with the scientific instrumentalists, every scientific belief as an instrument, then informative and technical progress coincide. There is, however, no need for a terminological ruling, especially as it is generally agreed that some scientific information may be of no technical use.

Just as positivist and pragmatist philosophers of science have emphasized the informative or technical dimension of scientific progress or change, so have others – in recent times particularly Ludwik Fleck and Thomas Kuhn – emphasized its explanatory dimension. Thus Fleck argues that science is a cooperative enterprise, undertaken by a scientific community (*Denk-Kollektiv*) in conformity to intellectual habits and presuppositions which together constitute the community's style of thinking (*Denk-Stil*). Kuhn, who acknowledges his indebtedness to Fleck, similarly emphasizes the rôle of what he calls "paradigms". For those who think in conformity to a style of thinking or an overall paradigm, only what conforms to it has explanatory value or makes the subject matter intelligible. What violates them lacks intelligibility – even if it may give information.[6] Fleck and Kuhn can be regarded as tackling for the special case of scientific thinking the problem which Collingwood tried to solve for all thinking.

The difference between Collingwood's notion of a system of absolute presuppositions and the notion of a categorial framework has been discussed earlier (see chapter 10, section 2 and chapter 14, section 1). The main difference between a style of thinking or paradigm on the one hand and a categorial framework on the other is that conformity to the latter, unlike conformity to the former, is definable in terms of logical relations. A scientific theory T conforms to a categorial framework F and, thus, has full explanatory power with respect to F if, and only if, the axioms and theorems of T comprise only concepts which are maximal kinds of F or species of them and if the logic underlying T is the logic of F. Thus Newton's kinematics conforms to a framework in which movable bodies are defined in such a way that (among other things) the motion of a body is continuous. To reject this framework principle is to deny explanatory power to Newton's kinematics. It is not to deprive it of its empirical predictive or retrodictive content, which depends not on the theory's conformity to a framework but on its being linked to empirical propositions which – via idealizations and de-idealizations – may be linked to mutually incompatible theories and categorial frameworks.

To distinguish between the informative and the explanatory dimension of scientific progress is not to deny that if of two theories neither is preferable to the other on the grounds of informative content or conformity to an accepted categorial framework, other – for example, aesthetic – considerations may tip the balance. Yet to conflate, e.g., aesthetic appeal with explanatory power is no less misleading than to conflate explanatory power with informative content, since both kinds of conflation tend to obscure the

---

[6] See especially Ludwik Fleck, *Entstehung und Entwicklung einer wissenschaftlichen Tatsache* (1935, reprinted Frankfurt, 1980), and Thomas S. Kuhn, *The Structure of Scientific Revolutions* (Chicago, 1962).

relation between the explanatory power of a scientific theory and its conformity to a categorial framework. They also obscure the distinction between progress within a categorial framework or system of metaphysics and progress of metaphysics – if such there be. For it may well turn out that while there is change and progress within a metaphysical system or from its point of view, there is metaphysical change, but no metaphysical progress.

5 On metaphysical progress, as opposed to progress within a metaphysical system

In times of metaphysical stability, that is to say, when the members of a community explicitly or implicitly accept a common – immanent and transcendent – metaphysics, the problem of metaphysical progress is unlikely to arise. For, whatever the difficulties in ranking the predecessors of the accepted metaphysics, its general superiority over them is usually taken for granted. And when its unquestioning acceptors turn their minds to intellectual history, they all too often remind one of Faust's famulus Wagner, who enjoyed contemplating "what wise men before us had thought and how at least we ourselves got so wonderfully far".[7] One might try to escape from this predicament by searching for a standard of metaphysical progress which is external in the sense that although it is applicable to metaphysical systems, its applicability has no influence on the acceptance or rejection of any of them. A person who employs such a standard would sometimes have to admit that he has accepted a meta-physical system which with respect to this standard is retrogressive rather than progressive. However, it is not difficult to see that in so far as a standard of metaphysical progress is external to its user's metaphysics it does not measure metaphysical progress and in so far as it measures metaphysical progress it is not external.

To begin with a trivial example, one could measure the change of metaphysical systems with respect to the extent to which they further cookery. A person comparing metaphysical systems in this way could legitimately speak of periods in which metaphysics did or did not further culinary progress. Yet unless he had an overriding passion for cookery, or its results, he would be unlikely to identify a culinary progress of metaphysics with a specifically metaphysical progress. A less trivial example of measuring metaphysical progress would consist in comparing metaphysical systems with respect to the extent to which they further scientific activity. One can well imagine some people – for example, some

[7] Goethe's *Faust*, part I, "Nacht".

Buddhist or Christian monks – for whom this standard would be no less external than the culinary. On the other hand, those who identify metaphysical progress with the furtherance of scientific activity do so because of their metaphysical convictions.

A comparison of successive metaphysical systems by ranking them according to the extent to which they conform to an accepted morality is of particular historical and philosophical importance. This is so because everybody has a metaphysics and a morality and because his morality may come into conflict with his metaphysics. Thus a person may have accepted a metaphysics which, he believes, favours scientific and technical activity, in particular the production of weapons which will cause intolerable suffering, so that furthering that production in any way – for example, by arguing for his metaphysics – is grossly immoral.

A person acknowledging such a conflict between his metaphysics and his morality might react in one of the following ways: he might, with some logical positivists and some metaphysical pessimists, regard the moral standard for measuring metaphysical progress as no less external than the culinary. Against this, he might regard it as a metaphysical task to solve any real or apparent conflict between metaphysics and morality. This he might attempt either by declaring the primacy of morality over metaphysics and by introducing suitable moral qualifications into his supreme cognitive principles; or, less radically, by declaring the moral dimension to be one of a number of dimensions of metaphysical change. (In that case he would be faced with the difficulties mentioned in sections 3 and 4 of this chapter.) He might lastly make the conflict a subject of speculation about transcendent reality and, for example, declare conflicts between metaphysics and morality as a species of the merely apparent evil which his theodicy shows to be illusory.

Each of these attempts at providing a criterion of metaphysical progress either begs the question by locating the criterion for the ranking of successive metaphysical systems in one of them; or else replaces the question of the criterion of metaphysical progress by the different question of a criterion of some nonmetaphysical progress served by metaphysical change. To put it more moderately, whereas a person's criterion of metaphysical progress belongs to his metaphysical principles, his criteria of the extent to which metaphysical change serves some other kind of progress do not belong to these principles.

To the distinction between progress within a person's metaphysics, i.e., within the constraints of his supreme cognitive principles, and progress of metaphysics, there corresponds, as has been mentioned (section 3), the distinction between progress within a person's morality, i.e., within the constraints of his supreme practical principles, and progress of morality. The problem of moral progress (from one morality to another), if any, falls outside the scope of this essay. Yet it should be obvious from a comparison of supreme cognitive with supreme practical principles that – as in the case of metaphysics – a person's criteria of moral progress belong to his moral principles, whereas his criteria of the extent to which moral change serves some other kind of progress do not belong to them.

CHAPTER 17

SOME SPECULATIONS ABOUT
TRANSCENDENT REALITY

In examining the structure and function of categorial frameworks one is exposed to the danger of confusing peculiarities of one's own categorial framework with features common to all of them. In examining the nature of transcendent metaphysics one is exposed to similar dangers, especially the danger of putting too much weight on one's own transcendent speculations, on the interaction between one's own immanent and transcendent metaphysics and on the interaction between one's own transcendent metaphysics and morality. How far have these dangers been avoided in the present inquiry? In order to provide some relevant evidence for an answer, it seems appropriate that the inquirer give some indication of his own categorial framework, his own morality and his own transcendent metaphysics and that in doing so he refer to himself in the first person.

My own categorial framework can, and will be, sketched in a few words. This is so because it does not greatly differ from the metaphysics immanent in modern common sense and science and because I adhere more firmly to those parts of it which constitute the core rather than the periphery of logic, mathematics and the other disciplines which were identified as potential sources of supreme cognitive principles. An indication of my morality can, and will be, given in even fewer words. In so far as ethical considerations enter my speculations about transcendent reality, they concern the structure of morality (as sketched in chapter 2) rather than any specific moral convictions, such as my own. When it comes to the formulation of my transcendent metaphysics, some elaboration will be necessary. This is so not only because my speculative conjectures about transcendent reality, in particular my metaphysical perspectivism, differ from the dominant, contemporary systems of transcendent metaphysics, especially all versions of scientific realism and dogmatic theology, but also because they are to a considerable extent suggested by the results of my inquiry into the structure and function of metaphysical systems.

The chapter begins with a brief sketch of my categorial framework and a bare indication of my moral convictions (1). It then describes the strategy which will be employed in the formulation of transcendent theses and in their justification (2). There follow speculations about the relation between the world of intersubjective experience and transcendent reality (3) and about the nature of human freedom and creativity (4). The chapter ends by giving some reasons for my failure to understand and, hence, to accept or reject beliefs in the existence or nonexistence of an infinitely perfect being and of immortal souls (5).

1 Some brief remarks about a particular categorial framework and a particular morality

In accepting a categorial framework one relies heavily on the intellectual labour of others. Its division within a society corresponds to its division into specialists and nonspecialists in certain fields, such as mathematics, physics and the other sciences as well as history and the humanities. The nonspecialists in a certain field are and, indeed, must often be content to rely on the judgment of the experts without being able to check it for lack of intellectual ability, time or interest. Nonexperts may, of course, become experts and experts may lose their expertness by failing to keep informed about developments in their field. The commonsense and the specialist knowledge of a community are not strictly separated, but in continuous interaction. This is so especially in the sciences since their idealizations are often idealizations of commonsense propositions and since their results often seep in modified form into common sense.[1]

While it is obvious that, in accepting a particular categorial framework, I had to rely heavily on the intellectual division of labour, it does not seem necessary to account for the extent of this reliance in various fields. Nor does it seem possible to separate such reliance from possible misunderstandings. The influence of other philosophers on the formation of my categorial framework consists mainly in my reaction to their nonsophistic rhetoric in favour of their own categorial framework, as opposed to any of their claims to have discovered a method which is capable of establishing the unique necessity of a particular framework (see chapter 15). The influence of other categorial frameworks on my own must be distinguished from their rôle as examples and, hence, as a means of finding out what is common to them. That Plato, Aristotle, Leibniz and Kant have played a greater part in shaping my categorial framework than Descartes, Spinoza or Hegel does not imply that their metaphysical systems have been – or, at least, should have been – less relevant to my arriving at a general conception of the structure and

[1] For details of this interaction see *Experience and Theory*, chapter 12.

function of metaphysics and, hence, of a categorial framework.

The logic underlying my categorial framework is finitist and "inexact" in the sense of admitting inexact attributes, i.e., attributes having borderline cases and, hence, attributes sharing borderline cases with their complements. This logic underlies *inter alia* thinking about empirical arithmetic and empirical continua. It admits a variety of idealizations, which enable one to construct various versions of pure arithmetic, especially the classical system of real numbers, as well as other ideal mathematical structures, studied for their own sake and their usefulness in science. The principal idealizations of the finitist inexact logic involve "exactification" and various kinds of "infinitization". Where the purpose of the idealization permits a choice, I am aware of a preference for potential over actual infinities and for actual infinities of smaller, over actual infinities of greater, cardinality. (For details see chapters 5 and 6.)

The maximal kinds of my categorial framework, i.e., the highest kinds of independent, intersubjective particulars, are material things, animals and persons, admitting possible borderline cases between material things and animals and between animals and persons. I thus do not regard animals as a species of material objects, i.e., as living material objects. My reason for rejecting this classification is that I am not aware of any reductive analysis of "living" which I should feel inclined to accept. I can, however, imagine that such an analysis might be given in the future and make me change my mind. I am aware of a strong inclination to reject the classification of persons as a species of animals. But I readily admit that biological evidence, philosophical argument and even further reflection might make me change my mind, provided that the maximal kind of animals could be so conceived that the possibility of 'being an animal with human personality' would not conflict with my conception of being a person. A somewhat crude and emphatic way of indicating my position might make use of a distinction between 'having a (material or animal) body' and 'being a body': at present I have some doubts about the alleged equivalence of the statement that an animal has a material body and the statement that it is such a body. And I know of no convincing reason for regarding the statement that a person has an animal body as equivalent to the statement that the person is such a body.

The three maximal kinds share certain structural features characteristic of objects which, though changing in the course of time, yet for some of it persist as the same individuals rather than merely as members of the same class of objects. The individual objects of each of these maximal kinds consist of spatio-temporal object-phases which are unified and, thereby, individuated into distinct, more or less enduring individuals through a relation of interrepresentation, satisfying specific requirements of resemblance and continuity as well as certain pragmatic requirements. Since I have been on the whole successful in communicating my beliefs about, and my practical attitudes towards, individual material objects, individual animals and individual persons to other members of my community, I have good reason to hold that the relation of interrepresentation which is used by them for each of these kinds is rather similar to mine. I should, on the other hand, not be surprised if a member of a different culture did not share my requirements for interrepresentation – if, for example, a Hindu sometimes identified animal-phases and person-phases as phases of the same individual (see chapters 7 and 8).

The maximal kinds of my categorial framework are linked to special disciplines. Thus, being a material object, or a state of a system of such objects, is linked to physical science in the sense of being identifiable with some of its entities for the purpose of physical prediction and explanation. In acknowledging this linkage I also acknowledge the physicists' competence to change their theories on their behalf and mine until I can check their results, which in some cases may be never. In a similar way my concept of an animal is linked to biology. I have in particular no objection that in biology my notion of an animal's having a body is identified with the notion of its being a body. I also regard it as sometimes useful to identify the notion of a person with that of an animal body or of a machine, as is done in psychology and the study of artificial intelligence. Yet when in these fields the concept of a person is treated *as if* it were the concept of a machine, the danger of confusing a limited *as-if* identification with a description seems to me not only greater than in physics and animal biology, but also to lead to much more serious confusions.

For reasons given in the introduction to this chapter, very little needs to be said about my personal morality. It can be roughly described as a version of Judaeo-Christian morality, provided account is taken of my being an agnostic (see section 5 below). My conception of social justice implies a preference for representative democracy in Mill's sense over other forms of government, as well as approval of the strengthening of institutions which protect society from violations of personal freedom, from illness, political oppression, economic exploitation and undereducation. While each of these *desiderata* is a legitimate topic for a large treatise, I can for my present purpose rely on their commonsense interpretation or interpretations.

2 From immanent to transcendent metaphysics

During anybody's lifetime questions about the relation of his experience to a reality which is independent of it and about the nature of this reality are likely to occur and – sometimes at least – to cause intellectual discomfort. Attempts at removing it include the employment of a variety of more or less effective remedies such as seeking and finding distractions or the acceptance of more or less obscure answers, especially when they are given in poetic or otherwise aesthetically satisfying form. Sometimes the discomfort is removed or reduced only when the further step is taken of transforming some of the more or less obscure answers into theses and of supporting them by argument. Although the general nature of theses about transcendent reality has been characterized and exemplified and although the general nature of arguments in support of metaphysical theses – immanent as well as transcendent – has been characterized as nonsophistic rhetoric, it will be useful to say a few preliminary words about (some of) my transcendent theses and my strategy of defending them.

Each argument will proceed in three stages: a preparatory indication of a more or less obscure belief about mind-independent reality expressed in a form which falls short of expressing a thesis; the transformation of the belief into a thesis about transcendent reality; and last, the final stage or argument in the narrow sense, involving a premise or conjunction of premises, a conclusion (i.e., the thesis to be defended) and an inferential relation connecting premise and conclusion. The more or less obscure beliefs which are to be transformed into theses and the theses to be justified can in provisionally vague fashion be described as versions of metaphysical perspectivism and of moral indeterminism. The premises will be either statements about a certain categorial framework, a class of categorial frameworks or any categorial framework, or else they will be statements about a certain morality, a class of moralities or any morality.

The inferential relation which connects premise and conclusion might be called "metaphysical plausibility" since it bears some resemblance to subjective probability. In both cases the relation is nondeductive; and different persons may assign different rankings or values to it (be prepared to lay different bets). Yet whereas judgments of subjective probability may be confirmed or refuted by events, no such test is available for judgments of metaphysical plausibility. Thus the proponent of an argument to the effect that, say, the acceptance of any categorial framework or any morality makes a certain thesis about transcendent reality more plausible than its negation can – as is the case with all nonsophistic rhetoric – only exhort his interlocutor to consider premise and conclusion and to make up his own mind about the degree of their plausible connection. Such an exhortation need not be idle, since it may draw attention to otherwise neglected evidence.

Depending on whether the premises are statements about categorial frameworks or moralities, one might distinguish between epistemic and ethical premises of arguments based on metaphysical plausibility and, accordingly, between epistemic and ethical plausibility-arguments. The distinction would be decisive in circumstances in which a thesis about transcendent reality appears on epistemic grounds more plausible than its negation, but on ethical grounds less plausible than its negation. Yet as far as the strategy to be adopted in the following arguments is concerned, such circumstances will not arise for the simple reason that – for me – a thesis which is on epistemic grounds more plausible, but on ethical grounds less plausible than its negation or vice versa is metaphysically implausible.

Arguments based on metaphysical plausibility, whether their premises are epistemic or ethical, also have an aesthetic aspect which should not be neglected. It consists in their proponent's intention or hope that the feelings evoked by his more or less obscure premetaphysical beliefs in their original poetic or other form are adequately represented by the feelings evoked by the metaphysical theses which have taken the place of the premetaphysical beliefs. It is certainly my intention that the aesthetic satisfaction given by my premetaphysical beliefs be preserved in their transformation to theses. The aesthetic aspect of metaphysical arguments and theses was acknowledged by positivists and others who held that metaphysics is intellectual nonsense which can, at the very best, be no more than poetry. The criticism is among other things based on the mistaken assumption that what has aesthetic meaning therefore lacks intellectual meaning (see chapter 13).

In the case of metaphysical perspectivism and of moral indeterminism, an originally obscure belief can, as I shall try to show, be transformed into a thesis which is clear enough to be capable and worthy of a defence by a metaphysical plausibility-argument. There are other originally obscure beliefs which invite but resist such a transformation. I, for one, cannot achieve it for any belief in the existence or nonexistence of an infinitely perfect being or for any belief in the existence or nonexistence of immortal souls. Since the reasons for my failure, not merely to accept or to reject these beliefs, but even to grasp their meaning in a satisfactory manner, are fairly clear to me; and since they are likely to throw some light on my philosophical position, a brief indication of them will serve the purpose of this chapter.

3 A speculation about the relation between appearance and transcendent reality

Even the most radical realist distinguishes between the world as it appears to him and the world in itself, which exists independently of his perceptions and the application of his concepts and, thus, *a fortiori* of his categorial framework. What makes him a radical realist is his belief that the world as it appears to him does not differ from the world in itself. A more moderate realist will assume a more or less close resemblance or that, even though the resemblance is as yet not very close, there is good reason to hope that – for example, as the result of scientific progress – the resemblance will become ever closer. The more moderate realist thinks that just as we now see reality only "through a glass darkly", or, to give a more literal translation of the original Greek, "through a mirror in a riddle or puzzle-picture", so we shall eventually see it "face to face" (Corinthians, 1:13). Whereas Paul in his letter to the Corinthians accords the privilege of seeing reality, as it is in itself, not to mortal men but to their immortal souls, the moderate realist accords it to mankind as represented by some members of a future generation (see chapter 11, section 2).

The belief in the accessibility to human beings of the world in itself, which is common to St Paul and the realist believers in scientific progress, is also held by philosophers who believe that at least some aspects of transcendent reality are in principle accessible to everybody, if he only would employ the right method for gaining access to it. As has been noted earlier, this allegedly right method consists according to some philosophers in replacing conceptual thinking by a nonconceptual apprehension of reality through mystical experience; according to others in replacing ordinary thinking by some kind of superthinking, e.g., of ordinary logic by a superlogic which rejects the principle of noncontradiction (see chapters 11 and 12). It may even consist in drawing inferences from propositions about the world as it appears to a person to propositions about the world as it is in itself. Thus Kant, who insists that the world in itself is not knowable but, at best, a topic for a rational faith, nevertheless deduces from the world as it appears to us that it is a world consisting of a plurality of noumena and that to every empirical self, i.e., every person in the world of intersubjective experience, there corresponds one intelligible or noumenal self in transcendent reality.

(To know that the unknowable reality is not one *noumenon* but a plurality of *noumena* is to know more than merely that there is a transcendent reality.)

An objection to asserting the accessibility of transcendent reality, which I find persuasive, has been put forward by the sceptics. Sextus formulated it by saying "that the same impressions are not produced by the same objects, owing to the differences in animals".[2] Just as the world as apprehended by subhuman species differs from the world as apprehended by human beings, so could, I believe, the world as apprehended by human beings differ from the world of posthuman beings, if biological evolution is a process which has not stopped with the emergence of mankind. If one assumes, as is done in this essay, that different groups of human beings apprehend the world under the constraints of different categorial frameworks, it seems natural and sensible to distinguish between a transcendent reality which is mind-independent and thus independent of being apprehended under the constraints of a categorial framework and the world as it appears "through a categorial framework". It seems equally natural and sensible to regard the appearance of the world through a categorial framework as a perspective of the world in itself. In order to distinguish such a perspective from other ways of apprehending the world, it might be called a "categorial perspective".

The metaphor that transcendent reality is seen through a glass darkly or the less metaphorical statement that it is apprehended through a categorial framework can be reformulated and justified by an argument. Its premise is that different categorial frameworks can be – in a more or less distorted manner – represented by each other. If this were not so, no acceptor of a categorial framework could "understand" another's categorial framework or argue for its rejection in favour of his own (see chapter 9, section 3, chapter 14 and chapter 15). That different categorial frameworks are more or less distorted representations of each other suggests that each of them is a distorted representation or perspective of transcendent reality. This speculative assumption is internally consistent, as well as consistent with my own categorial framework. It is, moreover, consistent with my assumption that my own categorial framework is preferable to any other, known to me, or at least that no categorial framework, known to me, is preferable to mine. An important point in favour of "speculative framework perspectivism" is that it helps to explain why even a rejected categorial framework may contribute to a fuller understanding of reality. The reason can be indicated very briefly by means of an analogy. Although a portrait of a person may give us a more adequate representation of him than a caricature, the

---

[2] *Outlines of Pyrrhonism*, I. 40.

caricature may nevertheless constitute a valuable addition to our knowledge of him.

4 A speculative defence or moral indeterminism

If I blame myself or somebody else for having acted immorally, I imply that I or he could have acted differently – and this not merely in some logically possible world, but in the actual world in which the immoral action has been committed. I regard myself as free to act morally or immorally and distinguish this moral freedom from what Kant so well describes as "the freedom of a roasting spit which, once having been wound up, performs its movements by itself".[3] I similarly distinguish my freedom to act morally or immorally from any dependence of my actions on the occurrence of merely probable events or, as Einstein puts it, "on a dice-playing God".[4] In other words, I consider my apparent choosing between a moral and an immoral action not to be a mere appearance or illusion, which it would be if all my apparently chosen actions were determined by initial conditions outside my control or sphere of action, together with either causal or probabilistic laws of nature. (On the concept of action see chapter 8, section 2.)

In defending speculative perspectivism it was not necessary to show that it satisfies the necessary consistency conditions which every thesis of transcendent metaphysics has to satisfy, namely, internal consistency and consistency with its proponent's categorial framework. Those who reject the thesis will, I think, reject it on other grounds. The situation is quite different in the case of any defence of moral indeterminism. For its opponents not only claim that it fails to satisfy the conditions of internal consistency but, frequently, use this alleged fact as a premise in an alleged deductive proof of some version of moral determinism. Indeed they sometimes argue that moral indeterminism is not only logically but linguistically meaningless. (For the difference between these types of meaninglessness see chapter 13, section 4.) Because of this, the argument in favour of moral indeterminism has to be preceded by showing that it is linguistically meaningful, internally consistent and consistent with my own categorial frameworks as well as many others which share its respect for science and logic.

My moral freedom, as I conceive it, enables me to choose effectively between alternative courses of action and, hence, of nature, e.g., between switching on a light or pulling the trigger of a gun on the one hand and not

---

[3] *Critique of Practical Reason* Akademie Ausgabe edn, p. 174.
[4] *Albert Einstein, Hedwig and Max Born Briefwechsel* (Munich, 1969), p. 204.

performing these actions on the other. The difference between my choosing effectively and my merely seeming to choose effectively is that in the former case my action is not causally or probabilistically predetermined by events which involve me in no way or which may even precede my existence.[5] There is no empirical test by which it could be decided whether I can ever choose effectively. But does it even make linguistic or logical sense to say that I am sometimes capable of choosing effectively to bring about an event with certainty or to increase the probability of its occurrence without my having been causally or probabilistically determined to choose what I in fact choose? Does it, in other words, make linguistic or logical sense to say that I am a creator?

It does make linguistic and logical sense, if one distinguishes between the creative power of, say, the biblical God and the creative power of man – the "little God of the world" (*der kleine Gott der Welt*), as Mephistopheles calls him in Goethe's *Faust*. [6] God's creative power, as described at the beginning of the book of Genesis, is twofold. It is the power of creating something out of nothing (*creatio ex nihilo*) and the power to create order out of complete or comparative chaos (*creatio ex tohu bohu*, as it might be called). The latter kind of creative power can be meaningfully ascribed to man – both by those who believe that God in creating man after his own image gave him this power and left some chaos in the world to be increased or decreased by man; as well as by agnostics and atheists who see no reason why they should replace, for example, their conception of a Goethe or Mozart as a little God by a conception of two completely programmed *homunculi* without effective choice. To hold, as I do, that the concept of man having the power to create order out of comparative chaos or to increase it is internally consistent, is not to hold that the conception of man as a *homunculus* without effective choice is not also internally consistent.

Having indicated why I regard the speculative assumption of man's power of creation out of comparative chaos and, hence, of his power to make effective choices, including effective moral choices as internally consistent, I must now indicate why I consider the assumption to be consistent with my and similar categorial frameworks.[7] To argue for such logical compatibility in our time is easier than it was, for example, at the times of Leibniz, Hume or Kant. For these philosophers held logical and scientific beliefs and corresponding metaphysical beliefs which, at least prima facie, excluded the possibility of effective choice.

---

[5] For a discussion of effective choice, see *Experience and Conduct*, chapter 5.   [6] "Prolog im Himmel".
[7] Compare my *Kant's Conception of Freedom*, Brit. Ac. Dawes Hicks lecture, 1967, and chapter 14 of *Fundamental Questions of Philosophy*, 4th edn (Brighton, 1979), for a more detailed discussion.

If one holds, e.g., with Leibniz, that every proposition – whether or not it refers to a future event – is timelessly true or false, then man has no effective choice between making any proposition true by one action and false by another. But if one rejects the principle of excluded middle – for example, by admitting inexact predicates and borderline cases – one will find no difficulty in assuming that a proposition which depends for its truth or falsehood on an effective choice is not timelessly true or false, but becomes true or false if, and when, the effective choice is made. Again, if one holds with Hume or Kant that in nature all events are causally determined, then there is in nature no room for effective choice – although one may with Kant assume that there is room for it in the *noumenal* world. If, however, one rejects the validity of the unrestricted principle of causality, one may prepare the ground for admitting effective choice. Yet, as has been pointed out earlier, replacing Kant's roasting spit with Einstein's dice-playing God will not do. What has to be restricted is not the deterministic or probabilistic character of the scientific laws of nature, but their range of applicability. The possibility of this restriction is implicit in my account of scientific theories as idealizations which *in certain contexts and for certain purposes* can be identified with descriptions of commonsense experience. And, in my view, actions involving effective choices are in general not identifiable with events not involving them (see chapter 7, section 4).

Having indicated why, contrary to what seems to me the view of the large majority of contemporary philosophers, I regard the thesis of moral freedom as internally consistent and consistent with my and other categorial frameworks, I may add a brief pragmatic argument in its favour. The premises are: (i) I and the addressee of the argument agree in our desire that men should conform to a greater rather than to a lesser extent to their morality; (ii) there is no empirical test to establish whether we are or are not morally free; (iii) if we are not morally free then assuming moral freedom makes no difference to the morality or immorality of our actions; (iv) if we are morally free, then assuming moral freedom rather than its absence is likely to counteract the tendency to excuse immorality by denying the absence of effective choice and thus to increase the likelihood of greater conformity to one's moral convictions. The metaphysically plausible conclusion is to accept the assumption of moral freedom. The inferential relation is one of ethical plausibility. The argument as a whole is *not* a deductive or inductive argument, but an example of nonsophistic rhetoric, i.e., an argument in favour of a thesis of transcendent metaphysics which I have accepted by giving reasons which I find acceptable.[8]

---

[8] The argument formally resembles Reichenbach's pragmatic argument in favour of induction. See his *Wahrscheinlich-Reitslehre* (Leiden, 1935).

5 Some reasons for a failure to understand beliefs in the existence or nonexistence of God and the existence or nonexistence of immortal souls

Before attempting to put forward a metaphysical plausibility-argument in favour of a moral indeterminism, it was necessary to show that the concept of moral freedom is internally consistent and consistent with the categorial frameworks of the proponent and the addressee of the argument. My reason for being unable to propose an argument for or against the existence of the God of Jewish, Moslem and Christian philosophers, or indeed for the internal consistency of their concept of God, is simply that the meaning of the concept is not clear to me. To indicate my position, I shall refer to the arguments adopted by Thomas Aquinas in the first part of his *Summa Theologiae*, as well as to some comments on them made by Father F. C. Copleston, SJ, in the twelfth chapter of *A History of Medieval Philosophy*.[9]

Thomas first raises the question whether God exists and – having answered it to his satisfaction in the affirmative – then raises the question what God is, i.e., what the meaning of the term 'God' is. Copleston rightly says that Aquinas in explaining the concept of God combines the negative way of explanation (the *via negativa*) with the method of analogy. The negative method is based on the conviction "that the divine essence in itself transcends the grasp of the human mind",[10] whence we cannot attribute any of our positive, but only some of our negative, concepts to God. Thus we can characterize God as being infinite only in the sense of not being finite and not in any sense which goes beyond our understanding of the separate and combined sense of the words "not" and "finite" (see chapter 12, section 3).

Copleston, again rightly, says that an "exclusive adherence to the negative approach seems to lead in the direction of agnosticism"[11] and that, consequently, Thomas is forced to apply positive concepts which are applicable to man "analogically" to God. The analogical modification consists in a transition from finite human attributes to infinite divine perfections, e.g., from 'humanly or finitely good' to 'perfectly or infinitely good' or from being 'humanly or finitely creative' (like Goethe's little God of the world) to 'perfectly or infinitely creative' (in the sense of having the power of creation out of nothing). I find the required transition from a human attribute to a divine perfection unacceptably vague and obscure and, hence, the question whether God exists infected by the same vagueness and obscurity. The transition from human attributes to divine perfections recalls, and is meant to recall, the transition from the concept 'finite

[9] F. C. Copleston, SJ. (London, 1972)   [10] Ibid., p. 196.   [11] Ibid., p. 196.

number' to some *positive* concept 'infinite number' – a transition which, as we have seen (chapter 11, section 5), is highly controversial and can be made in a variety of mutually incompatible ways. Yet even if I did understand the transition from mathematical finiteness to mathematical infinity in, for example, Cantor's sense, I would not, I think, be thereby enabled to understand the transition from nonmathematical, finite human attributes to nonmathematical, infinite divine perfections.

My difficulty in understanding the meaning of a perfection extends also to various versions of the ontological argument for the existence of God, including the following elegant and formally correct version, which seems to me a fair interpretation of the proof propounded by Anselm in chapters 2–4 of the *Proslogion*. It is based on the premises (i) that there is a relation 'x is more perfect than y' which establishes a strict linear ordering (after the fashion of 'x is numerically greater than y') among all existent as well as merely thinkable entities; (ii) that being an existent x (a living thing or a thing which forms part of the actual world) is more perfect than being a merely thinkable x; (iii) that there is a most perfect x (be it existent or merely thinkable). The third premise together with the other two does imply that the most perfect being exists. But the premises do not help me either singly or in combination to fathom the meaning of 'perfect' or 'most perfect'. A particular obstacle to my attempts at understanding is the second premise, which for me removes Anselm's meaning of 'more perfect' from any ordinary meaning of 'humanly preferable'. I, for one, cannot accept that what exists (e.g., a person living his life in constant pain and unhappiness) is always preferable to what is merely a thought (e.g., the mere thought of such a person).

Basing agnosticism about God's existence, as I do, on a failure to understand the meaning of the perfections which allegedly constitute his nature may well appear not only unusual but also perverse. For it seems to imply that Anselm, Thomas Aquinas and many other outstanding thinkers who attempted proofs of God's existence did not know what they were talking about. But this is decidedly not a conclusion which I wish to draw. For I assume that these thinkers all have had a – veridical or spurious – experience of an entity which could to some extent be described as possessing the perfections which I cannot grasp. The difference between them and me is that they were acquainted with something with which I have no acquaintance, that they can see something to which I am blind. I do not exclude the possibility of becoming acquainted with what they try to describe and, as a result, of understanding its characteristics. Until that time, which may never come, I lack the concepts and the experience which would enable me to venture a speculative conjecture about God's existence or nonexistence and to support it by a speculative plausibility-argument.

What I have to say about beliefs in the existence or nonexistence of immortal souls resembles what I just said about the existence or nonexistence of an infinitely perfect being. I see no difficulty in admitting that the minimal characterization of a person which I attempted earlier (chapter 8) can be supplemented by assuming that 'being a person' logically implies 'being a soul', i.e., an irreducibily mental particular. I can *understand* characterizations of the soul by means of negative attributes, e.g., the attribute nonmortal. But I do not understand the meaning of positive attributes such as 'immortal' in the sense of 'living before birth', 'living after death', which remind me of the perfections, i.e., attributes of God arrived at not through the *via negativa*, but by analogy to human attributes. In trying to understand the transition from 'human life' to 'eternal life', I am as little helped by recalling the transition from 'mathematically finite' to 'mathematically infinite' as I am in trying to understand the transition from 'humanly wise' to 'perfectly wise'. Yet I do again admit the possibility that certain experiences, which others have had and I so far have not had, might at some time in the future make me regard my present failure to understand the meaning of 'the soul's immortality' as a kind of blindness.

I, naturally, sometimes wonder how understanding and accepting a belief in the existence of a perfect being and of immortal souls would affect my categorial framework and my morality. Since I would probably regard these beliefs as speculative interpretations of experiences which, at best, can be characterized only negatively or analogically, the new framework would, I assume, not differ greatly from my present one. My morality would, I think, not change in content, though I might be enabled better to overcome any moral weakness. My transcendent metaphysics would, very likely, change out of all recognition. And the mere possibility of a theodicy would help to alleviate any feelings of despair and inadequacy in the face of human misery and wickedness and would serve as a most welcome ground for cosmic optimism.

SUMMARY OF THESES

Chapter 1   On the cognitive organization of experience

1. The cognitive organization of a person's experience, which determines his immanent metaphysics or, more precisely, his categorial framework, involves a distinction between particulars and attributes; a deductive organization and epistemic stratification of his beliefs; an interpretative stratification of his beliefs, of which the objectivization of subjective beliefs is a species; in some cases a distinction between dependent and independent particulars and attributes and the admission of various types of auxiliary concepts.

2. The distinction between particulars and attributes allows for borderline cases between 'being a particular' and 'being an attribute' and for radically different results, as shown, for example, by Leibniz's and Kant's conception of space and time.

3. The deductive organization of a person's experience rests on the minimal requirement of consistency or the "weak principle of noncontradiction", which takes the form 'Not every proposition is true' or 'There is at least one attribute which has positive cases, to which it is correctly applicable and not correctly refusable; and negative cases, to which it is correctly refusable but not correctly applicable'.

4. The minimal requirement of consistency constitutes the core of a variety of logical systems which differ from each other by additional principles.

5. A person's beliefs are epistemically stratified if, and only if, they contain at least two sets of beliefs, say, α and β, such that α dominates β in the sense that whenever the person acknowledges that a belief belonging to α is inconsistent with a belief belonging to β, he rejects the latter and preserves the former.

6. A class of a person's beliefs, say, α is supreme if, and only if, it cannot be decomposed into two classes, α_1 and α_2, such that α_1 dominates α_2, and if α dominates the class of beliefs not belonging to it.

7. A person's logical principles – but normally also some nonlogical ones – belong to his class of supreme principles.

8. A perceptual concept P is interpretative of another such concept Q if, and only if, P and Q are co-ostensive and if while P logically implies Q, Q does not logically imply P. (In case there is a concept A such that P logically implies and is logically implied by Q *and* A, A is the "*a priori* difference" between P and Q.)

9. Judging something that is subjectively given in perception as also objectively given – to confer objectivity on it – is a species of interpretation.

10. A perceptual *a priori* concept (e.g., 'substance'), which is the difference between two co-ostensive concepts and is applicable to what is given in perception, must be distinguished from an idealizing concept (e.g., 'Euclidean triangle'), which is not so applicable.

11. The distinction between dependent and independent particulars and attributes, expressed in Aristotle's doctrine of substance, may lead to results which are different from his.

12. The concept of a categorial framework, as determined by the application of the above methods of cognitive organization, is not put forward as the only or ultimate analysis of 'immanent metaphysics', but as a useful piece of equipment for the present inquiry.

Chapter 2   On the organization of practical attitudes

1. A person's practical pro-attitudes, anti-attitudes and attitudes of indifference differ from his pure attitudes in being directed towards practicabilities, i.e., possibilities which he believes to be realizable by his actions.

2. A person's practical attitudes may be (and, if he has moral convictions or principles, are) stratified in the sense that he may have a practical attitude towards his having a practical attitude.

3. To the concepts of domination of (classes of) beliefs by (classes of) beliefs and of supreme beliefs, there correspond concepts of domination of practical attitudes by practical attitudes and of supreme attitudes.

4. To the concept of logical inconsistency there correspond three different notions of practical inconsistency of which "practical opposition" resembles its cognitive counterpart most closely: two practical attitudes of a person are practically opposed if, and only if, they are not jointly realizable. They are complementary if, and only if, in addition one of them must be realized.

5. The other two kinds of practical inconsistency presuppose practical stratification: two practical attitudes of a person are "discordant" if, and only if, one of them is an anti-attitude directed towards the other. Two practical attitudes of a person are incongruent if, and only if, each of them is either a pro-attitude directed to two opposed attitudes of the person or else each of them is an anti-attitude directed to two complementary attitudes of the person.

6. A practical attitude of a person is personally universal if, and only if, it is directed towards everybody's having a certain attitude towards a practicability; it is, in addition, circumstantially general if it is directed towards a kind of practicability rather than a singular one.

7. A general morality is a practically consistent conjunction of supreme, personally universal and circumstantially general practical attitudes. (In the absence of circumstantial generality, one may speak of a "concrete morality".)

8. A general morality is deontic, in so far as it is directed towards everybody's continued acceptance of a code of conduct. It is axiological in so far as it is not so directed.

Chapter 3   On aesthetic attitudes

1. The organization of a person's pure attitudes corresponds to the organization of his practical attitudes, provided one keeps in mind that the former are directed towards logical possibilities, as opposed to practicabilities.

2. Aesthetic attitudes (in the narrow sense, needed here) are directed towards aesthetically representative objects – aesthetic representation being a species of

representation which covers the identifiability of a *"representans"* and a *"representandum"* in legal, linguistic, scientific and other contexts.

3. The *representans* of aesthetic representation or, briefly, the "aesthetic object" is a person's conduct or product in so far as it evokes a certain feeling; the *representandum* or "aesthetic meaning" is the feeling which the object is intended to evoke; the aesthetic object represents or expresses the aesthetic meaning for a person who treats the feeling evoked *as if* it were the feeling whose evocation was intended.

4. The "feelings" in question are grounded in specific states of mind in such a manner that a change in these states would amount to a change of feeling.

5. If a person identifies in a certain context (e.g., on attending a play, or listening to a symphony) the feeling evoked with the feeling the evocation of which he regards as intended, he may have a pro-, anti- or indifferent attitude towards the representation. To this attitude his attitude towards the aesthetic object or the aesthetic meaning may, or may not, be relevant.

6. It may be that he further has a personally universal pure attitude towards his aesthetic attitude. If in addition the attitude is circumstantially general and not the object of a higher practical or pure attitude, he is in possession of an evaluative, critical principle. (The complexity of aesthetic representation makes the occurrence of reasonably wide circumstantial generality unlikely.)

7. The artist – unlike the mere critic – is capable of grasping aesthetic meanings independently of the fully realized aesthetic objects; of creating aesthetic objects; and, in the process of creation, of adjusting aesthetic objects and aesthetic meanings to each other.

Chapter 4   Immanent and transcendent philosophy

1. The principles determining a person's conception of logical consistency (and hence of logical deducibility), together with the other supreme principles which constitute his categorial framework, are his standards of cognitive rationality.

2. Similarly, the principles determining a person's conception of practical consistency (and hence of practical deducibility), together with the supreme principles which constitute his general morality, are his standards of practical rationality.

3. To acknowledge a plurality of categorial frameworks and moralities is to acknowledge that the concepts of cognitive and practical rationality are relative to them. To draw attention to features of these systems which limit their possible differences is to exhibit the limits of this relativity.

4. Before inquiring into some of the sources of supreme cognitive and practical principles and before exemplifying some of them, it is possible to draw attention to the following common features of categorial frameworks and, similarly, of moralities: a common structure resulting from the common organizing principles; a common stock of beliefs and practical attitudes on which the structure is imposed – including common assumptions about human beings; the ability of their acceptors to understand divergent beliefs and practical attitudes and to argue about them (see below, chapters 9 and 15).

5. Apart from characterizing the structure and function of categorial frameworks

and moralities immanent philosophy also has the task of exemplifying categorial frameworks and moralities and of inquiring into the various sources of supreme principles.

6. Transcendent philosophy speculates about the nature of transcendent reality.

7. A person's transcendent philosophy – if it is expressible in concepts – must be internally consistent and consistent with his immanent metaphysics.

8. The statement that transcendent reality is accessible to mystical experience, or in some other nonconceptual way, is internally consistent.

Chapter 5   The principles of logic as supreme cognitive principles

1. It is important to distinguish a logical principle from the empirical fact of its being accepted or rejected: that (almost) everybody accepts the weak principle of noncontradiction is no less an empirical statement than the statement that not everybody accepts the principle of excluded middle.

2. It is possible to exhibit the syntax and semantics of a logic which violates Frege's principle of exactness and to show that it is – or, at least, much more closely then Frege's logic resembles – the logic underlying commonsense thinking.

3. Constructivistic logic, which is another possibility, differs from classical logic by identifying logical truth and falsity with decidable truth and falsity. (Such a logic – for example, in its intuitionistic form – appeals to mathematicians who reject nonconstructive proofs, i.e. proofs yielding pure existence theorems.)

4. Logical theories also differ in being finitistic or infinitistic and, in the latter case, in accepting specific concepts of infinity selected from a great variety of such concepts.

Chapter 6   On mathematical thinking as a possible source of immanent metaphysics

1. Mathematical structures differ from nonmathematical structures in their abstractness and high degree of generality and idealization – as can be seen by comparing the notions of "empirical arithmetic" and "empirical continuity" on the one hand with corresponding mathematical notions of arithmetic and continuity.

2. Empirical arithmetic is based on a notion of counting which allows objects to be identified through misclassification; which ignores whether the aggregate which is assigned a number is a class or a complex; and which leaves undefined the fundamental sequence equinumerousness with whose subsequences enables one to assign numbers to that which is being counted.

3. A pure arithmetic removes these defects in one of a number of different ways which involve "exactification", i.e., the replacement of the inexact empirical concepts by exact ones; and "infinitization", i.e., the introduction of one of the many concepts of 'infinite sequence of natural numbers'. (The nature of the infinitization largely determines the nature of the real number system, e.g., of the density, continuity and differentiability of real functions.)

4. Empirical continua, as characterized, for example, by Aristotle, consist of subcontinua and of common borders between adjoining subcontinua, where the common borders exist only *qua* common borders (and not – as do the subcontinua – as independent parts).

5. The logic of inexact attributes is a suitable means for describing empirical continua, because the common border between two subcontinua can be expressed by the common borderline cases of an inexact attribute and its complement.

6. The application of pure numerical mathematics to empirically discrete and continuous phenomena is – like the application of mathematical structures to nonisomorphic empirical structures in general – a species of (idealizing) representation.

7. Mathematics can be the source of supreme principles of immanent metaphysics, for example, the Kantian principle that space is Euclidean.

Chapter 7   *On predictive and instrumental thinking about nature as a possible source of immanent metaphysics*

1. The supreme principles which determine a person's categorial framework include, apart from "formal" principles of logic and (usually of some) mathematics, also "substantive" ones, in particular constitutive and individuating principles associated with kinds of entities which, while undergoing change, yet retain their individuality.

2. Material objects – which may, *but need not* constitute a maximal kind in a person's categorial framework – consist of material-object-phases the unification of which into distinct, individual material objects must be distinguished from both the classification of the objects and of their phases.

3. Being a material-object-phase implies being perceptually uniform, being intersubjectively perceivable, consisting of some material and having a certain structure.

4. The phases of an individual material object represent each other for certain purposes and stand to each other in an equivalence relation – x *Interrep* Uy – from which the unified object is abstracted.

5. In addition to this relation, the class of material-object-phases has to satisfy various requirements of resemblance, of continuity and certain pragmatic requirements.

6. The requirements may come into conflict and may have to be weighed against each other in various ways which sometimes call for "equitable" *ad hoc* decisions.

7. A natural, as opposed to a merely logically correct, classification of material objects has to serve the purposes of prediction and explanation by natural laws relating different classes of material objects.

8. The transition from commonsense predictive and instrumental thinking to special scientific theories consists in concentrating on certain features and neglecting others and is achieved by various idealizations and other modifications of the commonsense conceptual net.

9. Commonsense, as well as scientific, predictive and instrumental thinking are sources of supreme principles of immanent metaphysics and raise problems about transcendent reality.

Chapter 8   *On thinking about persons and mental phenomena as a possible source of immanent metaphysics*

1. Many judgments of fact, especially those involving the application of intersubjectivity-concepts, and many evaluations, especially moral judgments, involve a reference to oneself and other persons.

2. Any concept of 'being a person' implies 'being a reflective subject', 'being an agent' and 'having access, as well as being accessible, to other persons'.

3. A reflective subject is the unification of temporally distinct reflective (awareness of being aware of . . .) phases in the physical, cognitive, evaluative and active dimension of awareness, such that the unification satisfies, apart from the formal requirements of interrepresentability, also certain requirements of resemblance and continuity, as well as certain pragmatic requirements.

4. Reflective awareness of an action involves being aware of a chosen bodily conduct; having certain beliefs about and practical attitudes towards its "retrospect" and "prospect"; amd believing, or at least acknowledging the prima facie impression that the chosen bodily conduct is "effective" in bringing about the prospect.

5. The effectiveness of chosen bodily conduct is defined in terms of causal, probabilistic or some other kind of predetermination in such a way that it does not prejudge the issue between various theses of transcendent metaphysics about the nature of moral freedom.

6. The facts of social life demand a considerable convergence of an agent's actions as they appear to him and as they appear to others.

7. Access to the beliefs and attitudes of others can be understood as a step-by-step interpretation of bodily conduct or its results.

8. An account of mental attributes can, in the spirit of Brentano, be given in terms of names, attributes and sentences which occur in modo obliquo (indirectly or as inseparable parts of attributes).

9. It is possible to show that under certain assumptions any statement ascribing a material (mental) attribute to a particular is logically equivalent to a statement ascribing a more or less complex mental (material) attribute to a particular. Examples of such assumptions are "the assumption of intersubjective harmony between minds" on the one hand and "the assumption of intrasubjective recording" on the other.

10. Mentalism, materialism or dualism may or may not be linked to intersubjective science or common sense and thus constitute topics of immanent or transcendent metaphysics.

Chapter 9   On thinking about social phenomena and history as a possible source of immanent metaphysics

1. A social group is an open, on the whole only gradually changing, aggregate of persons who share some of their more or less stable beliefs, attitudes and acknowledged rules of conduct, which in being shared determine to some extent what the members of the group expect from each other.

2. Social belief-systems, attitude-systems and social institutions – like the groups characterized by them – have a certain stability on which predictions about the groups can be based.

3. Sharing a belief or attitude with another person involves understanding it, which in turn involves ascribing mental attributes to the person by interpreting his bodily conduct or its results; relating these mental attributes to others which he is assumed to possess; empathetically comparing the mental attributes ascribed to the other person with one or more mental attributes possessed by oneself.

4. The greater the extent to which a person's action is an interaction with the actions of other members of his social group, the greater its complexity and the need for simplifying idealizations.

5. History differs from the natural and social sciences in not searching for regularities expressed in the form of empirical laws or idealizations.

6. It is conceivable that one day a physical science will be developed which is no less concretely descriptive than history or a social science which is as abstractly theoretical as classical mechanics.

7. In so far as thinking about social entities is not reducible to thinking about nonsocial entities and phenomena and in so far as the social entities are linked to the world of intersubjective experience, social thinking may be the source of supreme cognitive principles.

8. An example of a concept which, as usually explained, does not clearly belong to either immanent or transcendent metaphysics is the concept of progress.

Chapter 10   On delimiting a person's immanent metaphysics

1. To accept a proposition is to distinguish more or less clearly between the beliefs and actions appropriate to an acceptor and the beliefs and actions appropriate to a rejector of the proposition and to judge the acceptor's beliefs and actions appropriate to oneself.

2. To accept a proposition as true may mean the same as accepting it; that it conforms to a general and effective criterion of truth (which implies a vicious regress); that it conforms to a specific, effective criterion of truth (e.g., validation by the truth-table method); that it conforms to a general noneffective criterion of truth (e.g., correspondence to reality).

3. Assumptions about the last-mentioned type of criterion belong, since it refers to transcendent reality, to transcendent metaphysics.

4. The acceptance of a supreme principle may vary in strength – from absolute certainty to provisional acceptance.

5. In delimiting a person's categorial framework it is useful to introduce the relation 'f is fundamental to g', which is satisfied if, and only if, the acceptance of f is consistent with both the acceptance or rejection of g, whereas the acceptance of g is consistent with the acceptance, but not the rejection, of f. In terms of this relation the notions of core, periphery and other useful notions can be defined.

6. Whereas if f is fundamental to g, g cannot be made independent of f, there are weaker dependence relations where such independence can be achieved. Thus, even though pure arithmetic, geometry and other ideal mathematical structures originally emerge as idealizing representations of empirical structures, they can (e.g., in Platonic fashion) be separated from their original *representanda* (and, e.g., transferred into the Platonic heaven).

7. The interdependence of practical choices and unchoosable facts can also be abolished by assuming that choices of a certain kind or facts of a certain kind are illusory.

8. The demarcation between immanent and transcendent metaphysics admits of borderline and controversial cases, especially when it is not clear whether or not certain attributes are instantiated by – or linked through *as-if* identifications to – particulars judged to be intersubjectively given.

Chapter 11 Transcendent metaphysics and the application of concepts

1. Among the general theses about transcendent reality are answers to the question whether or not it differs from the world of intersubjective experience and, if so, how far it is accessible to description and interpretation by means of concepts.

2. If a philosopher holds that transcendent reality is accessible only to non-conceptual apprehension, then he can *qua* philosopher do no more than try to remove conceptual and propositional obstacles to such apprehension.

3. There are various ways of conceiving transcendent reality as being approximated by empirical reality and, thus, by sharing at least some features with it.

4. Locke's distinction between primary qualities, which are "in the bodies whether we perceive them or not", and the secondary qualities, which are "nothing in the objects themselves", is taken from the science of his day and exemplifies versions of transcendent metaphysics based on an opposition between science and common sense.

5. The distinction between thinking (in some of its aspects) as "finding" the world of intersubjective experience and thinking as "making" it, is another source of transcendent metaphysics – for example, the factualism of Leibniz and the constructivism of Kant.

6. From concepts which are applicable to intersubjective experience or idealizing concepts which through *as-if* identifications are linked to them, one must distinguish the so-called perfections which are applicable to transcendent reality only – for example, God's infinite goodness or power.

Chapter 12 Transcendent metaphysics and the limits of conceptual thinking

1. The scepticism of *Sextus Empiricus* implicitly acknowledges a distinction between particulars and attributes; a distinction between the subjectively given and that which is interpreted as intersubjective; an epistemic stratification in which the class of logical principles is supreme; and – hence – a deductive organization of beliefs. His *implicit* conception of the structure of immanent metaphysics thus resembles the structure made explicit in this essay.

2. In trying to understand the mystics' reports on their mystical experience of transcendent reality it is – as in the case of poets – important to distinguish between sentences expressing nonpropositional hints and sentences expressing propositions. (A self-contradictory proposition may in certain contexts serve as a nonpropositional hint.)

3. The journey undertaken towards a mystical grasp of transcendent reality by philosophers as different as Plato, Nicolaus of Cusa and Wittgenstein (of the *Tractatus*) consists roughly of three stages: the recognition of the philosopher's categorial framework; the denial that its principles of conceptual and propositional thinking are of any use in grasping transcendent reality; the alleged apprehension of transcendent reality and, sometimes, the attempt at conveying this experience.

4. The attempt at conveying the mystical experience of grasping reality is a species of evocative representation, which is different when attempted by non-metaphysical mystics (for example, St Teresa), who do not use metaphysical terms in representing their experience, and when attempted by metaphysical mystics (for example, Spinoza), who do.

5. Sometimes metaphysical mystics, as well as other transcendent meta-physicians, use technical concepts in their hints at the nature of transcendent reality, e.g., by replacing logical implication by "coherence" or some kind of ampliative or "dialectical" inference.

6. It is sometimes not clear whether, to what extent and at what stage of his work a transcendent metaphysician is crossing the border between transcendent metaphysics, which consists of statements, and attempts at a nonconceptual grasp of transcendent reality.

7. An inquiry into the nature of transcendent metaphysics must try to reach this border or at least acknowledge it.

Chapter 13   On antimetaphysical errors and illusions

1. Any person who organizes his thinking by the methods exhibited at the beginning of this essay and who, however weakly, accepts the resulting categorial framework has an immanent metaphysics. If he relates his beliefs as constrained by his categorial framework to a mind-independent reality, he also has a transcendent metaphysics.

2. The erroneous belief of not having a metaphysics may arise in a person who identifies "metaphysics" with some special system (or systems) of immanent or transcendent metaphysics which he rejects.

3. An important error, exemplified by Comte, is to identify metaphysics with prescientific thinking.

4. The Marxist opposition between "real science" or dialectical materialism and "metaphysics" as a "fog-formation of the human brain" is similarly inconsistent with the conception of metaphysics as exhibited in this essay.

5. The positivistic rejection of metaphysics as meaningless is based on confusing linguistic, logical and metaphysical meaninglessness.

6. In attacking metaphysics as complete darkness or as lying on the road to it, Wittgenstein fails to notice that in his own description of language-games he frequently attempts the characterization of structures which belong to immanent metaphysics and can thus be regarded as versions of more or less incompletely described categorial frameworks.

7. Wittgenstein's metaphorical condemnation of metaphysics – more precisely of transcendent metaphysics – as "language resting" overlooks the often-realized possibility that ideas (such as Democritean atomism) which started as such may later be put to work (for example, by becoming part of a scientific theory).

Chapter 14   On internal strains

1   A person's metaphysical beliefs may change as the result of internal strains or external pressures.

2. Internal strains range from the discovery or suspicion of internal inconsistency within the set of supreme principles to more or less indefinite discomforts.

3. Internal strains may result from conflicts between immanent and tran-scendent metaphysics. (An example of such a conflict and an attempt at solving it is found in Leibniz's *Theodicée*.)

4. Internal metaphysical strains may affect decisions as to which of a set of logical systems is to be regarded as primary or supreme and which as merely auxiliary.

5. Just as various disciplines, especially scientific disciplines, may be the sources of supreme principles, so may interdisciplinary conflicts be the source of metaphysical strains.

6. Among the methods of dealing with internal metaphysical strains are, apart from replacing certain supreme principles, their demotion to a lower stratum of beliefs or to simplifying fictions.

7. Wavering between supreme principles may in some cases be irremovable.

Chapter 15   On external pressures exerted by methodological and other arguments

1. Metaphysical arguments differ from deductive arguments in two important respects. They are intended to establish premises rather than to deduce conclusions from given premises. The method for establishing supreme principles is much less clearly defined or not defined at all.

2. Although Descartes's method of doubt does not yield a general, effective criterion of truth, it implies that every person's organized system of beliefs contains supreme beliefs.

3. Although Kant's transcendental method does not establish that there is only *one set* of Categories the application of which confers intersubjectivity (objectivity) on what is subjectively given, it shows that, and how, intersubjectivity is conferred by the application of (*a priori*) intersubjectivity-concepts.

4. Husserl's defence of his phenomenological method is based on the mistaken assumption that the only alternative to accepting it is the acceptance of psychologism. (The method of this essay, resulting in empirical propositions about non-empirical propositions, constitutes a third possibility.)

5. The dialectical method, as used, e.g., by Hegel, the "scientific" method, as used, e.g., by the early Brentano, and the "linguistic" method, as used, e.g., by Ryle, serve, at best, to make implicit assumptions explicit. They do not establish their uniqueness.

6. The arguments of those philosophers who do not claim to be in possession of some absolutely cogent method can be described as honest rhetoric, i.e., attempts at arguing in favour of supreme principles which they themselves accept, by adducing reasons which they themselves find acceptable.

7. Examples of honest metaphysical rhetoric are Socratic arguments, arguments from so far inconceivable alternatives and pragmatic arguments.

Chapter 16   On metaphysical pluralism, intrametaphysical and metaphysical progress

1. One of the main aims of the preceding discussion was to exhibit the general structure of categorial frameworks, another to show that a great many of them share "common cores" of principles and differ merely in the "periphery" surrounding them. Like any other attempt at characterizing a genus and, within it, some species and subspecies, this attempt at doing so is neither relativistic nor absolutistic.

2. The belief in biological, metaphysical or other kinds of progress is easily

defended if it is conceived as a linear ordering by means of a relation which cannot be fully understood – either because (as in the passage quoted from the first edition of Darwin's *Origin of Species*) it is not clearly defined or else because (as in various theological doctrines of Divine Providence) it surpasses human understanding.

3. If one distinguishes progress in different dimensions and admits the possibility that progress in one of them may strengthen or weaken progress in another, then an overall measurement of progress may be difficult and – sometimes – impossible.

4. Whereas agreement about *scientific* progress in the informative dimension (including predictions and retrodictions) and the technical dimension is on the whole reached with comparative ease, the position is quite different when it comes to judging progress in the explanatory or moral dimension.

5. Informative or technical progress which is due to a new scientific theory does not guarantee that this theory logically implies any of its predecessors or, even, that it is consistent with any of them.

6. A theory has full explanatory power with respect to its acceptor's categorial framework if, and only if, the theory conforms to the categorial framework, that is to say, if, and only if, the axioms and theorems of the theory comprise only concepts which are maximal kinds of the framework or species of them and if the logic underlying the theory is the logic of the categorial framework.

7. Whereas a person's criterion of metaphysical progress belongs to his metaphysical principles, his criteria of the extent to which metaphysical change serves other kinds of progress do not belong to these principles.

Chapter 17   Some speculations about transcendent reality

1. Since the author of an essay on the nature of metaphysics is in danger of confusing features which are peculiar to his own categorial framework with features common to all of them and since he is, similarly, in danger of putting too much weight on his own transcendent speculations, on the interaction of his own immanent and transcendent metaphysics and on the interaction of his own metaphysics and morality, it seems desirable that he should, however briefly, indicate his own position in these respects.

2. The logic underlying my categorial framework is finitist and inexact, admitting of various kinds of idealizing exactification and infinitization. Its maximal kinds are persons, animals and inanimate things – linked to the results of the sciences. (So far, however, I have been unable to regard animals as a species of material objects.) The constitutive and individuating principles associated with these maximal kinds conform in *general* to what has been said in chapters 7 and 8.

3. My personal morality implies a preference for representative democracy, approval of any strengthening of institutions which protect society from violations of personal freedom, from illness, political oppression, economic exploitation and undereducation. (I believe that my meta-ethics, as explained in *Experience and Conduct*, is more relevant to the topics of this essay than my personal moral convictions.)

4. My transcendent metaphysics is a version of perspectivism according to which various categorial frameworks are different perspectives of transcendent reality. (This perspectivism is compatible with a preference for my own categorial framework over others known to me.)

5. As to the issue between determinism and indeterminism, I believe (and am pleased) that a good case can be made for a strong sense of human freedom and creativity and for a conception of man as Goethe's "little God of the world" rather than a completely programmed *homunculus*.

6. I am an agnostic about the existence of a perfect being and of immortal souls because I do not understand the key terms used in statements and arguments in which their existence is asserted or allegedly proved. I do not, however, deny the possibility that some future experience of a wholly new kind may give meaning to these terms.

INDEX

234